CU00826090

The Common
Legal Past of Europe

Studies in Medieval and Early Modern Canon Law

Volume 4

MANLIO BELLOMO

The Common
Legal Past of Europe
1000-1800

TRANSLATED BY

LYDIA G. COCHRANE

The Catholic University of America Press

Washington, D.C.

Library of Congress Cataloging-in-Publication Data
Bellomo, Manlio.
   [L'Europa del diritto comune. English]
   The common legal past of Europe : 1000–1800 / Manlio Bellomo ;
translated by Lydia G. Cochrane.
     p.   cm. — (Studies in medieval and early modern canon law)
   Includes bibliographical references and index.
   1. Law—Europe—History. I. Title. II. Series. KJ147.B4513 1995
349.4—dc20
[344]
94–17652
ISBN 0–8132–0813–0 (cloth).—ISBN 0–8132–0814–9 (pbk.)

to my wife
to my children

Contents

Foreword

With vigor and passion rarely found in a scholarly work, Manlio Bellomo introduces new vocabulary and a sweeping new interpretation of Western European legal history. He wrote his history of law for Italian law students. This English edition will make it available for students in the Anglo-American legal tradition.

This book is a textbook, but a textbook with a sharply argued thesis that will interest scholars and students. Bellomo begins by describing a "wave of codification" that swept over Europe in the eighteenth and nineteenth centuries. He contends that codification has proven to be an imperfect instrument with which to foster legal reform and encourage flexibility in a legal system. Europe's reliance on codification has introduced legal ambiguity, rigidity, and uncertainty into all the European legal systems. He believes that a new common law for all of Europe—a political process now underway in the European Common Market—would provide a much better vehicle for legal change and development.

From the modern age Bellomo looks back to when Europe had a common law that transcended national and legal boundaries. This system of law reigned from the twelfth to the seventeenth century. He tells the story of the birth and evolution of that common law—a story that Bellomo thinks could provide a model for how a European common law might be born again. The term "common law" sounds strange to most English-speaking historians when applied to continental legal systems. We speak of common law as being the legal system that evolved in England from the eleventh century to the present. This historical fact and terminology introduces problems for English speakers. The jurists of the twelfth and thirteenth centuries also spoke of common law, a *ius commune*. Their common law consisted of Roman, canon, and feudal law. This *ius commune* was taught in the law schools of Italy, France, Spain, Germany, England, and other European countries until the seventeenth century.

In France legal historians have called the *ius commune* the "droit savant"; in Germany, the "Juristenrecht" or "das gelehrte Recht"; in the Anglo-American world, "learned law." Bellomo argues that the terminology itself is not only wrong but misleading. Since "learned law" reeks of the classroom, scholars have dismissed it as unimportant for the growth of legal systems in European kingdoms, principalities, cities, and corporations—systems that Bellomo calls the *iura propria*. Consequently, scholars have ignored the *ius commune* because it was the law of the schools, the law of the jurists, the law of the ideal, not the real world. Bellomo demonstrates that this misconception has trivialized the importance of the *ius commune* and Balkanized the histories of national legal systems. With carefully chosen examples he illustrates how the *ius commune* permeated every crack and crevice of the *iura propria* from the thirteenth to the seventeenth centuries. It created the concepts, the institutions, the procedures, the documents, the doctrines without which the *iura propria* would have evolved very differently. Bellomo explains that every historian who ignores the *ius commune* when writing about local legal systems distorts and misunderstands the *ius proprium*. Bellomo's powerful admonition, which forms the backbone of this book, is a warning to everyone writing about European law.

In Lydia Cochrane's elegant and lucid translation, Bellomo's argument and thesis are sharpened for English readers by using *ius commune* for the Italian "diritto comune." On the rare occasions when Bellomo uses "diritto comune" to mean "common law" in a general sense of a law common to one territory or people, she uses "common law." The English version of the book has also added short explanations that will help the non-Italian reader to understand sometimes difficult and alien legal terms and concepts. In addition, to make the book more useful for English-speaking students, citations to English-language works have been added to the notes and the bibliography.

KENNETH PENNINGTON

Preface to the American Edition

The concept of the *ius commune* is almost unknown in Anglo-American scholarship, and the term "common law" sounds strange to most English-speaking historians. However, the fusion of Roman, canon, and feudal law produced a *ius commune* and a common jurisprudence in Europe between 1100 and 1800.

That does not mean that Europe had one unified complex of norms adequate for the juridical practices of cities and rural areas in every region. In reality, the situation was more varied and more articulated. All local institutions (for example, a kingdom, a principality, a free city, a feudal or territorial lordship, a corporation, a confraternity, a monastery) had their own juridical norms, and they respected them and applied them (or violated them) whether they were promulgated by a sovereign or by a deliberative assembly or whether they had been fashioned and transmitted orally from generation to generation in the form of customs. All of these various norms belonged within the *ius proprium*—that is, law proper to particular, individual institutions.

These norms varied greatly; they differed from place to place and from one level of society to another. This means that the unwary traveler of the time or the incognizant historian today might have found or still find the legislative panorama in Europe an inextricable confusion.

English "common law," the law proper to the British Isles, was simply one small part of this entire picture. Like the other normative systems, it too was dispersed and intermingled with many local experiences, and it too was known and applied within a limited territory.

Nonetheless, men of the Middle Ages had unshakable certitudes to guide them, aid their understanding, and provide a notion of unity and order. They had ideals and thoughts that molded their intellectual attitudes and formed their traditional behavior patterns. They turned constantly toward absolute and eternal values, attempting to follow and practice them or, more simply, feeling a sense of guilt and remorse for their violation and for sin.

They lived within an entire system of thought, usually with little consciousness that it was a system. They believed that outside of history—hence free from the folly and malice of the realm of possible actions—there were primary and divine values not fully knowable by humankind because man was an imperfect creature condemned to an earthly mortal life when Adam and Eve fell and were driven from the Garden of Eden.

One of these absolute values was justice, not only as it might be revealed and realized in modest human laws but, above all, as it could be intuited in the daily exercise of faith and in the practice of the precepts that God had given to humankind.

Jurists and theologians, in particular after Irnerius and Gratian, knew that the two aspects of justice, the human and the divine, were as closely connected as the two sides of a coin. They were also aware that, as with the coin, the two faces were necessarily distinct. Medieval man lived out his life following dual guidelines. He imagined and intuited an absolute justice, but he was keenly aware that he could never know and even less possess that justice; he obeyed earthly laws, but he was conscious that they contained only the palest reflection of divine justice. The jurist, like the sailor far at sea, sought a pole star. He found it in the ancient and "sacred" texts of a great emperor of the past, Justinian, and in the new norms of the Roman pontiffs—that is, in the laws of the two supreme ruling powers of the earth. In comparison with these broader systems, the local laws set forth by a lord or a corporation seemed what they in fact were—instruments of one social group or faction for the defense of partisan interests.

Thus the jurist observed, knew, and even accepted the local experiences that made up the *ius proprium*, but the common man did not understand that the ideal content of the norms governing daily life was meager. The only (or the chief) problem facing very many people was the dramatic one of physical survival in the midst of hunger and shortages, sickness and plague, war and extermination. Still, everyone, even those who did not realize it, lived within one sole "system," in much the same way that one can live today in a "capitalistic system" without knowing the laws that govern capital and markets.

In the juridical system of that time, the norms of one place or one social level (*ius proprium*) were closely linked to the norms common to all who believed in Christ (*ius commune*). This was because the norms of *ius proprium* found in the *ius commune* usable concepts, principles, rules, and technical terminology, at times even drawing on it for a specific fragment of its substance. This was true even when the *ius proprium* reacted against or diverged from the *ius commune*; when this occurred, by choice or out of ignorance, it created a problem of comparison with, hence of relation to, the *ius commune*.

Thus for the keenest intellects and the greatest jurists in Europe of the Middle Ages, the *ius commune* turned out to be a formidable unifying force. It lay at the center of the law and was the symbol of its unity. Just as Scripture was requisite for the cure of souls and the sacred texts remained valid even when in certain places or among individual sinners they might be neglected or violated, so the "sacred" texts of the *ius commune* were a necessity for the guidance of society and men's life in society, and those texts remained valid even when they were not applied or they were contradicted by norms of *ius proprium* or the customs of single communities.

Plurality was thus part of the "system," and the system itself was inconceivable and would never have existed without the innumerable *iura propria* linked to the unity of the *ius commune*. The greater imperfection of men's laws (the *ius proprium*) was related to the lesser imperfection of the laws of the rulers of the earth (the *ius commune*), but both laws, in varying measure, contained and divulged only a tenuous glimmer of the Justice that was absolute, divine, hence eternal.

With the advent of humanism in the sixteenth century, this system of thought and its practical applications fell into crisis. Gradually, with Descartes and Spinoza, with the natural law theories of Grotius, with the Enlightenment thought of Rousseau and Voltaire, and with Hegel's historicism, European thought ended its fallacious quest for earthly perfection. Such perfection—neither known nor knowable—did not, and, according to Christian doctrine, could not, appertain to human thought.

For over two centuries now, Europe has not had, nor could it have had, a common law conceived as a reflection of absolute Justice; it became clear that it was useless to try to bring within human history an imagined eternal Justice whose locus was outside history.

Still, no jurist can be resigned to being only a "man of law" of a transitory and occasional law, and even less of a factious, rapacious, or tyrannical law. Every jurist—if only in a fleeting moment in his professional life—has been or has wanted to be a "man of justice." When that moment arrives, the medieval "system of the common law" reappears in all its extraordinary potential as a great spiritual reality and a fundamental expression of civilization. Then the two sides of the coin, theology and law, still clearly distinct, confront one another reunited.

Trappeto (Catania), 1 October 1993

Preface to the 1991 Edition

The first Italian edition of this book was published in April 1988. The idea was to return to pathways well known to the specialists and point out the way to readers and scholars less familiar with them. Since the book reached five printings in three years it was perhaps not an untimely idea.[1] The testing it was subjected to has led to changes to bring it up to date and has made it clear that recasting many of the topics treated might help unravel some particularly complex and tangled problems. Hence this new edition, which includes an index of place names and an index of persons.

Although I hope that this book will continue to enjoy in its new guise the same good fortune it did during its first three years, I will look forward to making appropriate or necessary future revisions in the same spirit in which the book was first written and is now re-written.

Trappeto (Catania), March 1991

---

1. May 1988, May 1988, February 1989, June 1989, April 1991. The 1991 edition was reprinted in January 1993.

Preface to the First Edition

The idea of a book on the common legal past of Christian Europe first arose in Erice at the International School of Ius Commune, the directorship of which I have shared since 1987 with Stephan Kuttner, at Antonino Zichichi's "Ettore Majorana Center for Scientific Culture." It was further developed in Catania as a way to offer students of the "common law," the *ius commune*, an elementary guide to supplement their class lectures.

In both settings I have tried to adopt the viewpoint of readers who might, for a variety of reasons, want to know something about the *ius commune*.

A reader, for example, might sense that the various national law systems in Europe and the codes in which they have become crystallized (though not represented in their entirety) are in crisis. Or he or she might imagine a future in which national barriers will be in great part dismantled, in individual minds and in the collective awareness, and in which specific structures will become either anachronisms or a special province for speculation and fiscal legerdemain. A third and chief reason might be that he or she knows that every act in the present is linked to the past in much the same way that every individual action is connected to experience, from which it receives "form," "measure," and a sense of perspective and equilibrium missing in many who wander like amnesiacs from one disconnected, segmented day to the next, lacking both memory and imagination.

I hope to make a great epoch come to life again for people who are not professional students of the history of jurisprudence. In that great age between the twelfth and the eighteenth centuries, Europe knew and practiced innumerable "particular laws"—*iura propria*—but that age was also incontrovertibly the age of a sole, unique law, the *ius commune* or, more specifically, the *utrumque ius*, the Roman law and the law of the universal church.

This historical experience has now come to an end. Nonetheless, in the very act of becoming absorbed and surpassed by the internal logic of other perspectives, the real and ideal world of the *ius commune* stamped European law with some of the characteristics that to this day set it apart from other legal systems, in particular from the Anglo-American.

Another reason for returning once more to the *ius commune* is to give an account of the ideas that circulate among scholars today, some of which are universally accepted while others are challenged or are left to languish out of the spotlight. If we look to contemporary historiography for a work that will stimulate curiosity and debate on the historical processes that made European law what it is today, we will be faced with disappointments or a long search. The works that lay down the basic problems of the *ius commune* are either decidedly dated (Koschaker, Ermini, Cassandro), seem unaware of many events and ideas (Watson, Schrage), or present an interminable mass of materials and information primarily useful to orient the research of scholars and provide them with a crutch for their memories (Coing).

One work alone has withstood the test of time and has for that reason become a classic in legal historiography: Francesco Calasso's *Introduzione al diritto comune*, a work first published in 1951 and developed from the nucleus of his celebrated inaugural lecture, or "Prolusione di Catania," entitled "Il concetto di diritto comune" (1934). This incisive work immediately opened up vital and fertile new vistas to scholarship. For several decades now, entire generations of scholars have followed pathway indicated or intuited by Francesco Calasso and have produced valuable and relevant studies that go far beyond Calasso's expectations. These works share a concrete sense of the epoch and its history, creating a compelling overview of the *ius commune*.

This is why it has seemed to me appropriate to dissect a number of studies and point out their component parts for the benefit of readers who might find it difficult to locate them within a sizable body of literature or within specific individual works of historiography.

As this work goes to press I want to express my cordial thanks to Dottore Francesco Migliorino, who has given so generously of his time and aid in the final phases of this work.

Trappeto (Catania), April 1988

I

National Codifications
Triumph and Crisis

The Age of Codifications

There is a period in the history of European law that historiography calls "the age of codification" or "codifications," using the plural to stress the nationalistic connotations inherent in the connection between that phenomenon and the constitution or extension of the various European nation states, and using the singular to accentuate the unity of that phenomenon as a point of reference for an ideology and a method.

The time-span is not short: it includes all of the last century and a good part of our own. The "age of codifications" began in the eighteenth century with a few preliminary projects, some of them left in the planning stage, some put into effect. These compilations attempted to extract the most important provisions from the incalculable variety of particular norms of the nation states, with the idea that a body of selected precepts would be more useful than a disconnected congeries of sometimes contradictory dispositions. The attempt to bring order from disorder was by no means a new one; it had a famous predecessor, centuries before, in Gratian's *Concordia discordantium canonum*, or *Decretum*, of 1140–42. But the new attempt had a specific and particular historical significance, one that affected the outcome of later initiatives. After the sorting process that led to a "consolidation" in which a number of provisions were collected together, there came a concerted effort to draw up a body of rules articulated within an orderly and carefully crafted outline—a "code" authoritatively imposed to constitute the precept, mark the limit, and

I

state the guarantee it offered all the citizens of a state. Thus historiography usually shows a period of incubation and of "consolidations" preceding a period of revitalization and "codifications."

Scholars have scoured remote and in some cases insignificant corners of the eighteenth-century scene in search of attempted codifications conceptualized or realized at that time. They have rediscovered some figures with a conscious will for reform who operated in the context of a responsibly launched movement for renewal and who worked within organisms and magistracies that had the authority to act; they also encountered professorial dreamers and would-be philosophes closed within their private worlds fantasizing about a utopian new age and thinking their efforts had helped to bring them about. Even when these movements were conveniently labeled "consolidation" and "codification,"[1] historians have often confused the two phenomena in studying regions of Europe that did not and could not have experienced them. They have even done so despite a warning: "The code," Tullio Ascarelli wrote in 1945, "is characterized by a claim to construct a 'new,' 'complete,' and 'definitive' legal order that includes among its formulations solutions for all possible cases; it is precisely this characteristic that distinguishes it from the legislative consolidations of the previous epochs, whose only purpose was to reorganize the law in force."[2]

2. Precedents: The Experience of Consolidations

There were a number of legislative consolidations in Italy and in Europe. In the Kingdom of Sardinia (Piedmont, Liguria, and Sardinia; the capital was Turin), for example, "constitutions" were promulgated by Victor Amadeus II in 1723 and 1729 and by Charles Emmanuel III in 1770–71, the latter under the title "Laws and Consti-

1. "Consolidation" and "codification" are useful terms, now widely used for their clarity. They have also provided the title of a book that introduced the first term into juridical historiography and combined it with the second: Mario Viora, *Consolidazioni e codificazioni: Considerazioni sulle caratteristiche strutturali delle fonti di cognizione del diritto nei tempi andati, contributo alla storia della codificazione*, 3d ed. (Turin: Giapichelli, 1967). See also K. Pennington, "Law Codes: 1000–1500," in *Dictionary of the Middle Ages*, vol. 7 (1986) 425–31.

2. Tullio Ascarelli, "L'idea di codice nel diritto privato e la funzione dell'interpretazione" (1945), now in Ascarelli, *Saggi giuridici* (Milan: Giuffrè, 1949), 48–49.

tutions."[3] The terms *costituzioni* (constitutions) and *codici* (codes) were used interchangeably to designate the same phenomenon. This meaning persisted, to the point that even in our own century Vittorio Emanuele Orlando observed that "no objective difference exists between constitutional laws and ordinary laws,"[4] which means that even today "civil code" and "constitution" can be brought within "the broad process of codification,"[5] since the civil codes have incorporated "constitutions" and the concept of collections of legislative decrees within the meaning of "code."[6]

There were also early experiments in codification. The Senate of Venice ordered a "Feudal Code," drawn up in 1770 and promulgated in 1780, and another body of laws, the "Code for the Venetian Mercantile Marine," in 1786. Activity was even more intense in Tuscany, where at least two attempts to draw up a code deserve mention. The first, a project for a civil code (the "Code of the General Legislation of the Grand Duchy of Tuscany") limited by an outdated point of view, was a failure; the second, a penal code, proved a great success. Formally entitled "Reform of Tuscan Criminal Legislation," it is commonly known as the Leopoldine Code because it was sponsored and promulgated (in 1786) by Pietro Leopoldo, grand duke of Tuscany from 1765 to 1790 as Leopold I and after 1790 Holy Roman emperor as Leopold II.

Outside of Italy, the most important instances of a sovereign using his or her authority to back the idea of codification and to make it a reality occurred in Austria and Prussia.

In Austria, after the failure of the "Codex Theresianum" of Maria Theresa, which was completed in 1766 but never put into effect, Joseph II brought out a "Rules of Civil Procedure" (*Civilgerichtsordnung*) in 1782, followed by a penal code (*Allgemeines Gesetz über Ver-*

3. See Mario Viora, *Le costituzioni piemontesi (Leggi e costituzioni di S.M. il Re di Sardegna): 1723–1729–1770* (Milan, Rome, Turin: Fratelli Bocca, 1928; reprint, unavailable commercially, Turin: Società Reale Mutua di Assicurazioni, 1986).

4. Vittorio Emanuele Orlando, *Principii di diritto costituzionale* (1889), 5th ed. (Florence: G. Barbera, 1917), 140.

5. Pietro Perlingieri, *Profili istituzionali del diritto civile* (Naples: Edizioni Scientifiche Italiane, 1975), 63.

6. Michele Giorgianni, "Il diritto privato ed i suoi attuali confini," *Rivista trimestrale di diritto e procedura civile* 15 (1961): 391–420, quotation p. 399.

brechen und derselben Bestrafung) in 1787 and a Code of Penal Procedure (*Kriminalgerichtsordnung*) in 1788.

In Prussia, which extended over the greater part of the territories of northeast Germany, jurists steeped in Enlightenment culture (Thomasius, Coccejus, Schwarz, and others) made a number of attempts during the eighteenth century to draw up or give support to a code. A stable, concrete code came only in 1794, when Frederick William II (d. 1797) promulgated the *Allgemeines Landrecht für die Preussischen Staaten* (General Code for the Prussian States), commonly known as the Prussian *Landrecht*. It remained in force until 1900.

3. The Theoretical Roots of the Codifications

Codifications crowded the scene during the last decades of the eighteenth century. The motivations behind them varied, but they all belonged within the Enlightenment currents that "yearned for organizational reform"[7] and attempted utopian elaborations of new models for society, or that sprang from the sort of prudent reaction that always opposes movements for reform. A common thread ran through the welter of acts, thoughts, reactions, desires for change, and efforts to conserve the old ways that animated the various experiments: it was the notion that one must have "certain" rules; rules that were simple, clear, and in harmony with human "reason" and human "nature." "Rational" demands and "natural" needs were interpreted in ways that were far from uniform, however, and those who appealed to them often ended up in opposing camps—those who wanted radical and sweeping reform on one side and, on the other, those who wanted to consolidate a society divided into "orders," "estates," or "levels" and to assure stability to each of these groups, to guarantee its existence and guide it, in exchange for obedience to a sole and single law (the "code") willed and imposed by a recognized and incontestible sovereign authority.

Thus some supported the idea that it was up to the ruler, and to

7. As Piero Calamandrei put it ("smaniose di riformar ordinamenti"): Calamandrei, "Prefazione e Commento" in Cesare Beccaria, *Dei delitti e delle pene*, 2d ed. rev. (Florence: Le Monnier, 1950), 66–67, English translation by Henry Paolucci (Indianapolis: Bobbs-Merrill, 1963).

the ruler alone, to unravel or cut through the knottier problems of jurisprudence. The sovereign appeared, and in fact was, "illuminated" in that he was presented as giving rational order to social relations and "certain" rules for individual actions. In the broader picture, assigning this task to the sovereign implied diminishing the role of jurists, who were still genuinely active in all sectors of the judicial domain. It also implied an increase in the authoritarian centralization of the new sovereign.

One of the most significant theoretical statements in the Italian Settecento, Ludovico Antonio Muratori's *Dei difetti della Giurisprudenza*, published in 1742,[8] is shot through with this sort of thinking. Addressing his remarks to the sovereign, Muratori stated that confusion and irrationality were altogether too widespread; that jurists, singly and as a group, were too full of vain aspirations; and that they made exaggerated claims, presenting themselves or posing as high priests of justice, even of a justice both human and divine, like priests who defended and divulged the Divine Word.[9] Muratori appealed to the sovereign to take action to cut through an inextricably snarled system of justice created by the argumentative and quarrelsome verbosity of the jurists.[10] At the end of this work Muratori listed some of the spinier legal questions and the more dubious solutions, calling on the sovereign power to provide each of these with a sure law that would oblige the jurists, out of the obedience they owed to the sovereign's commands, to hold their peace.[11] As Muratori saw it, the call for a "sure law" covering each of the problems he listed was not yet a proposal for the elaboration of a "code"; the set of laws that he requested of the sovereign power would certainly have lacked the completeness, the homogeneity, and the capacity for generating further legislation that were to be typical of the nineteenth-century codes.

Furthermore, throughout the eighteenth century, even when jurists moved from exhortation to action, and even when the labors of

8. Ludovico Antonio Muratori, *Dei difetti della Giurisprudenza, Trattato* (Venetiis 1742).
9. Ibid., 1.
10. Ibid., 2.
11. Ibid, 161–80. Chapter 19 is entitled "Saggio di alcune Conclusioni intorno a certi punti controversi nella Giurisprudenza, proposto all'esame di chi ha l'autorità di far leggi e statuti" (Essay containing some conclusions regarding certain disputed points in jurisprudence proposed for the examination of whoever has the authority to make laws and statutes), 161.

learned commissions of jurists led to the elaboration and promulgation of a "code," such codes lacked one of the characteristics of all
modern law codes: the unity and equality of the juridical subject—the
people—for whom the code was destined. What is more, the figure of
the sovereign was still central to these schemes, like a keystone bearing the weight, assuring the equilibrium of the entire construction,
and intervening from time to time with specific legislative provisions.
In some eighteenth-century law codes—the Prussian *Landrecht* of
1794, for example—the general framework of the law imposed from
the top down confirmed an organization of society into three "estates" or "levels" (here, *Stände*), the nobility, the bourgeoisie, and the
peasantry. Each of these sectors had its own laws; legal capacity was
not uniform, and there were limitations and prohibitions, privileges
and exemptions, free men and slaves and servants. The organization
of these codes was indeed "rational" and "natural," but only to the
extent that they refrained from challenging the articulation of society
and the authority of the prince who ruled and governed the state.

This was one of the characteristics of eighteenth-century absolutism. The codifications and attempts at codification were the form and
the expression of that absolutism, and since they participated in its
nature they shared its fortunes. No group—neither the nobility, nor
the bourgeoisie, nor those who worked the land—recognized itself
wholly in all the codified norms, because these codifications mirrored
power and the ways in which power intended to safeguard society.
Any line of thought tending toward renewal or reform found little
room to maneuver; often the best it could hope to do was merely
exist. Yet it was precisely in the existence of such thought that ideas
took root that were to bear fruit after the French Revolution.

4. From the French Revolution to the Napoleonic *Code civil*

The tumultuous events of 14 July 1789 signaling the beginning of
the French Revolution produced a violent break with the past and
toppled the previous structures. The decapitation of a king was the
decapitation of an image of power, and, by imposed or self-imposed
exclusion, it brought with it the fall of the entire "order" or "estate"
of the nobility. After the Revolution, codes produced a unity of the
legal subject that replaced the plurality of legal subjects of the eigh-

teenth-century law codes. Henceforth it was not only possible but mandatory to legislate solely and in unified fashion for the "citizen" rather than for the "noble," the "bourgeois" and the "peasant."[12] The law was now equal for all, even though in reality individuals might have varying levels of wealth or well-being as well as different levels of culture, sensibility, and professional standing.

In 1804 Napoleon Bonaparte promulgated a code destined to enjoy an extraordinary success, the *Code civil*, which became the model for many other codes and which followed Napoleon's victorious armies, for some time mingling its destiny with the emperor's.

The vast changes brought on by the French Revolution encouraged the emergence of the bourgeoisie, a class that for some time had been gaining strength within the structures of traditional society. It was the bourgeoisie that bent to its advantage the revolution in which it had participated, but that also held in check and exploited the extreme and intransigent violence that had been loosed for an implacable destruction of the old structures of power and society.

Henceforth the bourgeoisie occupied the army posts gradually abandoned—by constraint or by choice—by the nobility. The bourgeoisie staffed the administration and the judiciary, a bureaucratic apparatus that had so grown in personnel, functions, and professional specialization (if not in efficiency) that it could endow its officeholders with a respected and coveted *noblesse de robe*. Unprincipled businessmen, a small but emergent part of the bourgeoisie, worked feverishly and garnered immense profits by supplying logistic support to the imperial armies and purveying to the needs of the military.

Thus the military apparatus, politics, Napoleon's campaigns, and the creation of empire that stretched beyond the frontiers of France to expand over much of Europe worked together to consolidate, buttress, and increase the spiritual and economic strength of the bourgeoisie. The army needed to be backed up by a civil administration ever more open to vast horizons; the professional competence of that administration was in turn challenged to search for practical solutions to the new demands of empire. The merging of the politico-military apparatus with the bureaucratic-administrative and econom-

12. This observation recurs repeatedly in Giovanni Tarello, *Storia della cultura giuridica moderna* (Bologna: Il Mulino, 1976), vol. 1, *Assolutismo e codificazione del diritto*; see, for example, 37ff.

ic-speculative apparatus in imperial France made it possible for the wiliest of the bourgeoisie to rise to the top. Such men found fertile terrain in the major state agencies for cultivating their prosperity, and they found a guarantee of security and stability in the social order that the empire had brought to pass.

The judiciary and the more prominent lawyers played an important role in the "era of the triumphant bourgeois."[13] Often the same bourgeois families used their interlocking relations and fortunate combinations of talent and vocation to place their kin in the army, the administration, and the judiciary.

With the nobility thrust aside or excluded and the common people stripped of political and economic responsibility, the bourgeoisie was on the threshold of its golden age. The Napoleonic *Code civil* was the image of its triumph. The simplification brought on by a unified juridical subject and the possibility of an equal status and a sole and identical juridical capacity for all (a capacity dynamically defined as an ability to act that could be blocked only for reasons of pathological incapacity, gender, or age) signaled the elaboration and imposition of a "model" to which every individual's reality must correspond. For example, either the legal construct of property effectively corresponded to a subject who was the owner of something—much wealth or little, movable or immovable goods—or it was an empty, abstract construct invoked by those who owned nothing but who moved and acted to have something, even perhaps to acquire a well-being that would enable them to live without having to work—a life-style that the new bourgeoisie inherited from a portion of the old nobility.

The "certainty of the law" became, and continued to be, the certainty of a social order. The vocation for justice became, and continued to be, a vocation for legality. For the judge, being a "servant of the law" was more important than being a "servant of the prince": it assured a degree of decorum, dignity, and respectability directly proportional to the abstraction of the law.

In every branch of public administration and throughout the world of the lawyers and the liberal professions, new, class-based, and ceremonial attitudes sprang up, borrowed from traditionally aristocratic ideals in decline but never rejected. Some of these—severity, self-con-

---

13. See Eric J. Hobsbawm, *The Age of Capital, 1848–1875* (London: Weidenfeld & Nicolson, 1975).

trol, detachment, courtesy, authority, paternalism, dignity of gesture
and demeanor—permeated the fabric of daily life in social comport-
ment and in parental and familial relations, affecting even the intimacy
of the home in relations between husband and wife and between par-
ents and children. No institution regulated by the French *Code civil*—
the subject, property, legal transactions, obligations, personal and pat-
rimonial relations within the family, succession—failed to reflect this
new world. No silence in the code failed to document the disappear-
ance or neglect of the old aristocracy and the juridical institutions it
found congenial, such as primogeniture, fideicommissum, the exclusion from inheritance of dowered daughters, and so forth.

5. Napoleonic Codes and National Codes in Europe

The age of codifications truly began with the *Code civil*, which in
common parlance became the "Napoleonic Code." In France and in
the parts of Europe occupied by Napoleon's armies the picture was
enriched with the promulgation of a *Code de procédure* in 1806, a *Code
de commerce* in 1807, a *Code pénal* in 1810, and a *Code d'instruction crimi-
nelle* in 1811.

The French may originally have hoped that the *Code civil* would be
extended throughout Europe, following the fortunes and the victories of Napoleon's armies. If such a hope ever existed, events showed
it to be illusory.

On first inspection those initial expectations seemed justified. The
Code civil was translated into Italian, and Napoleon extended it to the
Kingdom of Italy in March 1806, to the Principality of Lucca (1806–
13) in May of that same year, to the Kingdom of Naples (1805–15) in
October 1808 (with the exclusion of provisions on divorce), and to
the Grand Duchy of Tuscany in 1808.

In two areas, however, the Napoleonic Code met with opposition
and resistance. In Prussia the *Landrecht* of 1794 was still in effect, and
it continued in force until 1900, although it should be noted that it
lacked that fundamental characteristic of a code, the unity of the juridical subject for whom the code is destined. In Austria a modern
and excellent general civil code (the *Allgemeines bürgerliches Gesetzbuch*) was promulgated in 1811. That body of laws enjoyed a success
equal to that of the French *Code civil* because it too expressed the principle that the law must be equal for all citizens of the state.

In 1814, when the Congress of Vienna ushered in the period of the "Restoration," the *Code civil* seemed doomed. In Lombardy-Venetia it was substituted on 1 January 1816 by the Austrian Civil Code of 1811. In the Kingdom of the Two Sicilies (Naples was once more joined to Sicily) it was replaced by a new series of codes covering civil, penal, and commercial law and civil and penal procedure. All these were promulgated in 1819 under the title *Codice per lo Regno delle Due Sicilie*. The Duchy of Parma had a new *Codice Civile* in 1820. Tuscany turned back the clock to reinstate Roman and canon law and the "laws" of the Grand Duchy that had been passed before 1808. In Piedmont, and more generally in the Kingdom of Sardinia, which included Piedmont, Liguria, and Sardinia, the *Code civil* was eliminated (although not in Liguria). On the island of Sardinia itself, after a number of abortive attempts between 1817 and 1827, a body of *Leggi civili e criminali pel Regno di Sardegna*—not really a code but materials selected and organized for use in legal practice—was promulgated in 1827 and put into force on 1 January 1828. In 1837 a true *Codice Civile per gli Stati di Sua Maestà il Re di Sardegna*, usually referred to as the *Codice albertino*, was promulgated by King Charles Albert for the three regions that made up the kingdom of the House of Savoy. For its reinstatement of some institutions that had been eliminated from the French and Austrian codes (for example, the *exclusio propter dotem* of daughters from paternal succession) the Albertine Code can be considered one of the most important Italian manifestations of the Restoration, even though its incontestable character as a code made a notable contribution to the legislative revival in Europe.

Thus in Italy the French *Code civil* lost its value as positive law as the various pre-unification Italian states provided, in various ways, for the codification of their laws. Nonetheless (and this is true not only in Italy), the French code remained a model useful for two distinct but connected reasons. On the one hand, it continued to bear concrete and prestigious witness to the new idea of the code and to the "vocation of the century" for "the codified formulation of the law."[14] It expressed and incorporated a new manner of regulating and ordering society; it reflected and satisfied the triumphant bourgeoi-

---

14. In the words of the prime minister, Giovanni Battista Cassinis, in 1860: see Rosario Nicolò, "Codice civile," in *Enciclopedia del Diritto* (Milan: Giuffrè, 1958–), vol. 7 (1960), 240–49, esp. 241–42.

sie's need for stability and certitude, a need that it felt and imposed in order to guarantee its own existence, its role, and its political and professional victories. On the other hand, the *Code civil* suggested specific contents, definitions of institutions, and normative solutions, which meant that its written precepts could be borrowed for provisions to be inserted in the various codes that the European states were drawing up during the first decades of the nineteenth century.

This is what happened in Italy between 1863 and 1865. After the unification of Italy, the new kingdom under the House of Savoy thought it necessary to give a civil code to the nation—among other reasons, in order to express the new political reality in a uniform juridical discipline and to help standardize procedures that had varied from one region to another under previous legal systems. The commission charged with this difficult task, presided over by two successive ministers of justice, Giuseppe Pisanelli and Giuseppe Vacca, completed its task in short order. They had an excellent model in the French *Code civil* of 1804, and they followed it. In particular, the commission borrowed from its model the central and structuring idea that it is useful and possible, hence rightful, to promulgate a code valid for all citizens that provides a law that is the same for all; furthermore, that it is rightful to attempt to discipline the society of the nation in order to help it prosper in such a way that the individual within that society can be safeguarded and guided in his clearly codified rights and in every moment of his life and every aspect of his legitimate activities.

The Italian legislators also mined their French model for innumerable specific articles, with the result that entire sectors of Italian civil life came to be regulated by the new *Codice Civile Italiano* along normative lines broadly similar or identical to those of the French *Code civil* of 1804.

The first *Codice Civile* of a united Italy was promulgated on 25 June 1865 and put into force on 1 January 1866. It was followed in 1883 by a noteworthy *Codice di Commercio*.

6. Code, Interpretation, System

Codifications were rampant throughout Europe in the nineteenth century. Faith in them was extreme, and the fervor of the commissions and governments that set to work on them was as high as their optimistic expectations. What happened in the realm of legislation was mirrored perfectly in the realm of doctrine. A "code" proposed in both its intent and its operation as a complete body of provisions opened the way to interpretation of a logical and formal nature. In the earliest experience of the use of national codes during the first half of the nineteenth century, this demand for logical and formal comprehensiveness had a connection with the definition of the jurist, the judge in particular, since such men were and felt themselves to be "servants of the law." The jurist, however, had neither the obligation nor the capacity to innovate, nor could he modify, amplify, or limit the dictates of the code or of individual laws, but was expected only to understand them and to enunciate their content and their meaning, retracing the legislator's thoughts and coming to a faithful and "declarative" interpretation of the measure in question. These were the aims of the French school of exegesis, one of the chief spokesmen of which was Charles Demolombe. The French school concentrated exclusively on textual exegesis and refused consideration to the isolated datum.

Totally different methods—the methods of the *sistema iuris*—were also attempted, in particular outside of France. Broader interpretations were used to create norms for cases not expressly provided for in the code; failure to do this, it was argued, would result in an incomplete code.

Analogy, extensive interpretation, and arguments *a fortiori*, *a maiori*, and following other *modi arguendi in iure* served, on the one hand, as aids to a refined intellectual gymnastics and, on the other, as a way to enlarge the existing legislative provisions and to fill in possible lacunae. The idea of a "system" was thus joined to the idea of the "code" because both notions promised completeness, certainty, and definitiveness to codified law and because both notions reinforced the bourgeoisie's self-image as the dominant class in the modern national state.

The juridical system displayed its true potential both in the universities—in the theoretical training of new jurists—and in the forensic world of judges and lawyers. The criteria of juridical hermeneutics and the descriptions of juridical institutions became "dogma"—that is, "truths" that were indisputable and that indeed went unchallenged in the last century and a great part of our own century and are still accepted and propagandized as "truths" by weary votaries and inexperienced back-country professors. This nineteenth-century method and its results are usually known as "juridical dogmatics." For this school of thought, interpretation was divided into literal and substantive. Its object must be the individual norm, considered in isolation. The single norm could be analyzed in relation to the historical circumstances that produced it (the so-called "historical interpretation," which, parenthetically, bore no relation to the problem of the historicization of the law, which is something quite different) or in relation to the end or ends that it hypothesized and pursued. Interpretation must also consider the entire network of the "system" within which the individual provision was inserted. There were two reasons for this: first, each single provision reacted on the system, putting its elasticity to the test (that is, its capacity for including the greatest possible number of precepts), thereby contributing to shape the system; second (and a mirror image of the first reason), the system in turn reacted upon the individual norm to orient the interpreter's selection of possible meanings and his decision to pick one of those possible meanings as his own and as logically "true."

Legal science thus applied a refined capacity for logic to its own self-fashioning, and it produced increasingly analytical and complex results. It used abstraction to separate the "system" from social and political reality, because, in both the particular method by which that system was constructed and in that system itself, jurisprudence found the image of an order, the order of the hard-won stability of those who founded and shaped the system. When a class is victorious and gains domination over a society, as did the bourgeoisie during the nineteenth century, or when the absolutism of a sovereign or a dictator annuls or conceals social conflicts and the clashes and tensions among the various social groups, the space available for political action shrinks and the political import of every act and every thought is either passed over in silence, avoided, ignored, or eliminated. Those in power preach the uselessness of politics, while within the dominant social stratum (in the nineteenth century, the bourgeoisie) there develops an analogous but inverse lesson. At the same time the conviction spreads that a complex of social relations, solidly constructed in defense of the role and the spaces that have been conquered, needs only to be "crystallized," consolidated, and made juridically relevant and significant within the symmetry of an organic and complete "system" of thought.

The bourgeoisie expressed and defended itself with the "system" just as it had with the "code." It achieved its most incisive action in the political sphere at the precise moment that it removed society and politics from its intellectual range of observation.

7. Law, Code, and Juridical System in Germany: Thibaut, Savigny, and the Historical School

What happened in Prussia in the realm of the legislative and doctrinal questions that concern us here was truly emblematic, because in Prussia we can clearly see, like twin roots of a mighty tree, the two juridical phenomena of codification (which for the entire nineteenth century remained in the improper form of a "code," that is, in the form of the *Landrecht* of 1794) and of a legal system, which had become dominant by the end of the century.

The year 1814 was important not only for the history of German law but also for legal history throughout Europe. Two famous essays were published in that year, one by Anton Friedrich Justus Thibaut (1772–1840) and the other by Friedrich Carl von Savigny (1779–1861).

In the first of these studies (which was also first in date) Thibaut insists, as the title states, "on the need for a common civil code for Germany."[15] In this work, which shows the clear influence of two great models of recent date, the Napoleonic *Code civil* of 1804 and the Austrian civil code of 1811, Thibaut predicted swift national unification for a land whose unified legislation must operate as a stabilizing element as well as faithfully reflect national unity.

The second of these works was written in polemical opposition to the first. In it Savigny denied that a unified civil code was desirable and doubted, given the current state of Prussia, that the land could provide jurists capable of the task.[16] Prussia, Savigny stated, ran a serious risk of promulgating "an aggregate of single dispositions" rather

15. Anton Friedrich Justus Thibaut, *Ueber die Nothwendigkeit eines allgemeinen bürgerlichen Rechts für Deutschland* (Heidelberg, 1814). This work went through various editions; it is available in Italian translation in A. F. J. Thibaut and F. C. Savigny, *La polemica sulla codificatione*, ed. Giuliano Marini, texts translated by Margherita Peretti (Naples: Edizioni Scientifiche Italiane, 1982), 51–85; bibliographical references p. 50.

16. Friedrich Carl von Savigny, *Vom Beruf unserer Zeit für Gesetzgebung und Rechtswissenschaft* (Heidelberg: Mohr und Zimmer, 1814), available in English as Frederick Charles von Savigny, *Of the Vocation of Our Age for Legislation and Jurisprudence*, trans. Abraham Hayward (New York: Arno Press, 1975, reprint of London: Littlewood, 1831). For the various editions of Savigny, *Vom Beruf,* see Thibaut and Savigny, *La polemica sulla codificazione,* 92; the Italian translation of the essay is on pp. 93–197.

than "an organic whole," a course that would have an outcome different from, or even opposite to, the desired one.[17] Single laws aimed at circumscribed sectors, he stated, would better serve the end of regulating and ordering society. Savigny also stressed the irreducible and essential need for a legal science aware of its own strength and capable of organic development.[18] This is precisely why he entitled his study (usually referred to as *Beruf*, the key word in German) "Of the Vocation of our Age for Legislation and Jurisprudence."

It has been observed that Savigny's thought displays two partially conflicting tendencies that coexist "in a strong intellectual tension." On the one hand, Savigny was "oriented toward juridical theory and the ethics of liberty" and for that reason was sensitive to the cultural and political panorama within which the triumphant bourgeoisie took its place; on the other hand, he was "led . . . to support the cause of the historical rights of the Crown, of the Church, of the corporations [guilds], and of the privileged strata."[19] Threading his way between the bourgeoisie, which expressed itself in the codes and fought for national unity (rather, for the various national unities), and the traditional structures that supported the Prussian crown and the church, Savigny chose his own autonomous path, one linked to the demands of theory and connected with solid cultural traditions represented and symbolized above all by the authority of Immanuel Kant. The alternative seemed clearly drawn. On the one hand there were the mechanisms of the modern state—mechanisms that, throughout Europe of the late eighteenth and early nineteenth centuries, were primarily and principally constructed on the model (if not by the efforts) of the French military, bureaucratic, administrative, and legal structures, and that drew support from the broader circles of economic operators, speculators, and businessmen. On the other hand there were the men of law who crowded the courts from the lowest levels to the thresholds of the major magistracies.

17. Savigny, *Vom Beruf*, 157; Thibaut and Savigny, *La polemica sulla codificazione*, 194; quoted from Savigny, *Of the Vocation*, 178.
18. Thibaut and Savigny, *La polemica*, 197.
19. Franz Wieacker, *Privatrechtsgeschichte der Neuzeit unter besonderer Berücksichtigung der deutschen Entwicklung*, 2d ed. (Göttingen: Vanderhoeck und Ruprecht, 1967), in Italian translation as *Storia del diritto privato moderno con particolare riguardo alla Germania*, trans. Umberto Santarelli and Sandro Angelo Fusco, 2 vols. (Milan: Giuffrè, 1980), 2:59.

Savigny avoided choosing between the interests and the "vocations" of these two camps to follow his own, autonomous path. The "apparatus" that seemed to him the most important was his own professional group of scholars and academics. The university remained uppermost in his mind, and he benefited from two strokes of good fortune: the first was his appointment at the University of Berlin (just founded), which enabled him to leave the provincial University of Landshut in Bavaria; the second was the presence in Berlin of Wilhelm von Humboldt (d. 1835). Humboldt was a moving force in a vast restructuring of the model of the modern university, and he deserves mention here for a memoir destined to become famous, written, perhaps in 1810, on the occasion of the inauguration of the University of Berlin.[20] The basic thrust of this study was that the university must contain, defend, cultivate, and encourage "man's spiritual life" and man's vocation (which was both a duty and a need) for knowledge and study. For that reason the university was the institution best fitted for the formation of a "method" and for teaching or learning that "method." Beyond the undeniable influence these notions had on Savigny, and beyond their historical relevance for their contemporaries, they might well offer matter for meditation even today and still prove pivotal to the life and the structure of universities in all civilized countries.

Undeniably, Savigny's "activity as a reorganizer of universities and academies, placed within the context of intellectual and political circles in Berlin, should not be underrated."[21] Nor should it be thought episodic, unimportant, or aberrant within Savigny's own thought or within the objectives of that thought.

The kernel of Savigny's *Beruf* and of his polemic with Thibaut lay in the idea that it was not the task of the institution of legislative power to elaborate a "general code"; furthermore, it was not realistic to think that a "code" could be imposed on a people exclusively by following rational schemes often remote from the history of the society to which the "code" was attempting to give order. Savigny held instead that the legislator must limit himself to promulgating norms

20. Wilhelm von Humboldt, "Über die innere und äussere Organisation der hoheren wissenschaftlichen Anstalten in Berlin" (Berlin: 1810), in Wilhelm von Humboldt, *Gesammelte Schriften*, 17 vols. in 20 (Königlich Preussischen Akademie der Wissenschaften, Berlin: B. Behr, 1903–36), vol. 10, ed. Bruno Gebhardt, 250–60.
21. Wieacker, *Privatrechtsgeschichte der Neuzeit*; *Storia del diritto privato moderno*, 2:56.

for circumscribed sectors and must make his precepts fit within the determinations of legal doctrine—that is, he must follow the concrete and specific facts of "jurisprudence," a term that Savigny uses in a broad sense to refer both to the practical activities of judges and lawyers and the theoretical work of jurists. For Savigny, jurisprudence alone was in a position to define and comprehend the "spirit of the people"—the *Volksgeist*—and to give concrete form to that spirit by proposing and even redacting the texts of specific provisions that the legislator would then take responsibility for promulgating in the exercise of his exclusive legislative power. What is more, the legislator would have to take that responsibility; he could not act arbitrarily, nor should he have "extravagant anticipations" for the realization of "absolute perfection" as he might when he founded legislative projects of his own on "reason" alone.[22] The legislator must instead adhere to the content that jurisprudence constructed and imposed, interpreting "the spirit of the people" and attributing to himself the monopoly on that interpretation (a monopoly that had clear advantages in terms of prestige and power).

Thus doctrine (theory elaborated in the universities) became the vehicle for a precise and lucid political option, because it was doctrine that took responsibility for discerning the norms that various peoples, operating through custom, had created and respected, and because it was doctrine that took on the burden of interpreting and expressing the "spirit of the people."

What gave Savigny's thought homogeneity and enhanced the function of legal doctrine even more was the importance that he assigned to the *Volksgeist*. Savigny held that, in order to translate "the spirit of the people" into a legal precept, the jurist should not look to the people or to the society in which the people is always the principal actor but rather to the way in which the people had been viewed and represented by the jurists of the past, within the tradition of Western thought in general and German thought in particular. History had to offer certain and unchanging fact, not the events in which the people may have played the part of either hero or succubus, but rather the spirit of the people, as it had been historically configured, consolidated, and structured—the spirit of the people reexperienced and

22. Thibaut and Savigny, *La polemica sulla codificazione*, 95; quoted from Savigny, *Of the Vocation*, 178.

comprehended as it had been expressed by a succession of jurists through time, contributing to and shaping tradition by their writings. For Savigny, tradition was the determinant and conditioning historical "given" in the face of which neither the jurist nor, for even greater reason, the apparatus of state—not even legislative agencies eager to construct a code or the crown itself—could think or act arbitrarily.

These are the reasons that led historians to consider Savigny the founder of the "historical school of law."

The jurist emerged as playing an overwhelmingly important role in this view. Not by chance, that role found strong support in both the idea and the structure of the university, conceived and realized (following Humboldt and Savigny) as a center for training in methodology (rather than as a professional school) and as the focal point for a new elaboration of the law.

8. From the Historical School to the Pandectists

It is almost a corollary to Savigny's approach that although a "people" can live without a code, it cannot live without a legal "system" that serves to define all relations juridically by the guarantee that gives every individual the same legal status. The "norm"—that is, the specific solution offered by a provision—is marginal next to the process of legal status. If, for example, a relation between a man and a *res* is defined as *dominium*, any precept is marginal that provides in a specific manner, with more or less detail, for the various "faculties" already included in the theoretical figure of *dominium* in view of proposing all those "faculties" or even of admitting many and excluding some (which is what makes the norm marginal). Juridical "figures" were needed if relations were to be defined, and those constructs, in Savigny's view, had been created and were readily available (with the clarity and irreducible concision that was the secret of Roman jurisprudence) only in the Roman law—the law of ancient Rome and that same law as it had been revised and reinterpreted in the Middle Ages (the *ius commune*). As Savigny wrote, despite the "blind rage for improvement" of the eighteenth-century Enlightenment, one must not lose "all sense and feeling for the greatness characteristic of other times . . . all, consequently, that is wholesome and profitable in history."[23]

23. Ibid., quoted from Savigny, *Of the Vocation*, 20.

Thus Savigny moved quite naturally from his "historicist" thought to develop a "systematic" thought, and indeed his longest work, a classic and a monument in European legal science, is entitled *System of the Modern Roman Law*.[24] In this work the roots of an ancient thought—the thought of the great Roman jurisconsults and of the great jurists of the Middle Ages—were joined and mingled, thanks to an infusion of new vital fluids, with a new thought that resisted the rampant vogue for codification with a staunch defense of "jurisprudence" and its "function" and "vocation."

Savigny's thought gave rise to a scholarly movement whose members were known as "Pandectists," a name taken from that given to Justinian's *Digest* (*Pandectae*), which means a comprehensive legal work. The leading figures in this school were Karl Adolph von Vangerow in Heidelberg (1808–70), Alois von Brinz in Munich (1820–87), Karl Ludwig Arndts von Arnesberg (1803–78), the author of a well-received textbook on Pandects first published in 1852 that went through fourteen editions, Heinrich Dernburg (1829–1907), and, above all, Bernhard Windscheid (1817–92). These nineteenth-century jurists absorbed and interpreted the bourgeois spirit of their age with genius and acute sensitivity.

With the Pandectists the legal "system" crystallized and became the true object of juridical science. Laws became marginal to that science, which rigorously and absolutely excluded "the moral, social, and political conditions" of the community.[25] In this way, the Pandectists gave expression to a rigid formalism operating within a theoretical construction that was at its base ethical but was empty and neutral in its conformation. Thus the jurist-theorist interpreted and realized the need for "order" and "certainty" of the dominant social strata (the bourgeoisie, first and foremost), assured them "rules of the game"

24. Friedrich Carl von Savigny, *System des heutigen römischen Rechts*, 2d ed., 9 vols. (Berlin: Veit und Comp., 1840–56). See esp. Savigny, preface to *System*, vol. 9, *Sachen- und Quellen- Register zu von Savigny's System des heutigen römischen Rechts*, ed. Otto Ludwig Heuser; reprint (Aalen: Scientia, 1981). Vol. 1 of the *System* is available in English as *System of the Modern Roman Law*, trans. William Holloway (Westport, CT: Hyperion Press, 1979, reprinted from Madras: J. Higginbotham, 1867); vol. 2 is available as *Jural Relations: or, The Roman Law of Persons as Subjects of Jural Relations*, trans. W. H. Rattigan (Westport, CT: Hyperion Press, 1979, reprinted from London: Wildy & Sons, 1884).

25. Wieacker, *Privatrechtsgeschichte der Neuzeit*; *Storia del diritto privato moderno*, 2:135 n.25.

that could be freely utilized by anyone who had the (economic) means to do so, and guaranteed each component part of those strata sufficient liberty that individuals could choose their own ends, determine their own actions, and satisfy their own needs on the basis of personal "motives" extraneous to the system and therefore held to be extrajuridical. In this way, juridical resources were merely instrumental; out of respect for individual liberty this order did not focus on the motivations or the ends on the basis of which people acted, did not assign juridical relevance to those motivations and ends, and did not indicate what should or must be done.

What emerged was a framework that obliged the jurists only to see to it that the theoretical constructs had been respected and to judge whether or not the "rules of the game" had been followed. It also obliged them to take no account of the person who, as an integral being in a specific ethical, social, and economic setting, had performed an act or had been involved in a conflict of interest. "Pouvoir neutre, pouvoir nulle"—where power is neutral it does not exist— applied to judges. Thus the judiciary, one of the great branches of the apparatus of state, was seriously confined, limited, and conditioned by another sort of apparatus, the academic. Throughout the nineteenth century and even after, academic and university circles controlled jurisprudence in German-speaking lands; in fact, until as late as 1900, they succeeded in blocking codification of the law, a highly visible phenomenon that had achieved sweeping and lasting successes in other European lands. This explains the lofty dignity and enormous prestige that German and European universities enjoyed throughout the nineteenth century and for a good part of the twentieth century.

The Pandectists thus had an enormous and incisive influence on jurisprudence throughout continental Europe; they were responsible for consequences of fundamental importance in the historical long term. They created a European legal science that proved capable of overcoming the national barriers set up by the various national codes. They connected the new legal science with the old in a redoubtable historical continuum. They returned to the juridical methodology of the ancient Roman jurists and to the refined theoretical elaborations of a medieval jurisprudence that had both enriched European culture and civilization (by its rereading of the ancient Roman law and its interpretation of the medieval canon law) and had enhanced that legacy and defended it from the attacks of "enlightened" eighteenth-century utopians.

9. Critique of the Pandectists: Naturalist and Marxist Opposition

Some nineteenth-century thinkers were more cautious about excluding human and social conditions from juristic theory or else openly opposed the Pandectists. Among them a naturalistic school of thought urged jurists to take greater responsibility for examining what "nature" knew and produced.

Rudolf von Jhering (1818–92) was a leading figure in this movement. One of his works was a clever and well-received book made up of the "Confidential Letters of an Anonymous Correspondent on Contemporary Juridical Science," addressed to the editors of the *Preussische Gerichtszeitung*.[26] These letters were published in book form, along with other pieces, under the ironic title *The Serious and the Facetious in Jurisprudence* (*Scherz und Ernst in der Jurisprudenz*). The work launched a major critical debate on the "dogmas" of the Pandectists.[27]

An example may perhaps clarify the sense of Jhering's "joke." Jhering imagines a peasant riding on a cart loaded with manure or hay, and he pictures the man's joy as he heads for home. What have we "in nature" here, he asks rhetorically, if not the placid presence of the countryman on the cart and the skilled hand that guides the horses. We have, the jurists reply, revealing their different appreciation of the "serious" and the "facetious," the legal construct of "ownership" or "property," because one must qualify juridically the relation between the man and his cart and the load on his cart, and one must ascertain whether that cart and that manure or that hay are "the peasant's" and

26. Later renamed *Deutsche Gerichtszeitung* (1861–66).
27. Four of these pieces were published in 1880 in the *Wiener Juristische Blätter* as "Plaudereien eines Romanisten" (Chats with a Romanist); two unpublished essays were added, "Im juristischen Begriffshimmel: Ein Phantasiebild" (In the Heaven of Juridical Concepts: A Grotesque) and "Wieder auf Erden, wie soll es besser werden?" (Back to Earth: Remedies and Proposals) to form Rudolf Jhering, *Scherz und Ernst in der Jurisprudenz, eine Weinachtsgabe für das juristischen Publikum* (Leipzig, 1884), 4th ed. (Leipzig: Breitkopf und Härtel, 1891; reprint, Darmstadt: Wissenschaftliche Buchgesellschaft, 1988). I have used the Italian translation of this work, *Serio e faceto nella Giurisprudenza*, trans. Giuseppe Lavaggi, introduction Filippo Vassalli (Florence: G. C. Sansoni, 1954).

in what sense they are "his"—by ownership, by possession, or by detention. *Animus domini* is needed in order to establish that they are "his" by possession; otherwise the construct of ownership cannot become embodied in the real situation under examination. At this point the jurist risks losing heart, and Jhering makes his point by treating the question as a "joke": "What would you do, on seeing two carts loaded with manure or hay . . . to discern whether one is guided by a *detentor* and the other by a *possessor*?"[28] Jhering points out that the question was no joke for "poor Habermaier," who for lack of *animus domini* lost his lawsuit and "373 thalers and small change."[29]

The example illustrates the concerns of a theorist with doubts about the "completeness" of the theoretical legal construct and its adequacy to represent facts taken from nature; a theorist who, without renouncing the use of theoretical instruments (or "seriousness"), nonetheless seeks to use irony and facetiousness to comprehend the "nature" that lies beyond theory. Jhering developed this point of view in two weighty tomes written during the same years, *Der Kampf um's Recht* (The Fight for the Law; 1872) and *Der Zweck im Recht* (The Purpose of the Law; 1877–84), works that offered "a consideration of the law as an instrument for the affirmation of power and interests"— a dramatic conclusion if we think of the individual who expected guidance and justice from the law.[30]

Jhering's critique launched a new way of constructing legal reasoning on the basis of an evaluation of the interests involved, henceforth held worthy of inclusion among the things considered juridically relevant, not as the "goal" of the law but as its "object." The resulting "jurisprudence of interests" became a symbol and a banner for jurists who attempted to give juridical relevance to aspects of reality that the sometimes exaggerated formalism of the Pandectists had excluded from juridical observation.

A reliable hermeneutic criterion for the resolution of problems of interpretation emerged from this new position: beyond the literal dictates of the law and beyond the formal aspects of the legal construct used, one must look to the real interests involved and must

28. Jhering, *Scherz und Ernst; Serio e faceto*, 79.
29. Ibid., 80.
30. Wieacker, *Privatrechtsgeschichte der Neuzeit; Storia del diritto privato moderno*, 2:153.

evaluate those interests within the context of elements that, because they were juridically relevant, could point the way to a solution.

A second new development was more disruptive because it did not arise from within Pandectist thought and was not an autonomous and critical stage in the development of that thought. As a theoretical position that denied and radically contested the entire panorama of the dominant juridical culture, including both Pandectist thought and the critique of Pandectist thought, it found expression in the *Zur Kritik der Politischen Ökonomie* (1859) and *Das Kapital* (1867–72) of Karl Marx (1818–83), the fundamental texts of Marxist thought, which had been preceded (in 1848) by the famous *Communist Manifesto* of Marx and Friedrich Engels.

Marx stated that the entire sector of private law was destined to dissolve because the state must penetrate and regulate private life, thus blocking the autonomy of the private individual and eliminating the entire network of private-law institutions that typified that autonomy and also eliminating "freedom" of choice and the power connected with freedom of choice. For Marx, liberty and power were mere abstractions, since both "liberty" and "power" either meant something totally different in the abstract and in the real world or had no concrete existence. This was a direct challenge to the legal constructs that were both paradigmatic in the Western tradition and fundamental to the juridical structure willed and defended by the triumphant bourgeoisie in the nineteenth century: private property, the contract and legal transactions in general, obligations entered into voluntarily and by negotiation, the regime and the very idea of succession *mortis causa*, and the entire field of commercial law.

Anatole France gave a clear illustration of how, in Marxist thought, "freedom" and "power" (to transact, to exercise real rights, to inherit, and so forth) must be negated conceptually as inadequate to represent reality, and how they must even be considered as dangerous for the dominated classes as they were useful for the dominant class.[31] He had a revolutionary poet comment sarcastically that the new laws guaranteed "the majestic egalitarianism of the law, which forbids rich and poor alike to sleep under bridges, to beg in the streets, and to steal bread"—a highly ironic statement, given the improbability that

---

31. Anatole France, *Le Lys Rouge* (1894), chap. 7; cited in Wieacker, *Privatrechtsgeschichte der Neuzeit*; *Storia del diritto privato moderno*, 2:161.

any rich man would have the least desire to sleep under a bridge (even in Paris) or to beg in the streets for his daily bread.

10. The Triumph of Pandectist Thought and the German Civil Code

Despite the various schools of juridical thought assailing it, criticizing it from within or contesting it critically from without, Pandectist thought continued to hold firm at the center of German jurisprudence, and it had an enormous and lasting influence on all European law. Its idea of "system"—which was *sistema iuris*—had a strong impact not only on legal theorists but also on judges: it gave political, ethical, economic, and social neutrality to the logical operations that led to specific judicial decisions, but it also provided legal practitioners with a "textbook" that fast became the principal instrument for resolving legal problems.

That textbook was written by Bernhard Windscheid and was published in German in 1862 under the title of *Pandekten*. The title alone was significant and illuminating, because by echoing the traditional name for Justinian's *Digest* it expressed a clear preference for the portion of Justinian's compilation that focused on *iura* rather than on *leges*, thus reflecting a greater appreciation of jurisprudence than of the laws of the *Code*. Thus new and old were merged; the *sistema iuris* of the new jurisprudence emerged as consonant with the *iura* of the Roman jurists. Windscheid's *Lehrbuch des Pandektenrechts* had an extraordinarily large circulation in Germany (a seventh edition, revised by the author, was published in 1891) and not only in Germany. The work traveled across every national frontier and, translated into a number of languages, became an essential text throughout continental Europe.

Windscheid's textbook was of fundamental importance not only for its circulation throughout Europe and for the admiration that it inspired and the acceptance it received. In clear prose and enclosed within a reasoned and programmatically exhaustive summary, it set down the problems that the Pandectists had debated and the solutions they had reached. As a result, many of its parts and the entire systematic spirit that animated it were transfused into articles of law in the civil code drawn up for Germany in 1900, the *Bürgerliches Gesetzbuch*, or *B.G.B.*, as it is commonly known.

Bernhard Windscheid himself played a leading role in codification. As a member from 1880 to 1883 of the first commission for the codification of German law, he was able to cast the first draft of the civil code in the Pandectist mold and to propose the use, in certain specific areas of legislation, of the expository structure that was both his own and the trademark of the Pandectists. Windscheid's presence on the commission, his personal prestige, and his scholarly activities helped to solder the new civil code to the Pandectist "system" that dominated all sectors of jurisprudence—the university, the world of the lawyers, and the administration. As a result, the code was pivotal for the entire problematic area that concerned the jurist—although it still did not cover certain aspects of private life such as relations within the royal family, domestic labor, agricultural labor, subsoil rights, and questions related to mining.

ii. Nations and National Codes in Europe:
The *Testo unico* as a Model

If we turn to the larger European scene, we can see that in the early twentieth century it teemed with national codes. What is more, legislation in some sectors rapidly diverged, and it was further complicated (if not confused) by social motives and social demands often expressed in spontaneous riots or planned, organized conflicts. Political circles tended increasingly to seek compromise solutions. A new problem was thus posed, but there was at least a partial return to older ways in collections of norms that resembled the eighteenth-century consolidations more than the codes. In Italy such a collection was called a *testo unico*—a "one text."

The *testi unici* were not "by nature" as organic and systematic as the codes; unlike the codes, they were not burdened (and for good reason) with the task of proposing new principles, nor could they offer an opportunity to test new hermeneutic criteria.

To take only one example, a "Testo Unico sul lavoro delle donne e dei fanciulli" (Unique Text on the Labor of Women and Children) was drawn up on 10 November 1907 and published on 16 January 1908. The example is an important one, as this *testo unico* attempted to bring together and to strike a balance between two sets of social problems that were particularly acute in late nineteenth-century and early twentieth-century Italy. On the one hand, it dealt with juridical topics concerning labor that showed the effects of the labor struggles that were rampant (during these same years, the first "strike" actions in the newly consolidated industries of northern Italy were taking place). On the other hand, it dealt with the juridical topic of the "protection" of women and children—a question that jurists still spoke of in terms of "protection," disregarding the more radical demands for equality of the sexes advanced and defended by the feminist movements of the age. In the dominant point of view the preeminent and essential function of women was childbearing and the raising and guidance of children, which was why the human condition and the health of women deserved special regard in the home and, with even more reason, in the factory.

In the meantime the first rifts began to be apparent in the Italian *Codice Civile* of 1865 and in the *Codice di Commercio* of 1883, and some attempt was made to repair the damage with stopgap legislation in the form of bills. One such attempt was the law of 17 July 1919 (not coincidentally, soon after the end of World War I), which abrogated a number of articles of the civil code (numbers 134, 135, 136, 137, and part of article 1743) on marital authorization. Articles 13, 14, and 15 on the same topic were eliminated from the commercial code as well, and articles 252 and 273 in that same document on the "family council" were modified.

12. Italian Codes Today: Signs of Crisis

In Italy the last triumph of the idea of codification was celebrated during the twenty years of the fascist regime. The leading proponent of the movement was a skilled jurist, Alfredo Rocco, who, in the ministerial post of Keeper of the Seal, launched the last season of the Italian codes. Rocco considered the problem of codification to be an important element in his overall vision of society and the fascist state; to quote Alberto Aquarone, it played a decisive part in the "organization of the totalitarian state."[32] The *Codice Penale* was issued in 1930, at the same time as the *Codice di Procedura Penale*. Although as minister Rocco ranked well below King Victor Emmanuel III and President of the Council Benito Mussolini, the penal code is (quite properly)

---

32. Alberto Aquarone, *L'organizzazione dello Stato totalitario*, 2d ed. (Turin: G. Einaudi, 1965).

known as the "Codice Rocco." It supported the fascist doctrine of the state in two important ways: first, it presented the idea of an organic "code" as the expression of the social predominance of one class—the bourgeoisie—in the authoritarian and absolutist interpretation that dictatorship gave of the interests of that class; second, it provided an opportunity to translate the absolutist politics of dictatorship into specific articles of law.

The fascist regime put continuous and intense efforts into codification, which bore fruit in only a few years. The *Codice di Procedura Civile* was approved in 1940 and came into force in 1942. The *Codice Civile*, begun in 1938, was promulgated on its completion in 1942, when it replaced the civil code of 1865, absorbing and canceling the old *Codice di Commercio* of 1883. These were the last flickerings of the codification movement.

13. The Age of Decodification

In more recent history, when Italy, defeated in World War II, overthrew the fascist regime and replaced the monarchy of the House of Savoy with the Republic, the new Italian state needed to derogate or abrogate some of the provisions of the *Codice Civile* of 1942. Since then, much more devastating changes have taken place, profoundly impairing and in part overthrowing the original structure of the nineteenth-century codes and many of the principles embodied in them. The term usually used to describe these events, "decodification," gives a clear notion of their impact.[33] Their effects can be grouped in a few main categories.

First, the decodification movement "got around" the codes, compressing them or bypassing them by means of sweeping supplementary legislation in the form of bills on a vast number of topics. As early as 1933 Italy had laws concerning the bill of exchange (R.D. 14.12.1933, no. 1669) and the bank check (R.D. 21.12.1933, no. 1736) that the code of 1942 neither incorporated nor replaced, but from that date more and more special laws were passed covering broad areas of the law that closed up the gaps in the Codice Civile and cut off its capacity to

33. See Natalino Irti, *L'età della decodificazione* (1972). The second edition of this work (Milan: Giuffrè, 1986) includes an article, Natalino Irti, "L'età della decodificazione," that first appeared in *Diritto e Società* (1978).

expand. Among these were a law on bankruptcy (16 March 1942), laws on cooperatives (1947 and after), "Workers' Statutes" (1970), laws on industrial patents, and more.

Second, there were attempts to refurbish and recast the *Codice Civile*, either by the elimination of provisions that had been declared contrary to the Constitution of 1948 by the Corte Costituzionale, Italy's highest court, or by the abrogation or replacement of groups of articles. This was the case, for example, concerning provisions on divorce and family law. Third, some articles and some "institutes" of the *Codice Civile* were "frozen." They were neither abrogated nor declared unconstitutional, but their application was suspended when they were succeeded by special laws. For example, the rental of urban real property and leasing of rural properties were placed under special and temporary regimes that contravened the provisions of the *Codice Civile*.

It would be a mistake to neglect (and worse to ignore) the historical significance of these frequent and highly visible events. They document not only the need for more up-to-date regulation than was offered by the *Codice Civile* of 1942 but also the fact that the entire idea of a civil code had become outmoded. The civil code remained unmodified, and its old text was still applied only where it touched on topics of modest scope and usually of slight economic importance— the right to an external source of light or to windows facing neighboring property, the regulation of property boundaries, some questions of inheritance—or else it showed the influence of the need for new laws, as in the relationship of the classic constructs of societies of persons and of capital to the legal constructs of the cooperative and the *consorzio* (agricultural or industrial association).

The decodification of national law codes—by hemming them in with further legislation, by restoring and revising them, and by "freezing" certain articles—affected all the nations of continental Europe. The codes, originally conceived to bring unity to the various national laws, were submerged by the hundreds of thousands of pieces of legislation that were passed in each country (more than five hundred thousand in Italy alone, according to a survey made by the Corte Costituzionale). These were upsetting statistics in the literal sense that they overturned the codified system of law. Some scholars with a penchant for serious reflection were led to extreme conclusions. Natalino Irti wrote, "The *Codice Civile* cannot be recognized as having . . . the value of general law, [or as being] the seat of principles that are set forth and

'specified' by external laws." The best that could be said, Irti concluded, was that the code "functions henceforth as a 'residual law,' as a
discipline for cases not regulated by particular provisions."[34]

This conclusion probably goes too far, because both the jurist and
the citizen, for whom the law was created, have need of principles.
Nonetheless, it expresses clearly the malaise and disorientation of the
modern jurist. After the rational, reform-minded, and "enlightened"
eighteenth century and the age of the great nineteenth-century codes,
the jurist in continental Europe had been accustomed to thinking of
his own times as an epoch of order, unity, and the equality of the
citizens before a clear, unambiguous, homogeneous, and knowable
law. The modern jurist was persuaded that he had left the age of confusion far behind him and that he had eliminated the "defects of jurisprudence" that had been generated and fueled by a plurality of laws
and by the infinite number of ways in which they could be interpreted. He was so sure of this that he gave a pejorative sense to the adjec-
tive "medieval," which he applied to the entire period between the
ancient and the modern worlds (roughly the period from the sixth to
the fifteenth century). For over two centuries—the eighteenth to the
twentieth—any provision not linked to the order and certitude of a
unified code was "medieval." Moreover, although the German "historical school" (Savigny in particular) had warned that there were
limits, risks, and dangers in a purely "rational" organization of juridical problems, nonetheless the "Pandectist" sequel to that school had
worked, during the latter half of the nineteenth century, to sustain an
illusion of order, albeit in the name of a *sistema iuris* rather than a
sistema legis.

Our own decades are living examples of confusion, uncertainties,
difficulties, and unforeseen needs. As with all historical ages, even
these difficult decades require historical analysis.

14. From Decodification toward New Forms of Stability?

The fact that civil codes are outmoded and inadequate—in Italy
and throughout Europe—is, historically speaking, a reflection of a
new dimension and a change in the composition of the forces that
make up society today—forces that are diversifying within the old

34. Irti, *L'età della decodificazione*, 2d ed., 27.

bourgeoisie, that are seeking a new equilibrium, and that are attracting new elements and excluding some of the older ones. This is all taking place within political parties, labor unions, and associations, both public and secret, licit and illicit; within institutions and outside of institutions. At the same time the social and economic distances among entire sectors of the lower middle class and the world of labor are diminishing or disappearing, and power relationships (even economic ones) are being overturned. An emergent bureaucratic proletariat is discontent with its daily tasks but not with its ambiguous social status. It is a proletariat that neutralizes its internal tensions, its ambitions, and its expectations by bending and distorting its sense of the office that it exercises and by projecting the function of that office into the sphere of an abusive power rather than in dutiful fulfillment of institutional obligations; a proletariat that plans and realizes entrepreneurial adventures in a number of directions in crafts, commerce, and light industry.

The state, in the face of so many changes, is modifying the very nature of legislative action. It has rightly been observed that Italy has already shifted from a law perceived as establishing the "rules of the game" (the forms and procedures of acts, not their ends or their nature) to a law that guides the activities of individuals, offers incentives to entrepreneurship, and prefigures the development of entire sectors of the economy.[35] We have passed from a state that proposed no more than a "road map" and that left its citizens full freedom and responsibility to choose their routes (provided that they respected certain predetermined road signs) to a state that points to and at times prescribes the road that we must take and preestablishes its point of arrival.[36]

We need to "construct" a new manner of being a jurist and define a new role for the jurist. A systematic code, perceived programmatically and experienced as a projection of an arrived-at social order, is now being replaced by laws that chart a course or lay down a plan; laws that can be the result of lacerating, even ruinous, compromises among the social and economic forces that have won a voice in parliamentary debate. The last ripple of the long swell of cultural and academic power is dying out on this shore.

35. Ibid., 14ff.
36. See Franz A. Hayek, *The Road to Serfdom* (1944) (Chicago: University of Chicago Press, 1976); Irti, *L'età della decodificazione*, 2d ed., 15.

From the point of view of history, then, the age of codification is over. Now when a government manages to promulgate a code, as in Italy in 1988 with the *Codice di Procedura Penale*, the variety of social and political forces that it reflects, the tensions among them, and the compromises that leave traces coagulated in the code generate defects that soon lead to a need to retouch or recast the code or reshape specific articles, even to revise the overall thrust of the code or the specific provisions in entire sectors of it. We have been in the age of decodification for some years now.

When the legal historians, the admirers of positive law, and even the legal practitioners became aware of this fact, they realized that they had lost a secure haven, and with it a faith that had lasted for some two centuries. As late as the 1960s, one lingerer attempted to reconstruct the history of codification as an exemplary story of men who, thanks to their dedication, their instincts, and their political talents, their wisdom and their stability, rescued modern societies from the "discomfort" of a "confused state of legislation" that had been caused "above all by laws reforming local statutes and by princely laws" and by the "deformity of the . . . decisions" of judicial organisms.[37] Others have devoted years of study and reflection to "constitutions" and "codifications," and they continue to publish books and articles on these topics with an invincible faith that nothing has changed and that the history of those phenomena still holds the key for evaluating current experience. For them, the disorder and confusion of contemporary legislation and the obvious deformities in the sentences handed down by judges are all to be attributed to human malice, if not to ill will, ignorance, and uncouthness, whereas a model exists—the dual model of the code and the constitution—that is adequate per se because it was conceived and put into effect precisely in order to remove confusion, disorder, and malice.[38]

It is not the historian's task to predict the future or to say what the law will be like in the years to come. What is certain is that a new legal system is being created. Those who are forging it belong to the political, the economic, and the social spheres; they are legal prac-

37. Vincenzo Piano Mortari, "Codice: Premessa storica," in *Enciclopedia del Diritto*, vol. 8 (1960), 229.

38. For a recent example of this threadbare and reiterative historiography, see Carlo Ghisalberti, *Modelli costituzionali e Stato risorgimentale* (Rome: Carucci, 1987).

titioners, judges, and bureaucrats. Behind them one catches glimpses of some of the less somnolent professors in European and North American universities.

15. Ruins of the Modern Age: The "Codistic" Vision of the Law

The historian of the law has an obligation to emphasize certain perspectives and an interest in doing so. First, it is now clear that all rigid and fideistic "codistic" views of the law have lived their allotted span, marked and compromised as they are by exhausting their capacity to respond adequately to the composite social and economic situation today. Similarly, all "systematic" and "dogmatic" representations anchored to the text of a code are equally dated.

Second, it is just as clear that study of the age of codifications cannot take as its point of departure the Enlightenment hope (or utopia) of arriving at the best possible remedy for disorder and confusion in laws, decisions, or doctrines; nor can it rely on the complacent satisfaction that awareness and contemplation of a phenomenon offer those who seek a safe haven.

Third, it is also clear that continental Europe must begin from the beginning to seek juridical instruments adequate to repair the damage that massive numbers of laws, the difficulty of knowing them, and men's decisions can produce.

In this connection, the increasing curiosity and interest of European jurists and scholars in the juridical experience of Anglo-American lands—countries of Anglo-American common law—is an interesting topic that is beyond the scope of the present work but one whose historical relevance deserves more than passing note.

In the same connection, however, there is also historical relevance in a reconstruction of the complex experience of another sort of "common law"—*ius commune*—in Europe in the twelfth century. In a political and social climate of profound changes, that experience was not only the terrain on which extensive and repeated renovation took place on the European continent but also a secure point of reference in the tumultuous variety of particular systems of law (*iura propria*). For a number of reasons, reconstruction of this experience is now easier and has greater significance than some years ago. In the first place, the *ius commune* no longer bears the weight of the negative views of advocates of the consoling light of the new "codes," who saw nothing in medieval law but confusion and harrowing contradictions and who predicted that the new codes would be strongholds of order and certainty. The lens (which was at times a distorting lens) of the law as code, through which people were "constrained" to regard historical events in the Middle Ages and the early modern period, now lies shattered. What is more, people today recognize much of themselves and their own times, their doubts, and their problems in the concerns, the uncertainty, the violence, and the anxiety connected with justice during the Middle Ages. Thus an age long held to be remote and judged negatively—even the neutral term "medieval" was used in a pejorative sense—has now come back into fashion.

In order to clarify and solidify that experience in collective memory, we need to trace the historical conditions of an epoch that had no "jurists" and few written laws—the long age that began somewhere between the fifth and the sixth century and that ended in the eleventh century. Next we need to trace the changes that in the extremely rapid, intense, and creative crisis of the twelfth century led to faith and trust in the "sacred" texts of the *ius commune*, to the everyday practice of written law, and to the emergence of the figure of the "jurist." We also need to look at attempts that the same age made to strike a subtle and difficult balance among solutions always sought, with declared or implicit candor, in support of an absolute "Justice," but also defended, out of conviction or as an astute covert, tactical move, to safeguard and guarantee the political and economic spheres of operation of individuals, groups, or social strata.

2

Per pugnam sine iustitia
An Age without Jurists

The Gradual Disappearance of the Professional Jurist

At first sight it would seem to require a great effort to imagine an age without jurists. The idea becomes more comprehensible, however, if we heed Emperor Theodosius II and a passage in the constitution "De auctoritate Codicis" that prefaced the *Codex* of 438. The emperor says of jurists that "there are seldom any who have full command [*scientia*] of civil law," adding, "among so many dreary, bungling lucubrations it is difficult to find anyone who has received solid and complete doctrines."[1]

In the Western Roman Empire in A.D. 438 events had not yet reached the precipitous climax of the deposition of Romulus Augustulus in 476. Thus Theodosius was speaking of the lands that are now Europe.

We know that at the time there were vast stretches of thinly populated territories on the European continent, that civil life had shrunk to within a few cities, and that in rural areas, which were sometimes dominated by a town or an urban settlement, tradition governed the pace of work unless the peace was disturbed by bands of brigands on occasion joined by miscreant monks of dubious morality, utter vagabonds, and savage forest-dwellers. We know that the average lifespan was short and that people were considered lucky to live beyond the

---

1. Theodosius, *Const.* "De auctoritate Codicis": "Tam pauci raroque extiterit qui plena iuris civilis scientia ditaretur, et in tanto lucubrationum tristi pallore vix unus aut alter receperit soliditatem perfectae doctrinae."

age of forty; that illiteracy was the rule; that even a king—Theodoric, for example—found it difficult to write so much as the first letter of his name; and that everywhere hunger, brought on by famine, destitution, or ravaging armies, and death by sporadic epidemics or devastating plagues made simple survival the most urgent problem.

Only a few cities could lay claim to any splendor: Ravenna was first among these, followed by other cities of the coasts of the Adriatic (Rimini, Ancona) or the Ionian Sea (Otranto). Cities outside Italy included Marseilles, Arles, and Toulouse in southern France, Lyons in Burgundy, Toledo, Saragossa, and Seville on the Iberian Peninsula.

Rome was in full decline. The Senate, reduced to a shadow of its former power, was withering away, its horizons narrowed to local and provincial matters. The time when the voices raised in the Senate represented the most vital forces in the entire empire was only a memory. The cultural elites were in total collapse. In 533 there were perhaps three professors (one of them a jurist), all poorly paid if at all, if we can take Cassiodorus's word for it.[2]

2. Anthologies and Epitomes in the West: Doctrine and Legislation

In the early years of the sixth century some notice crops up of barbarian kings ambitious to link their names not only to the usual military victories but also to the important act of the promulgation of a "law." There were few if any jurists to put the royal designs into action, so the personnel available did the best they could. Some legal anthologies had survived, and they were refashioned for a variety of reasons—to provide a summary of their contents or to replace a document out of sheer necessity because its pages had worn thin. Thus Alaric, the king of Visigothic Spain and a talented ruler, chose one of these anthologies and in 506 "promulgated" and imposed it as the "law" in his kingdom.

2. See Pierre Riché, *Ecoles et enseignement dans le haut Moyen Age: Fin du Ve siècle, milieu du XIe siècle* (Paris: A. and J. Picard, 1989); Riché, *Les écoles et l'enseignement dans l'Occident chrétien de la fin du Ve siècle au milieu du XIe siècle* (Paris: Aubier Montaigne, 1979), consulted in Italian translation as *Le scuole e l'insegnamento nell'Occidente cristiano dalla fine del V secolo alla metà dell'XI secolo*, trans. Nicolò Messina (Rome: Jouvence, 1984).

According to that remote point of view, this *lex* was the Roman law of the Visigoths—the *Lex Romana Visigothorum*; nonetheless it was an odd "lex" from our point of view fifteen centuries later. For one thing, without concealing anything of its original physiognomy or its character as a private anthology, it was made up of snatches of the *Sententiae* of Paul and fragments of the *Libri responsorum* of Papinian, mixed in with a few imperial constitutions, either from before the Theodosian Code (and, on occasion, included in that Code) or after it. For another, it included a summary of all the *Institutiones* of Gaius—the *Epitome Gai*. Finally, the "legislative" texts (with the exception of the summary of Gaius), were supplemented by explanatory annotations—additions interpreting the various provisions (and indeed called *interpretationes*)—that we would now consider statements of doctrine rather than laws.

In short, examination of this document shows the limited idea that a king might have had of his own "law," even in a kingdom as extensive and important as the Visigothic. It was an idea extremely remote from our own.

The situation was no different in other lands of Western Europe, where norms were always stitched together in this fashion. Nor was there any difference between the way a "legislative" text such as the *Lex Romana Visigothorum* was put together and other anthologies that remained in the state of private compilations such as the *Lex Romana Burgundionum*, the so-called *Lex Romana Raethica Curiensis*, the *Epitome Sancti Galli*, the so-called *Edictum Theoderici*, the *Epitome fuldensis*, and others. In many cases it is difficult to establish whether the manuscript in question conveys a *lex* or whether it incorporates and documents the work of a private individual. One example of a puzzle of this sort is the *Epitome Sancti Galli*, also given as *Lex Romana Curiensis*.

Thus if there were "jurists" in Western Europe, they were capable of little more than knowing how to read, comprehending what they read as best they could. They did not bother to weed out what they did not understand; nor did they take the trouble to reflect on the materials they handled or to wonder whether an anthology could become "law." Nor could they have thought that their contemporaries would hold their labors in very high esteem since they were well aware that most people were ignorant and illiterate, tormented by hunger and cold, and decimated by violence and epidemics.

3. The East: The Great Legislative Compilation of Justinian

Compared to the West, the East was flourishing. It had splendid cities such as Constantinople (Byzantium), the capital of the Roman Empire of the East; it had famous centers of scholarship endowed with rich libraries such as Alexandria, Caesarea, Berytus (now Beirut). Many anthologies were made on these eastern Mediterranean shores that combined selected fragments of imperial edicts with passages taken from older Roman juridical doctrine. These were compilations of modest scope, usually written in Latin, although on occasion, as with the *Scholia Sinaitica ad Ulpianos Libros ad Sabinum*, they were written in Greek. The existence of the great libraries made possible the compilation of such modest anthologies. The jurists' persistence in producing works of that sort is documentary evidence of a legal culture with little learning and of one that relied on inferior authors. Perhaps it is no coincidence that these compilations are anonymous.

Nonetheless, what even a king as powerful as Alaric found it impossible to do in the West, Emperor Justinian managed to do in the East, beginning in 529. Admittedly, Constantinople still had a center of scholarship that functioned efficiently enough to hold firm to an idea of the law that resembled the Roman view of the law in its basic outline and its methodological approach. Thus the constitution "Omnem" drew a distinction between Berytus, "which has rightly been called 'mother of the laws,' "[3] and Alexandria and Caesarea, which it judged more negatively: "We have heard that even in those most splendid cities Alexandria and Caesarea and in others there are certain inexpert men who divagate and transmit an adulterated doctrine to their disciples."[4]

Thus Justinian had available a number of professors whom he could bring together to form a commission: Tribonian, who directed the legislative project; Dorotheus, a professor in that "most splendid city of Berytus"; Theophilus and Cratinus, who were active in the

---

3. Justinian, *Const.* "Omnem," par. 7, "In Berytiensium pulcherrima civitate quam et legum nutricem bene quis appellet."
4. Ibid., "Audivimus etiam in Alexandrina splendidissima civitate et in Caesariensium et in aliis quosdam imperitos homines devagare et doctrinam adulterinam tradere."

capital city, and still others. Nothing of the sort would have been imaginable in Western lands (Italy, Germany, the British Isles, France, Spain). This was the context in which Justinian's famous compilation of laws could be finished in only a few years.

The first step was to publish a "book of constitutions" that brought together in one *Codex* imperial edicts from a variety of epochs up to the reign of Justinian himself.

Next, in 533, a lengthy collection of *iura* was made, the *Digesta* (*Digest*, or Pandects), giving in fifty short "books" a condensed version of passages from ancient Roman doctrine. These were reproduced in the state in which they could still be known, and they often were full of post-classical interpolations and showed signs of having been manipulated and abridged.

In 534 a more complete revised version of the *Codex* (*Code*) divided into twelve "books" was produced. In that same year a textbook of jurisprudence in four "books," the *Institutiones* (*Institutes*), was elevated, by promulgation, to the level of "law." There were instances of similar operations in the West, for example, in the insertion of the *Epitome Gai* into the *Lex Romana Visigothorum*. These reflected a conception of the relationship between the legislative power and the authority of doctrine that permitted no distinction between the sphere of the creation of laws and the sphere of theoretical elaboration of the law.

Next came the *Novellae Constitutiones* (the *Novels*), which listed the decrees that Justinian promulgated until his death in 565. These were compilations made by at least two private individuals: one known as the *Epitome Juliani*, which included 122 constitutions, by Julianus, who was probably a professor at Constantinople; the other, anonymous and called *Authenticum*, which gave the full text of 134 constitutions.[5]

---

5. Today Justinian's laws are most commonly consulted and studied in the late-nineteenth-century German editions: for the *Digesta* there is the so-called *editio maior*, Theodor Mommsen, assumpto in operis societatem Paulo Kruegero (Krüger), 2 vols. (Berolini: apud Weidmannos MDCCCLXX). It contains a lengthy introduction by Mommsen describing the manuscripts used, editorial criteria, and so forth. The *Digesta* were first published in 1868 (the so-called *editio minor*, without Mommsen's introduction), but the edition most frequently used is the 1972 edition in one volume with the *Institutiones*, Paul Krüger (Berolini: apud Weidmannos), precisely because of the connection between the *Digesta* and the *Institutiones*. These form the first volume of the *Corpus*. The *Codex*, Paul Krüger (Berolini: apud Weidmannos, 1877), forms the second

Given the way in which they were compiled, the motivation behind the undertaking (it was linked to the utopian project of reviving the unity and splendor of the Roman Empire), and a broader cultural context that had already deteriorated in the East and had collapsed in the West, Justinian's legislative texts were like a jewel case guarding precious gems and removing them from use. They barely succeeded in conserving and safeguarding scattered and precious fragments of Roman law; despite the intentions and the illusions of Justinian and his commissioners, they served only to pass on an awareness of that law to later ages.

4. The Emperor's Lost Dream

Justinian's legislation found life impossible everywhere. In the East it was in large part extraneous to local customs and even to the ideology of empire. Never applied, in 740 it was formally replaced by a short collection of precepts (in only 144 chapters), *Ecloga tōn nomōn*, a work published in the context of a clumsy attempt at legislation on the part of Emperor Leo III.

In the West, Justinian's legislation was equally extraneous to the *regna* that had been constituted on the ruins of the Roman Empire. It was unknown in the Kingdom of the Visigoths (what is now Spain and part of southern France) in spite of an ephemeral conquest of the eastern portion of the Iberian Peninsula. It was unknown in the Kingdom of the Burgundians, in France under the Salian Franks, and in Germanic lands under the Alemanni and the Bavari.

It arrived in Italy in 554, when the Byzantine armies, after twenty years of devastating battles, reconquered the Italian Peninsula and united it once more with the Eastern Empire. It was the bishop of Rome, Pope Vigilius, who "supplicated" Justinian to pass a law to put his compilations into force, which he did with the promulgation of the *Pragmatica Sanctio pro petitione Vegilii*. Very few people in Italy had the time or the opportunity to become acquainted with that de-

volume of the *Corpus*. The *Novellae* (the third volume of the *Corpus*) was edited by Rudolph Schöll and Wilhelm Kroll (Berolini: apud Weidmannos, 1895). These three works, much reprinted, make up a *corpus* that circulates broadly to this day. The *Digesta* is available in English as *The Digest of Justinian*, ed. Theodor Mommsen with the aid of Paul Kreuger, trans. and ed. Alan Watson, 4 vols. (Philadelphia: University of Pennsylvania Press, 1985).

cree, however, because, beginning in 568, northern and central Italy were thrown into turmoil by the Lombard invasion and occupation, and because more Greek than Latin was spoken in the regions that remained loyal to Byzantium and connected with it, and the people there viewed with hostility laws deriving from a Rome that they remembered as a harsh and rapacious capital.

We know that only a very few copies of the *Institutiones* continued to be known, occasionally read, and modestly annotated. The *Codex* was dismembered: the last three books (dealing with the administration of the empire) fell into neglect; the text of the first nine books was abridged into an extremely rare and incomplete *Epitome Codicis*. The *Digesta* and the *Novellae* were totally lost, save for a few extremely rare fragments of the latter.

Thus in the sixth century, in the very years of its promulgation, the corpus of Justinian's laws moved into a long night that to some contemporaries must have seemed to herald its death. Today we know that its long night lasted roughly six centuries and that the long wait safeguarded the life of those laws.

5. The New Condition in the West

Western Europe came to be inhabited by a number of new and "barbarian" populations. Anyone who was not "Roman" was a "barbarian." The term's negative connotations came from a comparison of customs, always to the disadvantage of the "barbarians." When each of these peoples had become established in a territory of its own—at times after long wanderings—it felt the need of a "law" to give order to its social life. Two motivations joined to define this need and the means for satisfying: first, a desire to retain the "true" form of ancient oral customs that risked becoming contaminated or polluted by contact with Roman populations; second, a desire for a written text that would both preserve the ancient norms and make them known to the "Romans." For "barbarians" and "Romans" alike, the life of society was ruled by custom in unwritten norms known by experience and transmitted from one generation to another. Each of these norms was thought to remain identical to an original kept in folk memory, but in fact oral methods of conservation and oral transmission modified them incessantly, either by deliberate acts or by inattention and error.

The attempt to crystallize the contents of such customs in written form was thus only indirectly presented as the projection of a ruling power; it was more directly linked to the will of a community working to save its own patrimony of customs.

If we keep in mind that customary law was always highly uncertain in Europe between the sixth and the eleventh or twelfth centuries, that specific testimony was often needed to verify a precept (*inquisitio per testes*), and that written redactions of "Roman" customs were often lacking, we can better circumscribe the field within which the barbarian "laws" operated and better evaluate their historical importance. In reality the barbarian "laws" gathered together only a small part of a much vaster and more variegated store of popular usages. They left many customs unrecorded, and their frequent revisions and successive additions to them were insufficient to complete them. Among the "laws" of this sort that might be mentioned here were the *Lex Visigothorum* promulgated by King Recesvinde in 654 for the Kingdom of the Visigoths in Spain (also called *Forum iudiciorum* or *Fuero Juzco*); the *Lex Burgundionum* (also called *Lex Gundobada* or *Gumbata*) promulgated by King Gundobad between the last years of the fifth century and 501; the *Lex Salica*, in force throughout much of what is now France and continually revised from a nucleus that dated from around 511; the *Lex Ripuaria*; and, for Germanic lands, the *Pactus Alamannorum*, which we can date between 584 and 629, the *Lex Alamannorum* of between 712 and 725, and the *Lex Baiwariorum* of 743–44.

Analogous historical processes were taking place in Italy. In 643 the seventeenth Lombard king, Rothari, published an *Edictum* and stated in its preface that he had been led to this act because the *exercitales*, the arms-bearing men (hence the greater part of the young male population), felt a strong need for it. They wanted to have the genuine Lombard customs (*cawarfidae*), whose purity was threatened, set down firmly (*adfixae*) in a certain and authoritative written text. In reality a transformation was already taking place, accelerated by the use of the Latin language to translate the consuetudinary norms into legislative terms. The very idea of publishing the contents of customary norms in the form of royal edicts, thus changing their juridical title, contributed notably to changing them. The redaction of laws continued with Grimoald in 668 and, in particular, with the many *Edicta* of Liutprand from 713 to 735. Liutprand was the first Lombard

king to be converted to Catholicism, with the result that there was a
constant tension in his legislative acts between the more intransigent
and primitive point of view of some of his people attached to the pa-
gan tradition and the point of view of the crown and the parts of the
population that supported the monarchy and openly favored the
Christianization and Romanization of everyday customs and habitual
rites. This tension was particularly evident in a few specific cases. One
example was trial by duel. Single combat was an institution for the
settling of difference typical of populations who saw physical force as
the most adequate means for resolving conflicts of interest. In some
cases, the "judge" in the "trial" (who was not a jurist) was not expected to investigate what had occurred or to try to find the reasons
for it, which were discussed, tested, and weighed in accordance with
preordained formal schemes. Thus such "judges" were not charged
with "judging" in any usual sense but only with being present at a
contest and declaring the "right" of the combatant who, by his physical strength, skill, or luck, was the winner in the field. There was
nonetheless a tendency, vaguely expressed and more often discernible
in the statements of a king than in actual events, for the sovereign to
invite the "judges" to take into account the "laws" (that is, the *Edicta*)
or customary norms, to verify that they had been respected, and, in
case of violation, to oblige the contesting parties to respect them or,
after evaluation of the damages, to oblige the party responsible for
the violation to make reparation.

Further Lombard edicts were emitted under Rachis in 745 and 746,
under Aistulf from 750 to 755 (the *Regnum langobardorum*), and later
with the *leges*, *capitula*, and *pacta* of princes and dukes in Benevento,
Naples, and Spoleto, even after the Franks under Charlemagne had
taken possession of the Lombard kingdom.

6. Oral Laws: Custom; the *Verbum regis* and the Carolingian Capitularies

The laws of the "barbarian" peoples, and among them those of the
Lombards in Italy, were like an archipelago of tiny islands in the vast
sea of custom. Moreover, in a society that had almost totally lost its
centers for primary schooling and where illiteracy was rampant, it
would have been difficult for contemporaries to know the written text

of those laws. Only a few of the clergy, studying in extremely modest monastic or episcopal schools, learned the elements of writing and could manage to read the liturgical texts. "Grammar" had been deeply corrupted and both barbarian and Latin words had undergone deformation. Even syntax had become deformed. Everything was moving precipitously toward the highly mobile and uncertain turmoil out of which the new vernacular tongues (the Romance and national languages) arose in the various lands of Europe between the tenth and the twelfth centuries.

Even someone who knew how to read and write would have found direct acquaintance with a copy of the Lombard edicts extremely difficult. The later Lombard compilation called the *Liber Papiensis* had a limited circulation as well.

This was the situation that Liutprand sought to remedy. First he prohibited the *scribae* (roughly, notaries) from compiling *cartulae* (written acts documenting a juridical act) without direct vision and an actual reading of the text of the law, Lombard or Roman; next, he established that *cartulae* could be written if the legislative text was known at least from the report and testimony of someone who had actually seen it; finally, he established severe penalties for nonobservance of these measures.[6] This edict clearly shows that the very idea of a "law" was by and large beyond the ken of populations that had lived for centuries by orally transmitted customs, and for whom it seemed (and in fact was) a great novelty to rely on a written text, search out a copy of it, or at least have sure evidence of it from a trusted person who might have seen such a copy.

The orality of customary law, which was widespread in most sectors of European society from the sixth to the eighth centuries, emerged on higher levels during the Carolingian age from the eighth to the tenth centuries. In the later period, however, orality was combined with an attempt, in part new, to conceive of the "law" not as a text to certify popular custom but as the expression of a sovereign's will. Although it may have been a pale reflection of the Roman and Byzantine concept of *imperium*, this tendency dissolved and was lost in the practical process of the creation of oral norms. The "laws" of

6. Liutprand, *Edicta*, 91, ed. Friedrich Bluhme, in *Monumenta Germaniae Historica, Leges 4* (Hannover: Hahn, 1869), 144–45.

Charlemagne (768–814) and his successors, which were called *capitula* or *capitularia*, were always oral. What counted was the spoken will of the king, the *verbum regis*. Those who were privileged to hear the sovereign's commands could make notes, and they might write a "text" for themselves and for others that gave proof of the *verbum regis*. That text did not in itself constitute the law, however, hence the wording of the text could be modified, if the content of the precept was not altered—a condition that was violated, maliciously, by error or inadvertence, or perhaps when it proved convenient. As a result, current attempts at historical reconstruction are necessarily uncertain, as uncertain and diverse as the extant texts, not one of which permits knowledge of the true, genuine, original *verbum regis* that launched such a varied textual tradition.

7. The Concept of the Jurist: Significance and Limitations of a Generic Activity

That both customary and imperial norms were oral, that written texts of the barbarian laws were exceptional, that there were variations in content in orally transmitted norms or norms for which a written version was not readily available are all phenomena that we need to take into account when we consider the concept of the jurist in the early Middle Ages in Europe. Formally speaking, in this early period, the "jurist," as that professional category came to be defined in the twelfth century, did not exist and could not have existed.

There were no "jurists" in royal courts in which royal advisors worked modestly to enable some barbarian kings to give "laws" to their kingdoms. The written redactions of the laws that have come down to us show that the authors of those texts did not have a cultural heritage adequate to the task, either from the point of view of a command of grammar and syntax or from the legal point of view, and that they encountered grave difficulties when they transliterated into Latin—the language that was used and had to be used—terms from languages totally different from Latin. Obviously, this did not prevent some redactors of edicts from understanding their times well or from interpreting and lucidly synthesizing the particular motivations of the civilization to which they belonged.

On the level of activity we might call "legal," the concept of the jurist did not exist. It is true that the term *iudex* recurs in Liutprand's *Edicts*, but if we recall that for Liutprand the *iudex* was the person who certified the outcome of a judiciary duel, we will have to define this Latin word in conformity with the ideal representations that the populations in question assigned to it and according to the practice to which it corresponded. With the possible exception of the royal courts (which, in Italy, meant the royal court at Pavia), "judges" were simply "those who judge"; people who, in real life and at a specific moment and a particular time in their lives or their daily activities, found themselves in the position of having to adjudicate. Such men were not professionally engaged in that activity, and when, there was no one person charged with the responsibility of "judgment," an entire group—men able to bear arms, members of the landed aristocracy, or the clergy—could act as "judge."

Such a "judge" had little acquaintance with the customs of the place in which he lived, and if he had memory of them it was because he had become one of the persons who had lived longest in that locality (putting him among the *antiquiores loci*). He often had doubts, or doubts were suggested to him by the litigating parties affected by his decision, about the content of consuetudinary law or even about the existence of a specific norm. In such cases the "judge" might suspend the "trial" and call on the testimony of others among the older and more trustworthy men from the same place or a nearby place—that is, he might open an *inquisitio per testes* (investigation through witnesses) to ask such men what information they could offer on the precept that required clarification, thus guiding his decision.

These "jurists" did not "interpret" a norm or a law. Or rather—which amounts to the same thing—the possibilities for interpretation were so broad and gave so much liberty to the "judge" as to lose all sense of specificity or of following rules that might take textual form into account, look for substantive meaning, or seek the internal logic of the norm or of similar norms. It is difficult to imagine that the "judges" in Lombard or other European lands, many of whom were illiterate, were capable of posing sophisticated problems of that sort. It is easier to imagine them as respectable persons occupied in the exercise of arms (*milites*), in carrying out the responsibilities of religion (the clergy), or more generally in pursuing the peaceful labors of a landowner and proprietor of fields and houses—persons, in

short, who, out of necessity and because of the respect they enjoyed in
the community, took on the trappings of a "judge" and were indeed
"judges" for a day or an hour. If they were judges it was in a sense
unfamiliar to us, not as "men of law" but as "men of justice."

The role of the notary was similar. Actually, other terms are frequently used in the sources—*scriba* or *scriptor*, for example—to designate someone who knew how to write and could put his efforts at the
service of anyone who wanted to document an intended transaction
in writing—a barter exchange, a donation, a sale, a debt to be in-
curred, and so forth. These *scriptores* had modest talents when it came
to composing a text; their hesitant grammar and spelling made their
phrases unclear. Their capacities as "jurists" were even more modest,
if not nonexistent. They did not know the "laws," to the point that
Liutprand threatened them with severe penalties when they failed to
become acquainted with them or at least seek information from
someone who knew them, and they took the precaution of declaring
that they were "following the customs of the Roman laws" (*secundum
consuetudines legum Romanorum*). Furthermore, they were totally ignorant of both the concrete concepts that had been elaborated by Roman legal science and the concepts incorporated into the various barbarian norms (*gewere, wadiatio, thingatio,* etc.). This led them to
jumble together in one act legal concepts or terms whose names they
recalled, for instance designating the same legal act as a transaction, a
donation, a sale, or a barter exchange.[7]

8. The Law Is Not an Autonomous Science

Furthermore, there could be no "jurists" where there was no autonomous "legal science." The law, in fact, was seen as identical with
the arts of reasoning and expression, on the one hand, and with ethical standards, on the other.

This is a consistent point of view in both reflection and practice
throughout the early Middle Ages (sixth to eleventh centuries). First
and foremost, it is embodied in the *Etymologiae* of Isidore of Seville
(d. 636), a work that is a brief compendium of the culture of the age.

7. For examples, see Francesco Calasso, *Il negozio giuridico*, 2d ed. (Milan: Giuffrè,
1959), 91–96, 106–7.

This ideal encyclopedia of all *sapientia* was based on three basic disciplines known collectively as the "arts of the trivium"—grammar, or the rules of discourse, dialectic, or rules of reasoning, and rhetoric, which gave structure, form, and elegance to exposition. Law was regarded as subsumed under these branches of encyclopedic knowledge: technical terms and their primary meanings belonged to grammar; explanation of those terms and their logical concatenation belonged to dialectic; their explication was the province of rhetoric.

The law also meant rules for living, hence every precept (by custom, by edict, or by legislation) must operate in the realm of ethics, which gave discipline to life and was the earthly projection of divine order.

Thus throughout Europe men of the early Middle Ages were constantly involved in evaluating the actions that created custom, and in evaluating them according to divine laws, deciding whether they were just or unjust, and discussing them (dialectically, if need be) when doubt arose or when opinions diverged or clashed. Furthermore, they were motivated to do so not only because such acts had consequences of a terrestrial and social sort but also because they involved merits and responsibilities capable of saving (or losing) the human soul in the afterlife.

In short, the juridical realm took on a more varied coloring and became equated with the realms of ethics and theology. This was why ecclesiastics rose to prominence. The institutional responsibilities that they assumed made them the custodians and interpreters of the Ten Commandments and the Gospels, the holy texts and the earthly standards for divine justice, and their daily contact with the faithful, heightened by confession, required ongoing judgments of human actions. Within the communities of the time it seemed natural to turn to the parish priest, the bishop, the monk, or the canon not only for soul's salvation but also for protection of one's more terrestrial interests or for help and moral support in mundane business affairs (an opinion on the "just price" of a sale or the "just" choice of an heir, for example). It also seemed natural that the member of the clergy to whom one had turned for guidance would then be the person who took pen in hand to note on parchment the choices, decisions, and agreements of parties to a legal act. The man of the church was thus a divine judge and a terrestrial judge; he was a theologian, a "jurist," a rhetorician, and a "notary"; he knew and judged harmful human acts and illicit thoughts as "sins" but at the same time as "illegal" civil or criminal behavior.

This overall vision was crystallized and reinforced not only by the vast circulation throughout Europe of St. Isidore's *Etymologiae* but also by the renewed energy that the Carolingians infused into the cultural tradition of Western Europe, in particular in the age of Charlemagne and of the empire that was reborn (in 800) as "Holy" and "Roman." It was perhaps Alcuin of York's theoretical organization of the branches of human knowledge into one systematic outline that established the position and significance of that vision. Those branches of knowledge, then more properly called "arts" (which combined *scientia*—knowledge—and *sapientia*—wisdom), were divided into two overall categories: *artes reales* and *artes sermocinales*. The *artes reales* (the *quadrivium*) were mathematics, geometry, astronomy, and music; the *artes sermocinales* (the *trivium*) were grammar, dialectic, and rhetoric. Together they made up the seven *artes liberales*.

9. The Presence of the Church

In ecclesiastical circles, investigation of human nature, human behavior, and social order was able to exist and develop. This investigation was an all-out effort that included what the classical jurists, the Roman legislators, the "Fathers of the church" (the Latin and Greek patristic tradition), and the normative organs of the church had had to say about all aspects of individual and collective life. It also took into account the new pontifical decrees (*decretales*) and the decisions (canons) of the great assemblies of the church, the provincial and ecumenical councils.

Collections of norms from a broad variety of sources came into being in Europe, the texts of which circulated, in whole or in excerpts, in a number of ways, and at times these excerpts were collected and gave rise to new and different collections. The most prominent of these were the *Collectio canonum Anselmo dedicata* of the ninth century (ca. 882–96); the *Lex romana canonice compta*, revised on several occasions between the ninth and the tenth centuries; later (in the eleventh century), the *Decretum* of Burchard of Worms and the *Panormia*, the *Tripartita*, and the *Decretum* of Ivo of Chartres.

It is difficult to establish where many of these collections were written or by whom. The oldest among them generally circulated as anon-ymous anthologies, and, according to where they happened to take hold, they were added to, abridged, rewritten, or reorganized. At times they were faked for the demands of the faith or politics: one example of these is a collection attributed to a monk in Mainz, Bene-dictus Levita, a text made up of broadly counterfeited canonical sources and barbarian and Roman norms presented as Carolingian "laws."

In general, we can guess that these compilations came out of cen-ters for study or at least for reading and meditation; thus we should look toward great monasteries standing in rural isolation or perched on a hillside—Montecassino, Casamari, Nonantola, Bobbio, or Cluny—toward the great cathedral churches—Chartres, Ravenna, Metz, Aachen, Worms, or Mainz—or toward important collegial churches energized by the presence and activity of some learned canon. The vast network of city and country parishes had little to do with this movement, and most of the smaller dioceses were more likely to be caught up in city politics and in a difficult struggle with the local count and his court than to be occupied in the task of peace-ful elaboration of doctrine or to take even a minimal interest in ele-mentary instruction.

Thus we have very few points of reference in a continent that was sparsely populated, fragmented, and divided by nearly insuperable geographical barriers. Although such points were few in number, however, they were homogeneous, not only thanks to the universality of the church and its general structures but also thanks to the diffu-sion of the Benedictine Rule (and, to a lesser extent, the Rule of St. Columban) and to the mobility and "social" availability of the Latin clergy, who—unlike their Byzantine counterparts—sought the rela-tions offered by the collective life (in particular, through the activities of the canons) and integration into the community life of the monas-teries.

When the twelfth century ushered in a new age, terms were needed to designate those who knew how to read and write and those who did not: the first were always called clerks (*clerici*), even if their garb and their state were not religious; the second were called laity (*laici*). This distinction expressed a notion that had been current for centu-ries and that combined faith and *sapientia*, the responsibilities of the religious life and a dedication to both the spiritual and the civil life.

10. *Per pugnam sine iustitia*

Thus as late as the tenth century, Europe was still guided by two fundamental lines of thought that had permeated and guided civilization on the continent since the fifth or sixth centuries.

Anyone in normal daily life who thought his interests had been prejudiced or who foresaw that a ruinous act was about to bring him harm had only two ways to defend himself or win his cause: the force of arms, or the force of a reasoned justice founded in the human heart and animated by faith in Christ. Obviously, these two lines of recourse were not exclusive to the early Middle Ages, since in other epochs (and even in our own) they have been a temptation for someone in search of a defense. In those distant centuries, however, they had a prominence and a clarity that the historian must note.

When in 731 the anonymous drafter of the *Edictum* of Liutprand of that year wrote the lapidary phrase, "per pugnam sine justitia," at the close of the one hundred eighteenth chapter,[8] his point of reference was an ineluctable alternative: he knew that a right could be defended *per pugnam* (with armed force), which one should avoid, or *per iustitiam*, which was more desirable. To say *per iustitiam* was not the same as saying *per legem*, however. In that epoch "legality" was not known as a value, and the "law" was not looked to as an accepted, just, and rational way to prevent or resolve conflicts between individuals and order the life of the community. When, sporadically, a "law" did surface among so many customs, it only expressed the idea that the "law" must guarantee a free search for justice, either through the individual efforts of a judge or a notary or through the collective consolidation of customary acts, or else the "law" was an accidental, occasional, episodic but authoritative and written expression of the "justice" discerned in a particular instance (but this was a new concept that was consciously developed only in the twelfth century). *Iustitia* always held the central position. Men's instincts and their violence must be held in check and governed by the binding force of the supreme commandments of faith. Terrestrial norms were considered either as a corruption of *iustitia* or as a marginal actualization of *iustitia*. That was why it was impossible for an autonomous and distinct *scientia iuris* rooted in those norms to develop.

8. Liutprand, *Edicta*, 118 (ed. Bluhme, 156): "Quia incerti sumus de iudicio Dei, et multos audivimus per pugnam sine iustitia causam suam perdere . . ."

11. A Century of Great Crises and Radical Reforms:
1000–1100

Around the mid-eleventh century, signs of change were everywhere. In 1054 the church split into the Eastern and the Western churches, a schism that was to last for a millennium, that still exists, and that promises to continue. The break helped to accelerate change, but it was also a highly visible symptom of profound changes already in operation. A comparison between successive decades can be illuminating.

During the first half of the eleventh century, Rome was still the preferred abode of a rough and ignorant clergy given to simony and corruption. Pope John XIX (d. 1032), whose first concern was not his pontifical duties but improving the fortunes of his "house," the powerful Tuscolani family, was emblematic of the state of the clergy.[9] Strong reformist sentiments developed during the pontificate of Nicholas II (d. 1061). Among the champions of reform was Humbert de Moyenmoutier, who wrote an important treatise, *Contra simoniacos* in 1058. The most prominent reformer, however, was Cardinal Hildebrand, born perhaps in Rome, perhaps in Soana, near Grosseto. In 1073 he became pope as Gregory VII, and in 1075 he published a famous text, the *Dictatus Papae*, whose twenty-seven propositions outlined the prerogatives of the pope and of the hierarchy subordinate to him. Thus the most important act of this movement for reform, which came to be called "Gregorian" after the pope who was its most ardent proponent, was launched at the highest level of Christianity and from Rome.

Radical currents radiated from Rome throughout Europe. In many ways they were the most evident symptom of a reawakening, but they synchronized with other, equally far-reaching movements for renewal that preceded or coincided with them. These broad movements worked to reform canonical life by defining new "orders" of reformed canons such as the "Olivetans" of the Church of Sts. Peter and Paul of Oliveto, or the "Mortarians" of the Church of Santa Croce of Mortara. Monastic life was also being recast, thanks to the reinterpretation and spread of the Benedictine Rule that had begun with the Cluniacs at Cluny, in Burgundy, as far back as 910 and that

9. Luigi Salvatorelli, *Storia d'Europa*, 4th ed. rev., 2 vols. (Turin: UTET, 1961), 1:326.

was continued by the Camaldolese (from Camaldoli, near Arezzo) after 1012, by the Vallombrosans (from Vallombrosa, near Florence) after 1030, and by the Cistercians (from Citeaux, in Burgundy) after about 1098, and thanks to the decisive break with the feudal world urged by the Cistercian Rule of St. Bernard.

A historical reconstruction of the precise relationships between parallel phenomena is a difficult, if not impossible, task. It is even more difficult to state that one particular event was the determining cause of another. Nonetheless, one thing seems evident: in every field of human activity signs could be seen of a will for renewal; in only a few decades an extremely fluid state of affairs had opened the way to a new era. Historiography usually calls the centuries of this new era the "Renaissance of the twelfth century,"[10] or, more generally, the "Medieval Renaissance."[11]

12. Signs of a New Legal Science in the Roman Tradition

The ancient Roman legal tradition slowly began to influence law. An aptitude and a capacity for looking at everyday events and defining them juridically became part of the new cultural heritage and encouraged specialization in an activity that, thanks to intense and constant repetition, lent substance to the new professions of the practice and the theory of the law.

There are at least two works that testify to the new attitudes of the eleventh century, the *Expositio ad Librum Papiensem* and the *Exceptiones Petri*.

The first of these works was anonymous and was probably written in Lombardy around 1070. It was constructed as a series of annotations added to the *Liber Papiensis* and taken from the Lombard *Edicta* and the *Capitulare italicum*. For the first time in centuries, the names of "jurists" appear in these annotations: Bonfiglio, Bagelardo, Guglielmo, Sigefredo, Ugo, Walcausus. These men cite Justinian's legislative texts frequently and at length, and there are indications that the

---

10. See Charles Homer Haskins, *The Renaissance of the Twelfth Century* (Cambridge: Harvard University Press, 1927; New York: Meridian Books, 1960).

11. See Francesco Calasso, *Gli ordinamenti giuridici del Rinascimento medievale*, 2d ed. (Milan: Giuffrè, 1949; reprinted 1953, 1965).

author or authors were acquainted with the *Codex*, a work that had been forgotten for more than five centuries and was known only indirectly from a greatly abridged text that circulated sporadically, the *Epitome Codicis*, or from a slightly fuller version, the so-called *Epitome Codicis aucta*. The *Expositio* posed questions about dubious legal points and included references to disagreements among jurists.

The consistency of these annotations and the significance of their contents suggest the presence of jurists and legal circles already intensely pursuing specialized tasks. Exegesis was important not only (and not so much) for the interpretations it arrived at concerning individual norms but also (and even more) for the methodology that was its point of departure. At least three theoretical directions provided criteria for textual analysis, three directions that are known by the name given to their followers.

First there were the *antiquissimi*, who belonged to a past age but whose thought was mentioned on occasion for a specific contribution that it had made to the comprehension of a specific aspect of a norm. Then there were the *antiqui* and the *moderni*, who were distinguished by the method that they employed and believed in rather than by chronology, since they all lived at roughly the same time and were all part of the new generations of the second half of the eleventh century. The *antiqui* held that a norm could be interpreted only by comparing it to other norms in the same collection or by an appeal to principles common to a homogeneous body of precepts (edicts, capitularies, and so forth). As a consequence, they held that where no norm was provided or where the norm was dubious one should turn to the context of the dispositions in question and draw from them—and only from them—the needed norm or the most likely indication. The *moderni*, on the other hand, thought it possible and proper to return to Roman law either to understand Lombard edicts or Carolingian capitularies better or to fill in their eventual lacunae. They declared, in justification of their method, that this was possible "because the Roman law is the general law for everyone" (quia lex romana est generalis omnium), thus treating Roman law as meriting special attention. A bright future awaited this underlying premise.

A number of circumstances during roughly the same period (the eleventh and early twelfth centuries) show proof of a return to the study and the use of Roman law in the form it had assumed in the compilations of Justinian. In some areas of Italy—in Tuscany, and in particular in Arezzo and in Lucca—the technical quality of notarial acts showed a clear improvement. There were some composite works in circulation that presented the salient points of Justinian's compilation in simple terms. Furthermore, legal concepts began to reappear, not only in the theoretical works of jurists involved in constructing the new science of jurisprudence but also as essential working tools to enable practitioners to define adequately the terms in a legal act, conflicting interests, or situations that required surveillance.

The second work that manifested the new spirit was for all intents and purposes anonymous, since the author indicated in one of the variants of its title has not yet been identified. The work circulated either as *Exceptiones Petri* or as *Exceptiones legum romanarum*. The copies that have come down to us contain notable textual variants: at times the work is given as dedicated to a certain Saxolinus (a Tuscan, "Florentine civitatis magister"); other versions give a certain Odilo of Valence (a Frenchman, "Valentine civitatis magister"). As a result, historiographical debate on the work's land of origin, although lengthy and bitter, has not produced any sure results, and we still do not know whether the work originated in Tuscany or in Provence, although it is certain that it was used in both regions. Fragmentary documentary evidence of the work has turned up in various parts of Europe, and we can assume that these documents were either partial copies of the larger work or modest original sketches that were joined with others to form the full written version of the *Exceptiones*. There are many of these partial documentations: an "Ashburnham Book," a "Tübingen Book," a "Graz Book," a "Vercelli Book," and an "Admont Book."[12]

The eleventh century ended and the twelfth century began in a new cultural climate. More and more concentrated thought was devoted to legal norms and the behavior they regulated. At the same time, juridical theory helped to give a new quality and a new dignity to the work of practitioners, notaries first among them.

A new era was beginning for them too.

12. For the contents of this text and its editions in both the full and the abridged versions, see Manlio Bellomo, *Società e istituzioni dal medioevo agli inizi dell'età moderna*, 6th ed. (Rome: Il Cigno Galileo Galilei, 1993), 205–10.

3

Ius commune in Europe

Old and New Social Figures

In France in 1016, Adalberon, the bishop of Laon, wrote with conviction and satisfaction that Christian society was made up of "those who pray, those who fight, and those who labor" (*oratores, bellatores, laboratores*).[1] In this synthetic picture society was divided into three orders: the agrarian aristocracies, traditionally linked to bearing arms, the arts of war, and the exercise and responsibilities of religion; the clergy, in cities, towns, and rural areas and on the various levels of the official hierarchy (parishes, dioceses, and so forth), plus canons and monks; and finally the laborers, those who worked with their hands to cultivate the soil.

The idea of labor was secondary, and it was restricted to manual activities, principally those of the peasant (free, serf, or slave). Other ideals and values had priority over it, such as physical strength, warfare, or the religious life. It was widely believed that not only wealth and well-being but honor and one's good name were to be conquered and defended by the sword, either by individual force or with the aid of armed bands, and that material interests were to be safeguarded by physical ability and by solidarity within the family, the kinship group, and the socioeconomic group, or by political intrigue. It was agreed that one could also appeal to the imperatives of reason or morality or to the obligations that religion imposed on the faithful; but law, justice that becomes law and provides norms for civil life, skilled use of legal techniques, and even binding, constraining sentences were all

---

1. Adalbéron, *Carmen ad Rotbertum regem*, ed. G.-A. Hückel, in *Les poèmes satiriques d'Adalbéron*, Bibliothèque de la Faculté des Lettres de l'Université de Paris, 13, 2 vols. (Paris: 1901), 155–56.

things that remained outside the ideal framework and the vision of a three-part society, even if *iurisperiti*, judges, and notaries did exist.

Craft and commerce were also excluded from this ideal framework. Of course there had for some time been *negotiatores* who had built up fortunes, but they were regarded with suspicion or aversion. Trade was seen as a practice striving for undue and illicit gain; thus it was considered dangerous and harmful to both social well-being and the salvation of the soul.

In short, to look at society from Adalberon's point of view, one could see *milites*, clergy, and peasants attached to the land, but artisans and merchants, jurists and physicians were simply invisible.

The very lucidity of Adalberon's picture of society shows it to be the last reflection of a world about to enter a profound crisis of transformation. Only a few decades later, in the second half of the same eleventh century, signs of radical renewal were strikingly evident, as we have seen concerning the ecclesiastical world. Those signs became so intense and so widespread that they shaped a new civilization. Naturally, the new society continued to show vital behavior patterns, attitudes, traditions, ideals, and values that belonged to the epoch that was ending, but these now occurred within totally new historical processes, concrete situations, and theoretical configurations. The structure of "feudal civilization" was crumbling: the fief remained, but not the "civilization" that had made it the pivot and the nucleus of the feudal vision of life; many of the material and ideal elements of feudalism still remained, but they were gradually absorbed by the new and original communal and monarchical institutions; bent to other functions, they revealed different capacities.

This turmoil and this "rebirth" permeated all aspects of both everyday life and cultural life and all sectors of human endeavors. Adalberon's neat tripartite division was able to survive only in peripheral, isolated, and out-of-the-way areas where the society that had justified it had survived. In the cities and towns, in the central regions of Europe, and in the great monarchical institutional aggregates such as the *Regnum Siciliae*, everything was changing.

The new "vulgar tongues" emerged and spread. When the Italian, Spanish, French, German (and other) languages were born, after a long gestation during the tenth and eleventh centuries, it was an historical event without peer in the two millennia of Christianity. The canons of all manual and professional operations were overthrown in all fields: agricultural methods, craft techniques, trade and commercial operations, and the techniques of the artist and the scholar. Great stone cities were built, and with them and within them great fortunes were founded and augmented by skillful business dealings and by professional specialization, helped by notable and rapid earnings from an increased demand for city real estate and by higher profits from an enlarged urban market.

In the cities new sorts of persons were active and rose to prominence. Some were specialized jurists trained in schools that became famous and gave rise to the modern university. Some were medical doctors (called "physicians") who borrowed many of their positions and logical procedures for the analysis of reality from newly rediscovered Aristotelian texts, and who tested and refined their professionalism with direct observations. Some were scholars who acquired a growing social and political importance that reached its peak in the age of humanism in the fifteenth and sixteenth centuries. Some were artists—painters and sculptors in particular. Some were money brokers—exchangers of coins—and highly prestigious and powerful financial operators who laid the foundations for modern banking, and whose widespread, even international, business dealings gave a measure of economic and cultural unity to a nascent Europe.

A new idea of labor was in the air everywhere: labor was now viewed as including not only manual toil but the activities of the intellectual and the professional, the entrepreneur and the merchant.[2] At the same time, the age-old suspicion and sharp condemnation of trade and commerce declined. The benefits of commerce began to be appreciated, particularly in an age in which one region could be suffering a food shortage while others abounded in seasonal produce. People began to understand that commerce was essential for the existence and development of a market, and that if the market was to include specialized goods it could survive only if it was firmly linked to a flourishing international, or at least intercity, commerce.

2. See Manlio Bellomo, "Il lavoro nel pensiero dei giuristi medievali: Proposte per una ricerca," in *Lavorare nel Medio Evo*, Atti del XXI Convegno Storico Internazionale "Lavorare nel Medio Evo: Rappresentazioni ed esempi dall'Italia dei secc. X–XIV," Todi 12–15 October (Università di Perugia; Accademia Tudertina, Centro di Studi sulla spiritualità medievale) (Perugia: Benucci, 1983), 171–97.

2. From the Feudal World to Urban Civilization

In twelfth-century towns and cities, which were growing rapidly as their permanent population increased and their inhabited space was enlarged, economic growth, market specialization, an intensification of interpersonal relations, and new forms of political power produced new needs. Among these needs were theoretical models and practical instruments more adequate to new conditions than the models and means of the seigniorial, feudal, and rural world. We can glimpse a new conception of public power being tried out; attempts were made to modify the usual definitions and theoretical interpretations of intersubjective relations in the realms of both obligations and real legal situations; there was a new associative spirit that went beyond and often overthrew the feudal schemes of hierarchy and of personal and family status.

Its abstract and reiterated legal concepts made Roman law (which, incidentally, had strongly urban connotations) a mine of precious materials that jurists, as specialists arrogating to themselves a monopoly on the theorization of social relations, could recuperate and reutilize. With Irnerius they began to do just that.

Irnerius headed a school in which the task of reviving and reconstituting Justinian's texts was carried out enthusiastically and with the participation of young and brilliant students. They worked with a sense of urgency to provide theoretical responses, and with them collaboration and aid, to political movements and economic trends that were restructuring the city internally, refashioning its ties with the surrounding territory, and weaving a network of profitable connections between one city and another.

3. The Twelfth-Century Renaissance and the Autonomy of the Law

Irnerius's life spanned the years between the eleventh and the twelfth centuries (he died around 1130). He was a figure of mythical proportions, who symbolized the rebirth of European jurisprudence in Bologna[3]—a rebirth that, as we have seen, had begun around the

3. On Irnerius, see in particular Enrico Spagnesi, *Wernerius bononiensis iudex: La figura storica d'Irnerio* (Florence: Olschki, 1970). See also Manlio Bellomo, *Saggio sul-*

mid-eleventh century but had not found a way to express or manifest itself completely or in any one place.

The novelty of Irnerius's work lay mainly in the idea that the texts of the Justinian compilation (the *libri legales*, as contemporary sources called them) could be used to give a concrete response to anyone who might want to use the law rather than arms to defend his interests.

We do not know whether this idea was Irnerius's alone or whether it had occurred to others before him. Many indications suggest that a current of thought had arisen during the final decades of the eleventh century that had turned more and more toward Roman law, and that a need to know the original texts had kept pace with that interest.

In Bologna as in other cities, what is more, we have increasing evidence of *iudices, causidici, sapientes*, and *legum docti*, and there are a few personalities, remembered for various reasons, who stand out from the growing mass of people now occupied primarily or exclusively with legal problems. In Bologna we can find a certain Lambertus, whom Odofredus later called *antiquus doctor*, and a certain Ubaldus, who annotated a few passages in Justinian's laws.[4]

Pepo (or Pepone) was better known than those early figures, although little more than his name remains now.[5] He must have been famous in his day if nearly a century later an English writer, Ralph Niger (d. ca. 1210), could mention him favorably in a work written between 1170 and 1189 and give valuable information on him. Odofredus (d. 1265) said of Pepo that he was "of no fame," but this opinion was probably based on Pepo's scant production of scholarly works and on a comparison (that must have been striking) with the much richer and more mature scholarly activities of Irnerius. Odofredus avoids expressing an opinion on Pepo's work, however, and

l'Università nell'età del diritto comune (Catania: Giannotta, 1979; 2d ed., Rome: Il Cigno Galileo Galilei, 1992), p. 9n.; bibliography p. 9 n.7. For more recent bibliography, see Martin Bertram, "Neuerscheinungen zur mittelalterlichen Geschichte von Stadt und Universität Bologna," *Quellen und Forschungen aus italienischen Archiven und Bibliotheken* 67 (1987): 477–88.

4. See Giorgio Cencetti, "Studium fuit Bononie," *Studi Medievali*, ser. 3, 7 (1966): 781–833, now in *Le origini dell'Università*, ed. and intro. Girolamo Arnaldi (Bologna: Il Mulino, 1974), 115.

5. See Ludwig Schmugge, "Codicis Iustiniani et Institutionum baiulus: Eine neue Quelle zu Magister Pepo von Bologna," *Ius Commune* 6 (1977): 1–9. In general on Pepo, see P. Fiorelli, "Clarum bononiensium lumen," in *Per Francesco Calasso: Studi degli allievi* (Rome: Bulzoni, 1978), 413–59 and the bibliography cited therein.

he does not exclude the possibility that Pepo might have possessed a modicum of *scientia*: "quicquid fuit de scientia sua, nullius nominis fuit."[6]

In a context in which a number of "jurists" operated, then, Irnerius concentrated on the *libri legales* (Justinian's laws) which were in circulation in Bologna and other parts of central and northern Italy (at the least in Tuscany, Ravenna, Pavia, and Verona) but perhaps not yet in Provence or north of the Alps in general, where an interest in Roman law was nonetheless already fairly strong: "Up to now they [the *libri legales*] had been neglected and no one had studied them," Burchard of Biberach (d. after 1231), the provost of Ursberg from 1215 to 1226, declared in his chronicle.[7]

4. The Formation of the *Corpus iuris civilis* and the Writings of Irnerius: The Rise of Civil Common Law

Here and there, forgotten for centuries, separate or bound parchments bearing a text that reproduced (with uneven fidelity) the text of Justinian's lost ancient originals were saved from destruction. Toward the mid-eleventh century someone had the idea of rescuing them from their abandonment and putting them back into circulation. According to one imaginative report, something of the sort happened somewhere between Amalfi and Tuscany concerning a complete copy of the *Digest*. What is certain is that around the mid-twelfth century this exemplar, known under the name of *Pandectae*, was in Pisa and that it was and continued to be extremely difficult to get a look at it. Aside from this one instance, Justinian's compilation was nearly unknown. Fragments existed in Verona and Pavia. We know from later twelfth- and thirteenth-century sources, which give no details and present some uncertainties regarding some elements, that *libri legales* circulated in the late eleventh century in Tuscany, Bologna, and Lombardy.

---

6. Odofredus, *Lectura* in D.1.1.6, *de iustitia et iure*. 1. *ius civile* (Lugduni, 1550), fol. 7rb: "Quidam dominus Pepo cepit au[c]toritate sua legere in legibus. Tamen, quicquid fuerit de scientia sua, nullius nomen fuit."

7. Burchard of Biberach (Burchardus Biberacensis), *Chronicon*, ed. Oswald Holder-Egger and Bernhard von Simson, in *Monumenta Germaniae Historica. Scriptores Rerum germanicarum in usum scholarum* (Hannover and Leipzig: Hahnsche buchhandlung, 1916), 50:15–16: "Dominus Wernerius libros legum, qui dudum neglecti fuerant, nec quisquam in eis studuerat . . . renovavit."

What these books were we can only surmise, and even then only by lending weight and precise meaning to words that were written at a time so remote from the facts they recount that they should perhaps not be taken literally.

All of the *Institutes* and at least the first nine books of the *Code* seem to have been the first to reappear and attract scholarly attention. When Ralph Niger mentions that Pepo was *baiulus* of the *Codex* and the *Institutiones*, he is in all probability repeating a tradition founded in fact, thus setting the date of the first reappearance of certain portions of the Roman laws. If the *Epitome Codicis* was still known in the first decades of the eleventh century, now Pepo had access to a copy of the complete *Codex*, a copy that undoubtedly contained flaws and errors but was nonetheless fairly close to the original model composed in the ancient imperial chancery.

It took a good many sheets of parchment to pass on the laws of Rome. Some of these were loose because that was the way they had been found; others, sewn together, made up a "codex" (that is, a book) of two or three hundred folios. One "codex" was insufficient to contain all the laws, which is another reason why the *libri legales* were in a state of disorder. Very few copies existed, few were intact and complete, and all were extremely precious. They cost a great deal. Furthermore, the work required to put them back into order was immense.

Irnerius was the first to have the courage to recompose and restore them. Unlike Pepo, then, he was not satisfied simply to own a copy of the *Codex* or the *Institutiones* or to respect the physical existence of those documents. With the encouragement of Countess Matilda, the powerful feudatory of Tuscany (who may have provided financial aid as well as verbal encouragement), Irnerius "renewed the books of the laws and, reconstructing the order in which they had been compiled by Emperor Justinian, with the possible addition of a few words here and there, he divided them up."[8] Irnerius was not a jurist acting as a custodian for normative texts that he was lucky enough to have available and perhaps to own; he was a master of the liberal arts who made himself into a jurist in order to shatter the status of tradition, because tradition brought confusion and distortion.

8. Ibid., 16: "Dominus Wernerius libros legum . . . renovavit et, secundum quod olim a dive recordationis imperatore Iustiniano compilati fuerant, paucis forte verbis alicubi interpositis eos distinxit."

Work advanced slowly, thanks to the objective difficulties inherent in the task and its sheer length, but also because Irnerius was often obliged to leave Bologna to visit Matilda's court, to follow the emperor, Henry V, or to go to Rome to defend the antipope, Gregory VIII, in his struggle against Gelasius II. It seems from all the evidence that collecting the parchments and putting their contents into an order that reflected the original arrangement occupied Irnerius for the rest of his life. The entire work, including some portions that had been lost but had been rediscovered at the time, was once more recompiled, if not by Irnerius's own hand, at least in his own day and in his circle. First, many books of the *Digest* were added to the *Institutes* along with the first nine books of the *Code* from book one to the second title of book twenty-four (Dig.1–24.2). This came to be called *Digestum vetus*. (An old hypothesis, which may have some merit, states that at the time the *Digestum vetus* included all of book twenty-five as well.) Next, the final books were added, which in later tradition settled down to comprising books thirty-nine to fifty, but in Irnerius's time this portion may have begun in the middle of the last sentence of an earlier book, Dig.35.2.82, with the words *Tres partes* (though it is not impossible that it began with the twenty-sixth book). These additions were called *Digestum novum*. Finally the intervening books were added, from book 24.3 to book 35.2.82, perhaps without the section that came to be known, from its first words, as "Tres partes" (Dig.35.2.82-Dig.38.17). This portion was known as the *Infortiatum*. It was later extended when the "Tres partes" section was removed (if indeed it had ever appeared there) from the *Digestum novum* and placed after Dig.35.2.82, where it nonetheless remained a coherent whole. At that point the *Infortiatum* took on its definitive form as Dig.24.3 to Dig.38.17. The last three books of the *Code*, known as the *Tres libri* (Cod.10 to Cod.12) were also rediscovered, as were the *Novels* (*Novellae Constitutiones*), all 134 of which were collected together in a work considered complete and authentic, hence called *Authenticum*.

All the texts of the Justinian compilation were recopied onto new parchment folios and bound together so as to form new volumes, or codices. In this way, reproduced and emended where it seemed possible to do so (with the "addition of a few words here and there," as Burchard's chronicle tells us), they were distributed (Irnerius's *distinxit*) in five great folio volumes, each one of which contained some two hundred parchment folios (or some four hundred pages). A tradition was launched; under normal circumstances it continued to be respected until the much later printed editions of the fifteenth, six-teenth, and seventeenth centuries.

In this new and soon standard organization, books 1–24.2 of the *Digest* (the *Digestum vetus*) formed the first volume; books 24.3–38.17 of the *Digest* (that is, the *Infortiatum*) made up volume two; books 39.1–50.17 of the *Digest* (the *Digestum novum*) were volume three; vol-ume four contained the first nine books of the *Code*; the fifth volume (also known as the *Volumen* or *Volumen parvum*) contained the four books of the *Institutes*, the last three books of the *Code* (that is, the *Tres libri*), and the *Novels* in the version of the *Authenticum* (hence known as *Authenticae*) distributed into nine *collationes*.

5. Proliferating Texts and the Market for Juridical Books

Irnerius's restoration of the Justinian compilation was not the work of a scholar isolated from the world. It had profound reasons for its existence that gave it an extraordinary vitality. We need to take a closer look at those reasons.

First, however, we need to establish a few basic points. The texts that were rewritten and redistributed into five volumes began to be copied repeatedly and incessantly, and entire workshops of artisans and booksellers (*stationarii exempla tenentes* and *stationarii librorum*) worked at top speed and with increasingly well coordinated and re-fined methods to produce the numbers of copies that the market re-quired.[9] Moreover, the market was extensive, to the point that even today libraries in Europe and North America contain some two thou-sand copies, in whole or in part, of the various portions of the *libri legales*.

Every volume, or codex, of robust parchment worked and prepared for writing consisted of some two hundred folios, which means that about one hundred sheep were required to provide the raw material for one book! This made a book an expensive commodity, whose price reflected the costs of the parchment and its preparation, the cost of writing (entrusted to skilled *amanuenses*), and sometimes the cost of miniature, illumination, and binding, which further increased its

9. See Bellomo, *Saggio sull'Università*, 2d ed., 112–28.

value. A book was an inheritance, and like every legacy it was to be safeguarded, used with intelligence, and profited from.

It is impossible to think that all this occurred (Irnerius's recovery of the Justinian text, the production of copies of it, the formation of specialized workshops, the circulation of the books, the investment of large amounts of money, and the assumption of entrepreneurial risks) only because Irnerius thought it the proper scholarly thing to do to revise and reorganize the Justinian compilation, or simply because his contemporaries and successors were stricken with a pure philological or historical interest or with a yen to possess a book. Clearly, if their desire for knowledge had been predominantly or exclusively theoretical and intellectual, a professional concern for philological studies would soon have sprung up, and the need for an accurate "reading" derived from numerous comparisons of reliable texts would have led directly to problems concerning the authenticity of the text. Even if this had happened, we would still have to explain the very large quantities of books that were produced—numbers that seem far superior to the needs of even a large band of scholars. But for centuries nothing occurred that we could credit to any philological or historical interest. If there was (and indeed there was) concern to give the text a "certain" form, the reasons for doing so were all internal to a new way of dealing with legal problems.

Jurists, practitioners, and the professors in the schools all found a "certain" text useful: the value, validity, and reasonableness of an interpretation, in the courts as in the schools, could not do without the certainty that the text contained those precise words and not others, those passages, those precepts and not others. If during a debate someone could claim to alter the text under discussion, if someone could claim to present a text that differed by as much as a single word and could base his arguments on that altered text, then debate, colloquy, or the exchange of contrasting points of view on an interpretation would have become useless exchanges of soliloquies.

The jurist needed a dependable text, an *exemplar*. This was why structures were created that offered adequate guarantees, and why particularly reliable craftsmen-merchants (*stationarii exempla tenentes*) were entrusted with handling *exempla*—that is, autograph texts or authenticated copies that could be borrowed for payment of a fee.

This has nothing to do with any love for the past, nor with an admiration for the grandeur, the power, and the glory of Rome. It shows no desire for or interest in historical knowledge. Historians have even noted that the literary realm in the twelfth century was characterized by an "absence of the ancient classics and of vernacular literature"[10] among the usual reading matter of cultivated men and in the curriculum of the "arts."[11] It did not matter to the jurists who returned to the laws of Justinian whether Justinian had lived before or after Christ. Fanciful anecdotes circulated in the law schools about the origin of the "Twelve Tables" that contained the archaic laws of Rome. Thus if we read that "Roman law originated with the Greeks, like all other sciences,"[12] we know that the passage is a stylistic flourish written by an author who had only a vague notion of Greek and Roman antiquity, had little interest in improving his knowledge, and could not even understand Greek: "Grecum est, legi non potest."[13]

The proliferation of codices, their diffusion and their wide circulation despite their very high individual cost were thus related to other needs. Roman laws were useful to the jurist. Why? To satisfy what needs?

Before turning to this problem and attempting an explanation, we need to look at the larger question of the norms of the church as a universal organization embracing all the *fideles Christi*. We shall see a parallel, if not even more striking, development in canon law, with even larger numbers of copies that were produced and put on the market (and even larger numbers that remain today).

6. Gratian and the *Decretum*: The Rise of Canon Common Law

If it was thanks to Irnerius's efforts that Justinian's legislative compilation was brought back as a vital force in juridical circles, it was thanks to the efforts of another person of mythical proportions, Gratian, that the norms of the church were first successfully presented

10. Charles Homer Haskins, *The Rise of Universities* (1923) (New York: Peter Smith, 1940), 41.
11. Haskins notes that one professor in Bologna made fun of Cicero but declared that he had never studied him and came close to boasting of the fact that he had never read him (ibid., 11).
12. Accursius, the *constitui* to D.1.2.2., *de origine iuris. 1. necessarium*: "Sic ergo a Graecis habuerunt originem, sicut et quaelibet scientia."
13. See Bellomo, *Saggio sull'Università*, 2d ed., 15–17.

(after a number of attempts) in a homogeneous corpus reflecting the author's intention in a work that has become basic to European law.[14]

Gratian was probably a monk, and he may first have lived near Ravenna in the monastery of Classe. He later lived in Bologna, where around 1140 he finished drafting a monumental compilation of laws (some four thousand items), known in its manuscript versions as *Concordia discordantium canonum* but called by long-standing tradition the *Decretum*.

This work was not an official compilation, and although it came to be recognized as the base for subsequent church legislation, it was never promulgated into "law." We see here, as in other instances and on other levels (for example, with the redactions that put city customary measures into written form and gave them a sure base) that "legislative" phenomena at their origins and in an initial phase were defined by the initiative, the responsibility, and the authority of one private individual.

The *Decretum* has a complex structure that does not totally reflect its original organization. For some years at least—until the early 1150s—it lacked some parts that were added later (the titles *De poenitentia* and *De consecratione*), and it did not include some passages from the Justinian *Digest* and *Code* that were inserted later. Gratian also inserted into the *Decretum* brief annotations called *dicta*, in which he discussed the discordant legal texts or Holy Scripture, or he cited the institutes and principles of Roman law in order to compare them with the law of the church. At the same time, the *Decretum* was enhanced

14. See Peter Landau, *Kanones und Dekretalen: Beiträge zur Geschichte der Quellen des kanonischen Rechts* (Frankfurt: Keip, 1993). For a general introduction, see Peter Landau, "Gratian (von Bologna)," in *Theologische Realenzyklopädie* (Berlin and New York: Walter de Gruyter, 1977-), 14:124–30, and the annotated bibliography, pp. 129–30. On Gratian, see also Stephan Kuttner, "Gratian, canoniste du XIIe siècle," in *Dictionnaire d'histoire et de géographie ecclésiastiques*, ed. Alfred Baudrillart (Paris: Letouzey et Ané, 1912-), vol. 21 (1986), cols. 1235–39. There are at least two reliable editions of Gratian's *Decretum*. The first, made by the so-called *correctores romani*, was published in Rome in 1582; a more recent edition by Emil Friedberg appears in *Corpus Iuris Canonici*, 2d ed., 2 vols. (Leipzig: Bernhard Tauchnitz, 1879- 81), reprint, 2 vols. (Graz: Akademische Druck- und Verlagsanstalt, 1959). A partial English translation is available in Gratian, *The Treatise on Laws (Decretum DD. 1–20)*, trans. Augustine Thompson, with the Ordinary Gloss, trans. James Gordley; intro. Katherine Christensen. Studies in Medieval and Early Modern Canon Law, vol. 2 (Washington, D.C.: The Catholic University of America Press, 1993).

with notes called *paleae*, a word of uncertain origin that may refer to the author of the glosses, a pupil of Gratian's nicknamed Pocapaglia (Paucapalea), or "Little Straw."

Thus it probably was not Gratian's original intention to treat either problems of a theological nature (which is why the titles *De poenitentia* and *De consecratione* were missing) or the materials and the principles of Roman law (which is why citations to the *Digest* and the *Code* were added later). It is also probable that, as years went by, other jurists, influenced by the Bolognese schools of Roman law and by demands specific to the church, somewhat modified the shape of the 1140 version of the work. Gratian died around 1150; we can date the modifications to the *Decretum* from between that date to about 1170.

The original and central core of the *Decretum* was composed of materials that Gratian had selected either directly from scattered manuscripts or indirectly, extrapolating them from previous collections that had, in their turn, been taken either directly from the sources or indirectly from other works. His ideal (and in part real) library certainly included writings of Anselm of Lucca (*Collectio canonum*) and Cardinal Gregory of San Chrisogono (*Polycarpus*), the *Tripartita* and the *Panormia* of Ivo of Chartres, the so-called *Collection of the Three Books*, and the *Liber de misericordia et iustitia* of Anselm of Liège (or Lüttich). The *Etymologiae* of Isidore of Seville were known only in *excerpta*. Although Gratian certainly made use of the writings of the church Fathers (that is, of Latin and Greek patristics)—in fact they provide about a third of all the materials used—it is not clear whether or not he always read them in the full text. More probably he used anthologies such as the *Collection of the Three Books* that had selected and passed on significant fragments of such texts.

Around the middle of the twelfth century, Gratian's *Decretum* was taken as a "certain" and reliable text, one that could be referred to not only for the internal and structural problems of the church but also for a rule of life offered to or imposed on the *fideles Christi* throughout Christendom. Thus the work responded to the same need for "certitude" felt in the secular field, where it was satisfied by Irnerius's rediscovery and restoration of the laws of Justinian. There was a difference, however: although the emperors of the Holy Roman Empire continued to make laws, these norms were only very rarely inserted into the Justinian framework. This happened only in a very few, exceptional instances—for example, the *Constitutio* "Habita" of Frederick I Barbarossa, a few laws on heresy of Frederick II, and the entire text of the *Consuetudines feudorum* (*Libri feudorum*), a text that contained some imperial laws and that provided material for the tenth *collatio* of the *Novels*. Thus where civil law was concerned, the architecture and the contents of the compilations remained rigidly fixed, solid, and invariable. At the same time, "faith" in the Roman laws was reinforced and relived with a sense of trust imbued with a strong sacrality. The decretals of the popes and the canons of the church councils were immediately applied to everyday experience, added to the older laws, or substituted for them. They thus continually raised a problem that Gratian had attempted to solve by applying to norms of differing significance, taken from a variety of places and times, the four basic criteria of *ratio temporis*, *ratio loci*, *ratio significationis*, and *ratio dispensationis*. Doubts continually arose as to whether or not a legal precedent already existed for a specific problem or a case in point and, if so, whether that earlier law should be understood as having been abrogated (following the logic of *ratio temporis*); whether in some particular locality a rule might exist that contravened the general norm (*ratio loci*); whether the antinomy in apparently contradictory norms might not be worked out logically (*ratio significationis*); or whether clearly contradictory norms might not be treated as statements of a rule and an exception to that rule (*ratio dispensationis*).

In short, interpretive techniques and methods were developed that could be employed (and that were conceivable) in all cases because they referred to a dependable, "certain" normative text couched in "certain" words and not in others. As with the civilists, the juridical thought of the canonists excluded all intellectual requirements of a philological or historical nature; their sole concern was the need to consult a reliable and authoritative text.

7. The *Quinque compilationes antiquae*

There were other attempts to select from and systematize the vast legislative materials of the church. At times private individuals took on the task; later the church assumed direct responsibility for such operations and official collections were made, some of which were impressive works destined to last for centuries.

After Gratian, the jurists began to collect papal decrees. Soon they put together collections of papal judicial decisions (called decretals). One of the first collections to be used in the schools was the *Breviarium extravagantium*. It was the work of a private jurist, Bernard of Pavia, and was composed between 1188 and 1191, after the *Decretum* had crystallized into its definitive form (with the additions that we have discussed) and when other ways were being sought to update the legislative materials of the church. Bernard's *Breviarium* was divided into five "books," each of which treated a topic recalled by the mnemonic formula *iudex, iudicium, clerus, connubia, crimen* (judge, trial, clergy, marriage, crime). Another private jurist, John of Wales, produced a similar collection.

A third collection of papal decretals had official backing when for the first time a pope, Innocent III (d. 1216), thought it necessary for the church to act to guarantee the authenticity, the "certitude," and thus the trustworthiness of the measures, and also to reinforce the validity of the laws themselves by authenticating their inclusion in the compilation. The collection was promulgated in 1209 or 1210, and in the latter year it was sent to the professors of the flourishing and famous university schools of Bologna, a logical move, given the common mind-set and the many relations that linked the Holy See and the young *clerici* who studied law and their jurist "doctors."

A fourth collection was made by a prominent German active in Italy and known as Johannes Teutonicus (d. 1245), also a private jurist.

A fifth collection, published in 1226, was the work of Pope Honorius III (d. 1227). Honorius followed the example of Innocent III by sending his compilation to the schoolmen of Bologna with the recommendation that they not only use it in the schools and in the courtroom but also encourage its acceptance "by others, both in their decisions and in the schools,"[15] a message that he himself took to heart by sending the same compilation to the law school at Padua.[16]

Historians know these five works collectively as the *Quinque compi-*

---

15. Honorius III, *Compilatio V*, Proemio (in *Corpus Iuris Canonici*, ed. Friedberg, 151): "Mandamus, quatinus eis solempniter publicatis absque ullo scrupulo dubitationis utaris et ab aliis recipi facias tam in iudiciis quam in scholis."

16. Winfried Steltzcr, *Gelehrtes Recht in Österreich* (Vienna: H. Böhlau, 1982), 151.

lationes antiquae.[17] Although they were fated to disappear when they were absorbed, reelaborated, and replaced by the sweeping legislation of Gregory IX in 1234, they nonetheless document the decisive decades in European legal history between the late twelfth and early thirteenth centuries. In particular, they testify that, not only was the law of the church conceived of (as in Gratian) as a law common to all the faithful, but also it was proposed and imposed as the law in both the schools and the law courts. Gratian had relied on the spontaneous acceptance of the faithful, individually or collectively, and the fortunes of his work depended on their acquiescence, but with Innocent III and Honorius III this relationship underwent a radical change. The original objectives were not only respected but reinforced and strengthened: the "cultural" fabric that gave meaning to Gratian's efforts was completed and in part replaced by an intent that remained cultural but also bore the authoritative force of papal promulgation. This meant that the utilization of the works that were imposed on both the schools and the courts was conditioned and solicited not only by scholarly and methodological demands but also by the obedience due a "law" decreed by a pope.

If we were to ignore the two quite separate aspects of the problem we would be totally unprepared to grasp the reasons for the enormous success of the great laws of the church—and of Justinian's laws—in an age in which the law courts used the contents of common law, canon and civil (but not their underlying system or principles!), only as "residual measures" of last resort, to be consulted only when no law applying to the case at hand could be found. Nor could we grasp why the church insisted so vehemently on providing a law common to all the Christian faithful when it was evident (as is now indisputable) that the normative content of common law bore little weight in the law courts or in practice in the secular mechanisms that imposed order in the life of those same *fideles Christi.* Obviously, we need to broaden our horizons and to try to grasp the phenomena that we have begun to investigate according to a historiographic logic that goes beyond a consideration of only the most macroscopic aspects of judicial and notarial practice.

17. *Quinque Compilationes Antiquae,* ed. Emil Freidberg (Leipzig: 1882; reprint Graz: Akademische Druck- und Verlagsanstalt, 1956).

8. The Great "Codifications" of the Church: The *Liber Extra* of Gregory IX, the *Liber Sextus* of Boniface VIII, the *Clementinae* of Clement V, and the Formation of the *Corpus iuris canonici*

The church in the fourteenth century worked actively to create a universal corpus of laws and to give a physiognomy to its "common law."

In 1234 another great event occurred. Gregory IX (d. 1241), speaking in the name of the Universal Church of Rome, promulgated a ponderous collection of laws taken mainly from the *Quinque compilationes antiquae* (1188-ca. 1226), supplemented by Gregory's own decisions and decretals. The material was presented in 1239 "chapters" or articles and was divided into five books, following the design of the *Breviarium* of Bernard of Pavia, a structure that was to remain the model for the church's later legislative efforts. The drafting of this work was supervised by a great Catalan jurist, Raymond of Pennafort, a Dominican and the pontifical penitentiary, later canonized. The compilation was published under the title *Decretales*, but it was also called the *Liber Extra* because the measures it contained were outside of (*extra*) Gratian's *Decretum*.[18]

It is usually said that the *Liber Extra* resembles a code. Indeed, in it and by means of it two important principles were affirmed: first, the principle of exclusivity,[19] by which all norms or portions of norms not included in its corpus (or in Gratian's *Decretum*) were no longer automatically considered authentic (hence their application was not indisputably obligatory). The second principle was connected to the first: it was the notion of textuality, by which the decretals that had indeed found their way into the *Liber Extra* had special validity within the text in which they had been inserted and in the form and in the words chosen and used by Raymond of Pennafort. Undoubtedly, the legislative work of Gregory IX displays one of the most significant tendencies observable in legal circles and in twelfth- and thirteenth-century schools of law since the age of Irnerius—a tendency of both

18. *Liber Extra*, ed. Friedberg, in *Corpus Iuris Canonici*, vol. 2, cols. 5–928.

19. Peter Landau, "*Corpus Iuris Canonici*," in *Evangelisches Kirchenlexicon*, ed. Heinz Brunotte and Otto Weber, 4 vols. (Göttingen: Vanderhoeck & Ruprecht, 1956–61), vol. 1, cols. 773–777. Also Stanley Chodorow, "Law, Canon: After Gratian," *Dictionary of the Middle Ages*, vol. 7 (1986) 413–17.

practitioners and theorists to seek the sure haven of a "certain text," assumed as a point of reference in juridical debate. Whether or not that tendency was an original creation that came to be reflected in the consciousness and the thought of the age, and whether or not it manifested a new idea of a "code" as an organic and comprehensive, "complete" and "definitive" collection of laws is another problem. I doubt that this could have occurred, even in an age that admittedly often placed a high value on the authoritarian and sacral aspects of the universal powers of the pope and the emperor but that was nonetheless fully aware of the variety, fluidity, and composite nature of the laws, central and peripheral, of the church and of the local normative systems of cities, counties, duchies, principalities, and kingdoms. Furthermore, as is known, not only did new papal decretals continue to be produced and promulgated, circulated, and collected in a variety of ways in private compilations (at times they piled up in anonymous anthologies with no guarantee of authenticity), but also old canons and ancient decretals were reused, in whole or part, in a variety of ways.

Although there was indeed in the *Liber Extra* the idea of a unified and homogenous corpus that suggested completion and definitiveness, that idea had hermeneutic validity and force and was not realized in the dynamics or the gradations of the normative sources except in ways incompatible with the modern idea of a "code." As a "code," the *Liber Extra* would have to have done away with the local normative systems or at least have been given precedence over them in application; instead, outside the Papal States, the contents of its norms had validity and were utilized only as subsidiary law when there were no appropriate local and particular dispositions adequate to the solution of a specific judicial problem. They might not even have the force of subsidiary law if it was legitimate, in a particular case, for a judge to decide the case according to the place, the persons, his conscience, or his judgment of the equity involved.

Nonetheless, the popes continued to pursue the idea of a body of laws for all of the Christian world; of a corpus that would have unity and provide unity to the measures compiled; a corpus that would be sufficiently authoritative to constitute a necessary and fundamental part of the experience of the jurist—theoretical or practical—and to be an essential reference for legal practice or for administrative and commercial transactions. Several decades later (in 1298), Boniface

VIII followed the example of Gregory IX by promulgating a new and extensive collection of norms that came to be known as the *Liber Sextus* (to indicate that it was an addition to the five books of the *Decretales* of Gregory IX). It too was divided into five books, following the tradition of *iudex, iudicium, clerus, connubia,* and *crimen* inaugurated by Bernard of Pavia a century earlier.[20]

At the same time as the legal activities of the church were being extended and intensified and were gaining in specificity in both their exercise and their results, new projects for "codification" continued to arise. In Avignon, to which the papal see had been transferred (in permanent residence from 1305), Clement V launched a new official collection of the laws of the church. At his death in 1314 his successor, John XXII, completed and promulgated the work, but it took its name from the pope who had begun it, the *Decretales Clementinae* or simply the *Clementinae*.[21] The *Clementinae* included the constitutions of the Council of Vienne and the decretals of Clement V from 1305 to the year of his death.

At the start of the fourteenth century, then, there were great legal works that the church either appropriated (Gratian's *Decretum*) or promulgated (the *Liber Extra,* the *Liber Sextus,* and the *Clementinae*) in order to provide certain, homogenous, authoritative, and authentic texts for the community of the faithful in Christ, in particular for those who exercised jurisprudence in the wide variety of concrete local situations in the Christian world. These bodies of laws, which historiography calls "codes" but which only partially expressed a codistic view of the law, were known everywhere and everywhere taken as the basis of legality. But they had not yet been brought together into one body of law.

It was only later that people began to speak of a *Corpus iuris canonici.* In 1500 a French jurist, Jean Chappuis, put order into the various compilations, completing them with two additional texts and creating the grandiose edifice (whose basic elements already existed) that came to be known and was utilized for centuries as the *Corpus iuris canonici.* It contained the *Decretum* of Gratian (ca. 1140), the *Liber Extra* or *Decretales* of Gregory IX (1234), the *Liber Sextus* of Boniface

20. *Liber Sextus,* ed. Friedberg, in *Corpus Iuris Canonici,* vol. 2: cols. 929–1124.
21. *Decretales Clementinae,* ed. Friedberg, in *Corpus Iuris Canonici,* vol. 2, cols. 1125–1200.

VIII (1298), and the *Clementinae* of Clement V (1314 and following). Jean Chappuis also included some of the laws of John XXII that had been endowed with an *apparatus* of glosses, distributing them under various titles (headings) and publishing them as *Extravagantes Johannis XXII.*[22] Chappuis did the same for some papal decretals—in particular, the laws of Sixtus IV (1471–84)—that had proven sufficiently important to be included in private collections of canon law, and he published this collection of seventy-four laws under the title *Extravagantes communes.*[23] In 1582, Pope Gregory XIII had all of these collections printed after a commission had carefully examined their contents. This edition of the *Corpus iuris canonici* became the official Roman text that was never again altered until the present century.

Once formed, the *Corpus iuris canonici* had an extraordinary stability. It was in fact to remain in force in the church until 1917, when the Holy See itself was won over by the idea and belief that only in a modern "code" (the *Codex iuris canonici*) could the principles of order and authority be realized, universally imposed, and assured absolute precedence over all local bodies of law. The rapidity with which the Code of 1917 was replaced by a new code in 1983 shows how precarious and illusory it was for the church to place its trust in a single code conceived as a complete text.

9. Civil Law and Canon Law: The *Utrumque ius*

There was an urgent problem underlying the common law: there were two highest laws, the canon and the civil, a duality expressed by the term *utrumque ius*, "the one and the other law." Because both claimed to be the law common to the entire Christian world, the parameters of each one needed to be specified if they were to continue to coexist. The ancient laws of Justinian had little or nothing in common with the new constitutional structure of the Holy Roman Empire. The old magistracies had disappeared. The new magistracies, both central and peripheral, were different. All that was left—and it

22. *Extravagantes Johannis XXII*, ed. Friedberg, in *Corpus Iuris Canonici*, vol. 2, cols. 1201–1236; Jacqueline Tarrant, *Extravagantes Iohannis XXII* (Monumenta Iuris Canonici, ser. B, Corpus Collectionum, 6) (Vatican City: Biblioteca apostolica vaticana, 1983).

23. *Extravagantes communes*, ed. Freidberg, in *Corpus Iuris Canonici*, vol. 2, cols. 1237–1312.

was intensely alive—was a central conceptual nucleus once incorporated into the constitutions of ancient Rome and now revived and reinterpreted in the *figura* of the Holy Roman Empire. This nucleus was the very idea of *imperium*. *Imperium* was different and distinct from *dominium*; moreover, it was a notion that permitted no neutral and intermediate areas such as the idea of seigniory.

The laws of the church contained the same image of power but were directed to a different end. Whereas civil normative systems were conceived of and directed toward founding and guaranteeing the commonweal and the terrestrial existence of structures and persons, canon law was charged with creating the best conditions, in this world, for man to avoid losing his soul and to achieve salvation in the glory and beatitude of Heaven. At a certain point these two aims converged, but they tended to produce potentially conflicting results. Both regarded man in his terrestrial and juridical condition: for the empire, so that man, subjected to an *auctoritas*, might realize the common good in freedom and responsible autonomy; for the church, so that he might avoid the temptation of sin and enjoy the soul's salvation for all eternity.

In principle the basic distinction was and remained the ancient and highly lucid one that Pope Gelasius I had affirmed in 494: there were two *dignitates* that reigned over the world, the *auctoritas sacrata Pontificum* (sacred authority of the popes) and the *regalis potestas* (royal power). The first was constituted *pro aeterna vita* (for eternal life), the second *pro temporalium cursu rerum* (for the duration of the secular world).[24] Accursius expressed the same idea in juridical terms in a schematic and theoretical representation: "Nec papa in temporalibus nec imperator in spiritualibus se debeant immiscere" (Neither the pope in secular matters nor the emperor in spiritual matters has any authority),[25] thus reserving to the Roman pontiff dominion over the human spirit and to the emperor dominion over politics and the course of earthly events.

The problem was that, in fact, and in the administration of the two separate powers, the popes tended to occupy themselves with terres-

24. Gelasius I is quoted in Francesco Calasso, *Medio Evo del diritto* (Milan: Giuffrè, 1954), vol. 1, *Le fonti*, 140 n. 2.
25. Accursius, the *conferens generi* to Auth. Coll.I.6, *quomodo oportet episcopos, in principio*.

trial affairs precisely because many of these offered opportunities for sinning. For example, although mortgage contracts and rental contracts were undeniably terrestrial matters, and hence belonged within the emperor's sphere, it was nonetheless true that the payment of interest (a *usura*; usury) might be requested of the borrower or imposed on him. Because anyone who asked for or demanded interest sinned (since usury was prohibited for religious reasons), the pope had, or arrogated to himself, the power to intervene even in terrestrial affairs to dictate a measure that would serve to close off all roads to sin.

This is why Odofredus could write, with an incisiveness that tempered an irreverent and sarcastic tone, "Dominus papa ratione peccati intromittit se de omnibus" (The lord pope intervenes in all matters by reason of sin).[26] Several decades later, in the early fourteenth century, Cinus of Pistoia was equally decisive: "Ecclesia sibi usurpavit ratione peccati totam iurisdictionem" (The church usurps to itself all jurisdiction by reason of sin).[27] Many popes came in for repeated and sharp criticism of their acts and their legislative initiatives when they meddled in all areas of the law with the argument and the excuse of avoidance of sins.

It is certain that this occurred. If we turn to the *Liber Extra* of Gregory IX, promulgated in 1234, we have direct proof of the church's overstepping the line: in the field of criminal law, because the church claimed jurisdiction in such illicit acts as adultery and rape (X.4.7; X.5.16), bigamy (X.1.21), calumny (X.5.2), injurious libel (X.5.36), false witness (X.5.20), physical violence (X.5.36), and even homicide (X.5.12) and theft (X.5.18); in the field of private law, because there were legal institutions that the church considered particularly dangerous for the soul (because particularly conducive to sin) such as commodatum, or the free loan of chattels (X.3.15), deposit of funds (X.3.16), buying and selling (X.3.17), loans and *usurae* (usury; X.5.19), lending on gages and other securities (X.3.21), and donations (X.3.24). Still in the field of private law, because the family, which fell under private law, was the ideal community for the moral and reli-

26. Odofredus, *Lectura* in Cod.1.1.4, *de Summa Trinitate*.1.*nemo clericus*, no. 3 (Lugduni 1552), fol. 6rb.
27. Cino da Pistoia, *Lectura*, in Auth. *Clericus* post Cod.1.3.32(33), *de episcopis et clericis*.1.*omnes qui*, no. 2 (Francofurti ad Moenum 1578, reprint, Turin: 1964), fol. 18vb.

gious education of the individual, in the image of the Holy Family (Joseph, Mary, and the Infant Jesus), the church felt that certain structures such as consanguinity, kinship, and affinity (X.4.14) required regulation, as did some family-related activities. Hence the church not only felt justified in prohibiting adultery, bigamy, marriage between close relatives, and divorce (X.4.19), but also in fixing the time (X.4.2) and the forms of marriage rites, providing a specific regime governing the wealth of offspring who entered the clergy (X.3.25), and regulating donations between a father and his children and between husband and wife (X.4.20).

As is obvious, there was a wide spectrum of activities and norms within canon law that occupied spaces typical of legal institutions already regulated by Roman and Justinian law. But if superimposed areas of jurisdiction created many practical problems, they also helped to solve some. The rigidity of a discipline more than seven centuries old gave support to the church's laws, lending them basic, concrete legal concepts; at the same time, that rigidity was corrected, tempered, and bent to contain new norms marked by the supreme authority of the church, which served to make that authority coherent with the fluid events of extraordinarily creative centuries.

4

Ius proprium in Europe

Foreword: Setting the Scene

The two universal laws, the law of the ancient Roman Empire and the law of the church (the *ius civile* and the *ius canonicum*), designated together as *utrumque ius*, were completed between the twelfth and the fourteenth centuries. During that same long period, all of Europe lived under a broad variety of heterogeneous local juridical norms. We may give the generic name *ius proprium* to each of these norms.

There was no uniformity in the various particular norms (*iura propria*) to correspond to the unity of the *utrumque ius* (*ius commune*). Rather, their extraordinary diversity makes one suspect that the true face of medieval jurisprudence was uniquely, or at least principally, characterized by disorder, municipal rivalry and vengeance, and clashes between interest groups and social strata, all of which operated within the juxtaposition or opposition of several tiers of law emanating from the community, rural or urban (*consuetudines*), from the decisions of free or autonomous cities (*statuta*), or from the will of a sovereign or a powerful territorial lord (royal laws or the laws of a prince, duke, or count).

This is the image repeatedly presented in one school of thought in recent historiography,[1] whose members have devoted their energies to a frenetic and desperate search for specific and particular legal elements, which they study and reconstruct in isolation, thus offering a complete and exhaustive picture of a single legal phenomenon (*ius*

---

1. This view is still strongly held in a deeply rooted scholarly tradition in Germany. For this school of thought, juridical historiography is divided into "Roman law," "Ger-

proprium), without considering its similarities with other European *iura propria* and without investigating its connections with the discipline, the principles, or the doctrines of the *ius commune*.

This historiographical approach was carried to its sterile point of arrival by a long wave of polemical and negative evaluations of the *ius commune* that, for understandable historical reasons, were given or implied in relation to the *ius commune* by humanist jurists of the fifteenth and sixteenth centuries, by the theologians and jurists of the "Secunda Scholastica" in the sixteenth century, by natural law theorists in the seventeenth century, by Enlightenment thinkers in the eighteenth century, and by the backers of the eighteenth- and nineteenth-century codification movements who, out of faith or self-delusion, believed in the order and uniformity that a "code" would impose.

When any attempt was made to compare the *ius proprium* and the *ius commune*, only the "contents" of the various precepts were examined, which led to the obvious conclusion that the contents did not coincide and that the *ius proprium* and the great legislative corpora of the Empire and the church regarded and portrayed relationships differently.[2] Thus in this view the *ius commune* was simply considered positive law.

Some scholars have deduced from this that local legal traditions imbued with the spirit of the ancient barbarian populations "resisted" Romanization;[3] others have thought, more simply, that the phenomenon of the *utrumque ius* was secondary and relatively insignificant,

---

man law," and "canon law." Not only are there separate university chairs for these three disciplines, but even on a scholarly level the prestigious review named for Friedrich Carl von Savigny, the *Zeitschrift der Savigny-Stiftung für Rechsgeschichte*, is divided into three sections, *Romanistische Abteilung*, *Germanistische Abteilung*, and *Kanonistische Abteilung*. This helps to keep the three fields of study separate and to support the image of three "separate histories" of Romans, Germanic peoples, and ecclesiastics in German lands. Such a separation makes it plausible to study a system of law as "territorial" without qualifying it as *ius proprium*—that is, without any regard for the terms and capacities of its dialectical relationship with the *ius commune*. Rare exceptions aside, this is what happens, and it encourages the idea and the conviction that every scholar must keep to his or her own sector, because others are not considered pertinent.

2. For a recent and clear example of this historiography, see Ugo Nicolini, "Diritto romano e diritti particolari in Italia nell'età comunale," *Rivista di storia del diritto italiano*, 59 (1986): 13–172.

3. For example, this is one of the chief characteristics of the textbook, Jésus Lalinde Abadía, *Iniciacon historica al derecho Español*, 2d ed. (Barcelona: Ediciones Ariel, 1978).

and that Roman and canon law formed a modest "residual law" that
was applied only when local juridical norms lacked a measure to cover
a specific, practical legal problem.[4] Still others, speaking with conscious conviction or without sufficient reflection, have approached
the *ius commune* as if it were a terrain in which all manner of "archeo-
logical" finds were possible, while others who shared that conviction
but professed a total disinterest in juridical archeology have carefully
avoided the whole subject.[5]

Some expressions have become clichés: local law was "opposed" or
"counterposed" to the *ius commune*; local law was a "particular law"
or a "territorial law," and because local law was usually applied in the
law courts before the *ius commune*, it follows that it had greater
weight than the *ius commune* (following the common but erroneous
notion that a "practice" without theory is always of greater authority
as a guide for understanding concrete situations and for action).

Entire academic schools of thought have been founded on these
basic convictions. For years scholars insisted on a "hierarchy" among
norms, and although this notion has attenuated, it has not completely
disappeared.[6] They have concentrated on determining how the scale
of precedence was disposed in the schemes of each particular city or
realm; what they found was that judges were expected to apply the
local law first (the communal statute or the royal law in the case of
the *Regnum Siciliae* or Castile and León); second, the customary laws;
and finally, if no ruling could be found on either of the first two levels,

4. Historians of the law usually use the term "residual law" with caution, or else it
is implicit. It is explicit, however, in Giovanni Tarello, *Storia della cultura giuridica
moderna* (Bologna: Il Mulino, 1976), vol. 1, *Assolutismo e codificazione del diritto*, 29 n.
11: "Per 'diritto comune' s'intende un diritto residuale" (By *ius commune* we understand
a residual law)—a serious statement that does not come close to representing or expressing the complexity of the *ius commune*.

5. On this point, see Manlio Bellomo, "Personaggi e ambienti nella vicenda storica
del diritto comune," in *Il diritto comune e la tradizione giuridica europea*, Atti del Convegno di studi in onore di Giuseppe Ermini, Perugia 30–31 October 1976, ed. Danilo
Segoloni (Perugia: Libreria Universitaria; Rimini: distrib. Maggioli, 1980), 37–50, esp.
48ff. For specific bibliography, see Ennio Cortese, "Storia del diritto italiano," in *Cinquanta anni di esperienza giuridica in Italia*, Proceedings of the Congresso nazionale
organized by the Università di Messina and Casa Editrice Giuffrè, Messina-Taormina,
3–8 November 1981 (Milan: Giuffrè, 1982), 787–858, esp. 850ff.

6. A large number of studies have been published that follow this line of thought,
promoted by Ugo Nicolini. On this topic, see Manlio Bellomo, *Società e istituzioni dal
medioevo agli inizi dell'età moderna*, 6th ed. (Rome: Il Cigno Galileo Galilei, 1993), 381
and 381 n. 43.

the *ius commune*, equity, or some other law (such as the *Siete Partidas* on the Iberian Peninsula).

Some scholars in more recent times who have shared the intent to demonstrate how far "practice" was from the *ius commune* (on occasion they refer to it as *diritto dei professori*, *Juristenrecht* or *das gelehrte Recht*, *droit savant*, or *derecho docto*) have exaggerated the historical importance of judicial practices and of the *consilia* (records of courtroom proceedings and other related materials) connected with them. Today, although we clearly must acknowledge that the *consilia* are extremely valuable as testimony, it is equally clear that we need to be sensitive to their jurisprudence and their juridical significance. We need to examine the inner mechanisms, techniques, and methodologies used to formulate opinions and found their validity (or at least their defensibility) in some specific types of norms (always those of the *ius commune*) and not in others, but we also need to examine the significance of the *consilia* themselves as a means for defining the political and social role of the jurists who wrote them. When such aspects of the question are considered, the *consilia* demonstrate the contrary of what certain scholars have thought: in reality these questions prove that the *ius commune* was used massively and constantly in the *consilia*, out of the conviction that only in the *ius commune* must one, and therefore could one, find the arguments that were needed for trials.

It should immediately be noted that studies of this sort have enriched our knowledge: investigations guided by the intellectual joy of discovery have uncovered evidence of legal theory buried in the surviving documentation; analytical reconstructions have been made of the "hierarchy" of norms, in particular local, territorially limited entities (such as a *Regnum* or a *commune civitatis*); specific legal practices have been reconstructed. It is also clear that the overall vision that has resulted from such studies is identical in all the points of view just surveyed, since they all deny the *ius commune* any important role as a law capable of a real effect on local legal practice or doctrine, and their historiographical evaluations underestimate the multiple valences and capacities of the *ius commune*.

The problem, it seems to me, is thus to understand whether the reconstruction of the *ius commune* has any significance beyond a cultivated (and basically humanistic) pleasure in rediscovering an intellectual system of the past; whether our historiographical reconstruction of the law in the later Middle Ages can be based simply on the selection of particular data from one or more legal orders; whether one can see the *ius commune* uniquely as mere positive law; consequently, whether we can hold that the *ius commune* was only a secondary and residual law and, as such, was of scarce relevance in the local courts of law; whether or not we risk taking the point of view of the person or persons who ruled or hoped to rule a community or kingdom, and risk adopting the decisions they made (for political and social reasons) as the basis of our own historiographical evaluation.

We need to begin from a different perspective. The *ius commune*, unlike the many local laws, cannot be considered only as "positive law," even if, admittedly, it was positive law and hence also residual law. We can evaluate and appreciate other dimensions of the *ius commune* that came to be formed out of ideological and cultural beliefs, thanks to the concurrent existence and influence of idealized values; dimensions that arose or were adapted in concrete situations as instruments for the safeguard of corporative and group interests. We need to try to understand not only why tens of thousands of copies of the *Corpus iuris civilis* and the *Corpus iuris canonici* were produced and circulated but also why entire generations of students "became pilgrims for love of learning,"[7] and like "pilgrims" they made their way to the learned cities—Bologna, Padua, Perugia, Montpellier, Toulouse, Orléans, Salamanca—to attend schools of *ius commune* and become doctors *in utroque iure*, even at the price of considerable economic sacrifice and mortal danger (many in fact died far from their homelands). These are facts that we cannot ignore, nor should we consider them extraneous to the problems of the *ius proprium*. By ignoring them or holding them to be irrelevant we would have to claim that in the past thousands of young men were stricken with an inexplicable and widespread madness when they sold (or had their fathers sell) entire fiefs and mortgage their entire patrimony in order to buy—as they did—costly books of *ius commune* and travel *in terra aliena*—which they also did—to study the *ius commune* in the European universities of their time. Furthermore, we would have to assert that, once their studies had ended and they were functioning as judges or

---

7. This expression is in the *Constitutio* "Habita" of Frederick I Barbarossa: "Omnibus qui causa studiorum peregrinantur scolaribus . . . hoc nostre pietatis beneficium indulgemus." See the edition of this text by Winfried Stelzer, "Zum Scholarenprivileg Friedrich Barbarossas (Authentica 'Habita')," *Deutsches Archiv für Erforschung des Mittelalters* 34, 1 (1978): 125–65, quote 165.

lawyers, these thousands of young men did their very best to forget everything they had learned, lived solely on *ius proprium*, and used and applied only *ius proprium*, and that other young men who became cultivated and reserved jurists were content to spend a genteel and provincial old age cultivating an abstract, elegant, and scholarly jurisprudence. It is because it ignores the relationship between the *ius proprium* and the *ius commune* that French historiography refers to the *ius commune* as *droit savant*, that German historiography calls it *Juristenrecht* or *das gelehrte Recht*, and that Spanish historiography calls it *el derecho docto*, all ambiguous and at least partly misleading expressions. Even worse, Italian and Anglo-American legal scholarship have no word for it at all.

This is not the perspective from which I intend to view local norms—the *ius proprium*. The fact that the *ius proprium* existed and that its contents differed from those of the *ius commune* cannot mean, to put it simplistically, that the laws of Justinian and the laws of the church were everywhere essentially unheeded, that they were marginal to everyday practice in the law courts and notaries' studies, or that they were marginal to the legal civilization of Europe.

The panorama is extremely vast; I shall limit my remarks to tracing a few of the pertinent lines of thought in continental Europe, beginning with Italy and continuing to the Iberian Peninsula, France, and the German-speaking lands of central Europe.

2. Italy: Communal Legislation

At first, between the eleventh and the twelfth centuries, custom ruled everywhere. It governed the life of the communities scattered through the countryside (*consuetudo loci*), of isolated monasteries (monastic custom), and of towns and cities. Still, there was occasional awareness or memory of the ancient Roman laws, still to be restored, or of the patchy Lombard or Carolingian laws, especially as collected and recorded in the *Liber Papiensis* (where they were arranged chronologically) and the *Lombarda* (which divided them by subject matter). Nonetheless, even if he did remember them, anyone drawing up a *cartula* or taking part in a lawsuit thought of custom first. Notaries (*scribae*) thus used expressions that would be incomprehensible to a modern jurist—such as "secundum consuetudines legum Romanorum" (according to the customs of the Roman laws).

Toward the middle of the twelfth century, beginning in the lands of Lombard Italy, the situation began to show signs of radical change. The changes soon spread until they mingled with more radical legislative initiatives of the Italian communes (the statutes) that reflected the degree of independence won by the various local governments.

The first traces of this change take us to Milan and Bologna. An anonymous private citizen in Milan, the Lombard capital, wrote a *tractatus* in order to set down on parchment the customs of the city; also in Milan a feudal judge whose name has come down to us, Oberto dall'Orto (Obertus de Horto), first wrote down feudal customary law. This was the so-called "Obertine redaction" of the *Libri feudorum*.

In Bologna the city's orally transmitted customary norms were reported to have been written down *in curia Bulgari*—that is, within the complex of buildings and courtyards in which Bulgarus lived and taught. The literal meaning of *curia* is "court" or "courtyard," but in this case the term indicates the function as a private "judge" exercised by Bulgarus. Thus the redaction of customary norms, albeit "private," was connected with practical legal needs.

The redaction of custom tended to shift from private to public initiative—for example, in Milan in 1216, fragments of the old *tractatus* were collected and incorporated into official legislation in a document whose title nonetheless recalls its consuetudinary origin: *Liber consuetudinum* (Book of Customs).

This became current practice in the communes of north-central Italy. During the thirteenth century, it became more customary than it had been under the *consoli* of the earlier communal governments for the city leader, the podestà or the captain of the people, to have the customs that private individuals had already written down (thus removing them from the uncertainty of oral transmission) brought into a single corpus and copied in one book (*codex*). The same document typically included the measures (*statuta*) passed by the city's general assembly and the regulations laid down by the heads of the commune and accepted by the people, called *brevia* from *breve*, the oath sworn by both the city magistrates and the assembly to guarantee respect and obedience to the laws.

During the thirteenth century there were increasing numbers of city statutes, enlarged by new dispositions. The first *statuta* in Volterra appeared between 1210 and 1224; in Treviso between 1207 and 1263; in Padua between 1222 and 1228; in Verona in 1228; in Venice between 1226 and 1242; in Reggio Emilia between 1242 and 1273. In Bologna lengthy and organic statutes were drawn up between 1245 and 1267 for the Comune del podestà and in 1288 for the Comune del popolo, and so on. Recasting and updating the statutes was carried on at such a dizzying pace that proverbs sprang up: "Legge di Verona non dura da terza a nona" (Verona's laws do not last from terce to nones); "Legge fiorentina fatta la sera è guasta la mattina" (Florentine law made in the evening is spoiled by morning). One acute and critical observer, Boncompagno of Signa (d. 1235), gave a precocious and unsentimental analysis of the changeable city norms, writing that "these municipal laws and these plebiscites fade like the moon's shadows, and like the moon they wax and wane at the legislators' whim."[8]

Although the statutes purported to be "city laws" par excellence, for many decades they were limited in their range. What is more, they met with opposition and hostility on the part of broad segments of the city population, who saw little reflection of themselves and their interests in them. Not all the *residentes* of a city were considered part of the *commune civitatis*, hence "the communal statute, considered alone . . . appears as an act of will of a corporation"[9]—that is, of people who owned property and cultivated their agrarian and landholding interests. Any city dweller not included in the *commune civitatis* continued to fall under the jurisdiction and tutelage of the bishop. Furthermore, the many corporative bodies of the arts and trades, major and minor, generated their own *statuta* and relied on them for defense of their vital interests rather than on the statutes of the commune under the podestà. They did not relinquish this power to make their own rules even when they had their own *commune*, the Comune del popolo, toward the late thirteenth century. At the same time, one

8. Boncompagno of Signa, *Rhetorica novissima*, I.1, ed. Augusto Gaudenzi, in *Bibliotheca Iuridica Medii Aevi* (Bologna: In Aedebus Petri Virano olim Fratrum Treves, 1882; reprint, Turin: Bottega d'Erasmo, 1962), 2:253: "Sed iste leges municipales atque plebiscita sicut umbra lunatica evanescunt, quoniam ad similitudinem lune crescunt et decrescunt secundum arbitrium conditorum."

9. Enrico Besta, *Fonti: Legislazione e scienza giuridica*, 2 vols., in *Storia del diritto italiano*, ed. Pasquale Del Giudice (Milan: Hoepli, 1923–25; reprint, Frankfurt am Main: Sauer und Avermann KG; Florence: O. Gozzini, 1969), quotation vol. 1 pt. 2, 502.

of the many corporations, the *collegium* of the jurist "doctors," used its monopoly on knowledge of Justinian's laws and the universal law of the church as a formidable instrument for political and social control of city life and as a means for increasing and safeguarding the unique power of its members and reaping immense professional profits.[10]

In Italy of the communes, then, custom was interwoven with the statutes, and its fate was mingled with theirs. Exceptions were few: in Pisa, to note one, the normative texts of the *Constitutum legis* were kept separate from the *Constitutum usus* (which contained customary norms promulgated by the city government, hence given a new and different title of validity). Customary norms that continued to be transmitted and observed without being written down and, above all, with no modification of their nature—as events in Pisa showed—also remained separate.

In certain regions of northern and central Italy, laws produced and imposed by the authority of a prince or ruler were added to city laws and took precedence over them.

Piedmont and Savoy

In Piedmont and Savoy, Aosta and Vaud were both conspicuous for their imposing bodies of customary norms. But from much earlier days—the times of Pietro II, from 1266 to 1269, and of Amedeo VI, the "Green Count," in 1379—the central government had aimed at providing an overall, unified set of laws for the entire land; a law that, unlike city customs, hoped and claimed to be a general (or common) law. In reality the most significant results of these efforts came only with Amedeo VIII and his promulgation (in 1430) of a body of laws set out in the five books of the *Decreta seu Statuta*.[11]

The Papal States

The same sorts of things occurred on the two levels of the *ius proprium* in the Papal States, which cut across several regions and occu-

10. Bellomo, "Personaggi e ambienti."

11. For the *Decreta* and their relation to common law, see Isidoro Soffietti, "Note su deroghe apportate al Codice giustinianeo da parte di legislatori sabaudi," in *Studi in onore di Giuseppe Grosso*, 3 vols. (Turin: Giapichelli, 1968–70), 3:631–49. See also Soffietti, "Una norma dei 'Decreta seu Statuta' del duca Amedeo VIII di Savoia sul canone enfiteutico," *Rassegna degli Archivi di Stato* (1974): 1–12.

pied a large part of the center of the Italian Peninsula, from Latium north and east, passing through Umbria to the Marches, and including a part of Emilia.

On the lower or city level there were customary norms and city statutes as in Lombardy, Liguria, the Veneto, and Tuscany. Above the local norms (but as a law subsidiary to them) a broad-ranging corpus of laws, divided into six books, was promulgated in Fano in 1357 under the supervision of Cardinal Egidio d'Albornoz, the papal legate for Italy in the years in which the pope resided in Avignon. The title of this document was *Liber Constitutionum Sanctae Matris Ecclesiae*, but it was also known as the *Constitutiones Marchiae Anconitanae* or simply *Constitutiones aegidianae*.[12] Some two centuries later, when Cardinal Rodolfo Pio of Carpi made additions to it that were promulgated by Paul III in 1544 as *Additiones Carpenses*, this collection of laws was still showing signs of life.

The *Giudicati* of Sardinia

Sardinia's history was intimately connected with that of Europe, despite the judgment of many historians, the inadvertent neglect, and the deliberate omissions that have attempted to relegate that large Mediterranean island to the fringes of the major events of the period.

In Sardinia as elsewhere, cities and towns had their own customary norms, in part channeled into broader statutory texts, which were the symbol and expression of the vitality and the autonomy that the urban community had won and could enjoy. This was the case, for example, in Sassari and Cagliari.

Furthermore, as in the Duchy of Savoy (Piedmont and Savoy) and the territories of the church (the Papal States), there were attempts in Sardinia to create a unified legal system for local populations, but the project was realized only in a part of the island. The *giudicati* (small kingdoms—*regna*—headed by a monarch called a *iudex*) of Cagliari, Logudoro, and Gallura gave little sign of any such intentions, but in the *giudicato* of Arborea, the reigning *iudex*, Mariano (1353–76), drew up a first project for a general law, which was followed by a complete

12. There is a lengthy and fully documented work on Egidio d'Albornoz and his *Constitutiones*: Paolo Colliva, *Il cardinale Albornoz, lo Stato della Chiesa, le "Constitutiones Aegidianae" (1353–1357)* (Bologna: Real Colegio de España, 1977). See also "Il testo volgare delle Costituzioni di Fano dal ms. Vat.lat. 3939" in the appendix to that work.

corpus of laws promulgated in 1390–91 by Eleonora of Arborea, Mariano's daughter.[13] The thorough coverage and the maturity of this *Carta de logu de Arborea* enabled it to reach beyond the borders of the *giudicato* of Arborea to become a territorial law for all of Sardinia. Thus Sardinia had local laws on the two levels of the city and the region.

The *Regnum Siciliae*: Municipal Customary Law and Royal Law; The *Assisae* of Roger II; the *Liber Constitutionum* of Frederick II

These problems were particularly interesting and particularly varied in the part of Italy known as the *Regnum Siciliae*. The kingdom that took its name from the island of Sicily reached from Campania in the west and the Abruzzo in the east, south through Basilicata, Puglia, and Calabria to Sicily. Within the kingdom, founded by Roger II in 1130 and later ruled by other Norman, Swabian, Angevin, and Aragonese kings, there were cities and towns with rich civic traditions and prosperous economies. Among them one should mention Bari and Trani on the Adriatic coast and Otranto on the edge of the Ionian Sea; on the Tirrhenian coast, Naples, Amalfi, and Salerno; on the island itself, Palermo, Messina, Catania, Siracusa, and Trapani, a city famous for and made wealthy by the production of salt and the manufacture of coral objects.

Some cities, Amalfi for example, had seen their relations with the East shattered and their trade ruined by the installation of the Normans to the south of them and the construction of a Norman kingdom partially blocking Amalfi's long-standing connections with Byzantium. In spite of this, Amalfi made good use of the extraordinary potential that it had gained from the varied administrative and notarial experience that grew out of its traditional economic activities, and the city gave birth to entire "dynasties" of notaries and able administrators. Other cities—Bari, Messina, Palermo—had periods of intense development due in part to their strategic locations and their excellent seaports.

These cities demanded of the monarchy freedom to live according

13. Ennio Cortese, "Nel ricordo di Antonio Era: Una proposta per la datazione della 'Carta de Logu'," *Quaderni Sardi di Storia* 3 (1981–3): 39–50; Antonello Mattone, "Eleonora d'Arborea," in *Dizionario Biografico degli Italiani* (Rome: Istituto della Enciclopedia Italiana, 1960–), vol. 42 (forthcoming).

to their own ancient customs, a political course that the crown opposed and, when it could, tried to quash.

Some of the cities of Puglia obtained a first recognition of city rights when they surrendered to the new sovereign shortly after the consolidation of the new kingdom. Between 1130 and 1140, Roger II drew up explicit pacts with these cities, validated and documented by *carte di resa* (charters of surrender), in which the king promised to respect the local customary norms and the cities submitted to the crown. In 1140, however, the same Roger II violated these pacts and forced the judges of the kingdom to apply the laws of the realm (the *Assisae*) first, referring to customary norms only when they did not "most manifestly" differ from the sovereign's laws.

The cities of Puglia continued their dynamic development during the last decades of the twelfth century, when two Pugliese judges, Andrea and Sparano, redacted the customary norms of Bari (Andrea those of the Roman tradition and Sparano those of the Lombard tradition).

In Messina the first attempt to write down the city's customary norms (undoubtedly on the initiative of a private citizen, a judge or a notary) dates from the first two decades of the thirteenth century. After 1220, however, Frederick II, who was also Holy Roman emperor, began to exercise his sovereign powers as king of Sicily. He established a harsh policy of the containment or repression of local freedoms and local autonomy, and one particular law in the *Liber Constitutionum* of 1231 that he promulgated, the *Constitutio* "Puritatem," was to pose great problems of interpretation for later historiography. This constitution established a rigid hierarchy among the normative sources of the *Regnum*. Judges were to apply the laws of the kingdom first; if the royal law failed to provide a norm corresponding to the case under examination, the judges were directed to turn to the city customary laws, but only if such laws had been expressly held just and admissible (*bonae et approbatae*) by the king. Finally, if the judges found no applicable norm either among the sovereign's dispositions or among the *bonae et approbatae* customary laws, they might avail themselves of the *ius commune*. This, according to an explanation in the text but perhaps added after its publication and placed at the end of the constitution, comprised Lombard law and Roman law.

Historians who have grappled with the problems posed by "Puritatem" have not always dealt with both aspects of the problem. The text should be examined from the point of view of the local legal institutions of which the statute was an expression, but also from the point of view of that universal political entity, the empire, of which the *ius commune* was a projection. Furthermore, some historians have considered the local laws and the *ius commune* only within a perspective that reduces them all to simple positive law. By considering Roman law only as positive law, they have thus concluded that the *ius commune* was only a subsidiary law. Then, with a bold leap justified by a similarity between the gradations in the law imposed by "Puritatem" and the hierarchies of law present in many communal statutes of central and northern Italy, they have drawn the further (but hasty) conclusion that in all cases the *ius commune* was a subsidiary law, the study of which is thus all the more useless for comprehension of the complexities of local municipal statutes, since men of that time—whom one legal historian refers to as *gli omarini di media cultura* (the little men of middling learning)—had only the vaguest knowledge of the *ius commune*.[14]

Although it is true that, if we hold to the perspective of positive law, a gradation among sources of law leads to an acceptance of the notion that the *ius commune* was (in that perspective only) a subsidiary law, it is also true that the problem is wrongly posed in those terms because they are both limited and limiting.[15] A partial truth is not the truth. What is missing here is the other perspective, the one that enables us to view the *ius commune* not as a positive law but as a law that "eternally" (it was thought) radiated juridical logic, juridical concepts, and the terminology and mechanisms of legal reasoning—in short, the jurists', hence the judges', modes of being. Thus what

14. Carlo Guido Mor, "Considerazioni su qualche costituzione di Federico II," *Archivio Storico Pugliese* 26 (1973): 423–34, now reprinted in *Il "Liber Augustalis" di Federico II di Svevia nella storiografia*, ed. Anna L. Trombetti (Bologna: Patron, 1987), 293–303, quotation 294.

15. For an example of this approach, see Hermann Dilcher, "Kaiserrecht und Königsrecht in staufischen Sizilien," in *Studi in onore di Edoardo Volterra*, 6 vols. (Milan: Giuffrè, 1971): 5:1–21, available in Italian translation as "Diritto imperiale e diritto regio nella Sicilia sveva," in *Il "Liber Augustalis,"* 305–24, esp. 319. The example is telling because Dilcher's approach leads him to confuse the *ius commune* with the "laws of the coronation" of 1220 and to write, among other things, one phrase that is incomprehensible at best: ". . . leggi dell'incoronazione del 1220—che, secondo il diritto romano erano da considerarsi *ius commune* . . ." (laws of the coronation of 1220 which, according to Roman law, were to be considered *ius commune*).

seems secondary when one follows one interpretive line becomes essential and bears its full load when one follows a different and broader approach. This is true whether we are looking at events in the *Regnum Siciliae* as they related to levels of law in the *Constitutio* "Puritatem" or whether we examine what went on in any other part of Europe when a specific legal system imposed hierarchies of laws for the guidance of the judge. As we shall see, this happened in Europe even in regions of northern France, where Roman law was by no means in force as positive law but where it persisted as *ratio scripta* and informed every act and every opinion of the agents of justice because it penetrated the jurists' reasoning mechanisms and because its language was the vehicle for all ideas.

After the death of Frederick II in 1250, both during the course of the tumultuous events that ended the Swabian phase of the *Regnum* and when Charles I, the first Angevin king of Sicily, came to the throne in 1266, the cities once more began to weave the fabric of their liberty and their self-government.

Cities in both parts of the *Regnum* gave free rein to such initiatives after the Sicilian Vespers in 1282, an event that for roughly a century and a half separated Sicily (ruled by the Aragonese) from the continental Mezzogiorno (under Angevin French rule). The cities were abetted by the crown's lack of interest, by its weakness, and by the rapacious greed of Aragonese sovereigns such as Alfonso, called the Magnanimous (d. 1458), who were willing to recognize the cities' laws, old (that is, customary) and new (*capitula*), in exchange for substantial payments in gold coin—Florentine or Aragonese fiorini or Sicilian onze. Cities were also helped by the administrative policies of the Angevin crown, which saw that the kingdom would flourish by keeping a balance between the sovereign's central authority and the local liberties of the demesnial cities (that is, cities directly subject to the crown). In any event, in the late thirteenth, the fourteenth, and the fifteenth centuries the cities of the kingdom were intent on having their own law, first by the redaction of customary norms, then by *capitula* to which the sovereign, according to his interests, gave or withheld his *placet*. This sort of activity was intense in the demesnial cities that were directly subservient to the crown with no intermediate feudal lord. Although from time to time some cities and towns passed under the power of a feudal lordship, many remained as part of the king's demesne, as Martin of Aragon the Younger, king of Sicily, took care to remind the Parliament of Siracusa in 1398 as part of a royal "census" of the demesnial cities.[16]

The compilation of customary norms (*consuetudines*) was begun through private initiative. When the city adopted a private collection and made it its own, it sought to legitimize it by requesting confirmation from the king, who, if he so desired, then conceded the collection of customs "as a privilege."

The so-called "Ancient Text" of the *Consuetudines* of Messina goes back to the latter half of the thirteenth century. This widely known text served as a model not only in the neighboring areas of northeast Sicily but also in places as far away as Trapani. Trapani, in fact, took the *Testo Antico* of Messina as its own law in 1331, and, because there is no direct documentation of the original version, we know the oldest Messina customary laws through the *Consuetudines* of Trapani or by their reuse in even later and in part fragmentary texts.[17]

During the fourteenth century, increasing numbers of privileges were requested and granted for city *consuetudines*. Thus Palermo, Catania, Siracusa, Noto, Patti, and a number of other demesnial cities and towns, great and small, all enjoyed royal "privileges."[18]

The situation was different in the feudal cities. There, although the city dwellers used customary law to defend a stability that served them as a guarantee of their liberties, the redaction of custom took place within "pacts" that led to complex, difficult, and often violent relations between the local community and the feudal lord.

Royal legislation formed a counterpoint to the variety of the local legal norms. It too was *ius proprium* in respect to the *ius commune*, but it served a broader and more homogeneous territory than the *consuetudines* and the municipal *capitula*, thus it appeared as a territorial law endowed with a general authority that the municipal legal systems could not have. In the *Regnum Siciliae* as elsewhere (and earlier than

16. Francesco Testa, *Capitula Regni Siciliae*, 2 vols. (Panormi: 1741–43), 1:132–33.

17. See Lucia Sorrenti, "Le vicende di un 'testo vivo': un'antica redazione delle Consuetudini messinesi nel manoscritto Messina, A.d.S. 52," *Quaderni Catanesi* 15 (1986): 127–212.

18. With only a few exceptions (see previous note), little scholarly work has been done since the studies of Vito La Mantia, many of which were collected in La Mantia, *Antiche Consuetudini delle città di Sicilia* (Palermo: A. Reber, 1900). On these studies, see Manlio Bellomo, "Problemi e tendenze della storiografia siciliana tra Ottocento e Novecento," in *La presenza della Sicilia nella cultura degli ultimi cento anni*, Atti, 2 vols. (Palermo: Società Storia Patria Palermo, 1977), 2:989–1004, esp. 990 n. 4.

elsewhere) we can see the phenomenon of the dual levels of the *ius proprium* that we have already seen in Savoy, in the Papal States, and in the Sardinian *giudicati*. We shall see that it was fairly widespread north of the Alps as well.

The oldest royal legislation is the *Assisae* (Assize) promulgated by Roger II for Ariano di Puglia (now Ariano Irpino, in Campania) in 1140. These were norms, few in number, named for the assembly (*assise*) in which they began their official life. The king's will was what counted: the assembly, informed of his pleasure, served only to make known and publicize that will. William I (the Bad) and William II (the Good) also promulgated constitutions, in large measure now lost.

In Melfi in 1231 Frederick II promulgated his famous body of laws, referred to in the sources variously as *Constitutiones* or *Constitutiones Regni* but more commonly known as the *Liber Constitutionum* or *Liber Augustalis*.[19]

This legislative work, which may have been in large part drawn up by Frederick's secretary, the cultivated Pier della Vigna, is divided into three books. It is an "open corpus," however, to which *novellae constitutiones* of Frederick's were added, either as an integral part of the work or separately in an appendix. Not all of Frederick's later legal enactments found a place in the *Liber Augustalis*, however, a fact that shows selectivity at work and that ultimately gives special value and significance to the legislative texts that were included and demotes the excluded texts to a secondary or occasional status. In short, the *Liber Augustalis* contained the notion (which was to be typical of nineteenth-century "codifications") that the materials it subjected to unified treatment were to underlie the entire normative system throughout the land. This is, incidentally, an idea that was realized during those very same years, in sharp rivalry with the *Liber Augustalis*, in the *Liber Extra* of Pope Gregory IX, a work that gave the

---

19. For the various editions of Frederick II's constitutions, see *Constitutiones Regni Siciliae. Liber Augustalis, Neapoli 1475: Faksimiledruck mit einer Einleitung von Hermann Dilcher* (Glasshütten / Taunus: D. Auvermann, 1973). The introduction to this work, which appears in Italian translation in *Il "Liber Augustalis,"* 123–43 (see n. 14), gives information on the best editions of the constitutions. There is an English translation by James M. Powell, *The Liber Augustalis or Constitutions of Melfi Promulgated by the Emperor Frederick II for the Kingdom of Sicily in 1231* (Syracuse: Syracuse University Press, 1971).

church a universal normative system, the exclusiveness of which we have already seen. This rivalry created an internal ambiguity in the *Liber Augustalis*: although it undeniably was promulgated by Frederick II in his authority and dignity as *Rex Siciliae*, it nonetheless expressed the will of a man who was also emperor of the Holy Roman Empire. Francesco Calasso rightly emphasized the positive aspects and the constructive results of this ambiguity: expressions heavily freighted with meaning as strong projections of the *maiestas* and sacrality of *imperium* were inappropriate to the reality of a more modest royal legislation.[20] This ambiguity places the *Liber Augustalis* squarely at the center of the sources of the *ius proprium*, and it attributes a value, a dignity, and a quality to that *ius proprium* lacking in other local normative regimes.

Although the *Liber Augustalis* remained in force for centuries, it was not studied in the specialized juridical schools. It did not even figure in the curriculum of the *Studium* in Naples that Frederick II himself founded in 1224. This fact seems most singular if we judge it by the logic of those who see the sources of the *ius proprium* (royal decrees, customary law) in the *Regnum Siciliae* and the norms of the *ius commune* uniquely as "positive law." Moreover it is a fact that has always been ignored or eluded in all historical studies of the *Constitutio* "Puritatem" and left out of their overall view of the problems connected with the laws of the *Regnum*.

If we follow the current historiographical logic we cannot explain, on the one hand, why Frederick II imposed the *Liber Augustalis* as the primary and general law of the *Regnum* while relegating the *ius commune* to the lowest level of "subsidiary law" or, on the other, why he took the *ius commune* (Roman and canon) as the primary, even the only, law when he reorganized the law school of Naples in 1224.[21] He backed the programs of these schools and carried on an intensive and at times bitter political campaign to limit the influence of Bologna; at the same time, however, he tried to transplant to Naples Bolognese methodology and the study of the Bolognese texts of common law,

20. Francesco Calasso, "Rileggendo il 'Liber Augustalis,' " in *Atti del Convegno Internazionale di Studi Federiciani*, Messina 18 December 1950 (Palermo: Renna, 1952), 461–72. This study has been reprinted several times, most recently in *Il "Liber Augustalis,"* 53–64.

21. Manlio Bellomo, "Federico II, lo 'Studium' a Napoli e il diritto comune nel 'Regnum,' " *Rivista Internazionale di Diritto Comune* 2 (1991): 135–51.

rallying to his cause such southern jurists as Roffredus Beneventanus and others who had studied in Bologna and had personal experience with the teachings of northern schools either in Bologna or influenced by Bologna.

Such an approach is a dead end that will lead only to an impasse. It follows the reductive conviction that royal law and *ius commune* were merely positive law, with the corollary that the only problem worthy of attention is an investigation of the ways in which a judge fulfilled his duties by a search for the norm appropriate to the case before him. I do not believe that Frederick II ever had such a modest view of his own *maiestas*, nor do I believe that, even when he lowered himself to take on the figure and the functions of a king, Frederick II had any doubts about being always and at all times and occasions, also and above all, an emperor. Thus, thanks to Frederick's global concept of *imperium*, the *ius commune*—which the judge could do without and was even obliged to do without if an appropriate principle could be found in royal law—recovered its sacred character and its value as a paradigm and a model for the autonomy of the law, an image superior to legality, and an extreme limit set to any thoughts of insubordination on the part of the judges of the kingdom.[22]

The same was true of the precepts of Holy Scripture. Although it is quite true that the judge could not apply them in preference to local, royal, or customary norms, he still had to keep them in mind at all times. Although from the twelfth century on, law was distinct from both theology and ethics and each had its specific terrain, the distinction by no means involved an absolute separation, except perhaps for people of weaker conscience or in dubious affairs or the shady maneuvers of obscure minor lawyers.

This vision—a vision that permeates the *Liber Augustalis* and gives it life and significance—makes the corpus of laws of Frederick II stand out clearly from analogous collections (or "codifications") of the time. The only compilation that bears comparison with it was its rival, the *Liber Extra* of Gregory IX (1234). The pope's attempts to modify Frederick's legislative initiative, which was clearly forthcoming by 1230, become essential for understanding not only the motivations behind the *Liber Augustalis* and the significance of that docu-

---

22. The last point is clearly stated, and with the same general viewpoint expressed here, in Federico Martino, *Federico II: Il legislatore e gli interpreti* (Milan: Giuffrè, 1988).

ment but also, given that the two situations were parallel, for understanding the positive valence of the *Liber Extra*, which reached beyond the domains of positive law and the guidance to be given to a judge, to radiate throughout the entire realm of jurisprudence. In that broader arena the law was regarded as a norm to be applied, for which respect was compulsory, but it was also regarded as a source and corpus of human justice, a basis for theoretical elaboration, and an instrument for political power and for the pursuit of the economic and social interests of individuals, groups, and entire segments of society.

Thus, to cite just one example, if we must agree that Charlemagne's universal order fell apart because that first emperor of the Holy Roman Empire had no clear idea of *imperium* and *dominium*,[23] it is just as undisputable that Frederick II had a very clear grasp of those same notions. These were ideas founded on and incorporated into the dispositions and doctrines of the *ius commune*, thanks to the rediscovered importance of the ancient Roman law and Justinian law. They were a part of the European legal tradition of the first half of the thirteenth century, when the glossators' school had reach its height in the works of Azo, Hugolinus, and Accursius, some time before 1231 and the promulgation of the *Liber Augustalis*. They were the only possible roots from which the project of a "general law" for the exercise of *imperium* could spring—which was the point on which Frederick II and Gregory IX clashed.

3. Europe outside Italy

Outside Italy—the center from which the great European legal civilization of the later Middle Ages radiated—the most frequently recurring typologies of the *ius proprium* were substantially analogous to the Italian ones, even when they were marked by variants and differences and set off by a different terminology.[24] Local custom always

---

23. See Robert Boutruche, *Seigneurie et féodalité*, 2 vols. (Paris: Aubier/Montaigne, 1959–70), vol. 1, *Le premier âge des liens d'homme à homme*, consulted in Italian translation, *Signoria e feudalesimo* (Bologna: Il Mulino, 1971), vol. 1, *Ordinamento curtense e clientele vassallatiche*, 169.

24. On particular law in medieval Europe, see Sten Gagnér, *Studien zur Ideengeschichte der Gesetzgebung*, Studia iuridica upsaliensia, 1 (Stockholm: Almqvist and Weksell, 1960), esp. 288ff. For a more recent and more analytical work, see Armin Wolf, "Die Gesetzgebung der entstehended Territorialstaaten," in *Handbuch der Quellen und Literatur der neueren europäischen Privatrechtsgeschichte*, ed. Helmut Coing, 3 vols. in

played a prominent role, and accompanying it (or placed above it) there were statutes, royal laws, and compilations of laws and customs. Nonetheless, as with Italy, the *ius proprium* as a whole cannot be seen either as an all-absorbing and exclusive phenomenon, at most permeated by rivalry among local legal systems, or as a self-contained phenomenon, excluding its constant relationship with civil and canon *ius commune*.

That relationship existed in part because of the circulation of the various Western anthologies discussed in chapter 2, but also because some provisions of the *ius proprium* were identical, in whole or in part, to dispositions in civil or canon law that, thanks to specific application of the same principle since ancient and even extremely ancient times, had become ingrained in local practice. It was also a relationship that existed throughout Europe—albeit at the lowest subsidiary level—inasmuch as the *ius commune* permeated every nook and cranny of local positive law. The relationship existed, primarily and above all, for another reason: without the theoretical focus provided by the *ius commune*; without the doctrines and concepts that were its most significant patrimony; without the terminology of the *ius commune*, which was adopted, respected, or bent to represent functions that differed from the original ones but which was always kept in mind as a fundamental instrument of expression; without the principles and the values incorporated in the *ius commune*—without this entire "structure" of thought, form, culture, and mind-set, we can understand neither the letter nor the spirit of the local laws. Indeed, we must think that such a "structure" was essential in the act and in the moment when jurists (or simple lawyers) composed the texts of the *ius proprium*.

4. The Iberian Peninsula: *Fueros*, *Usatges*, and Royal Laws; The *Siete Partidas*

On the Iberian Peninsula the *fueros* were the most prominent form of local law. *Fuero* is a term that has a number of meanings in the

---

8 (Munich: Beck, 1973–87), vol. 1, *Mittelalter (1100–1500): Die gelehrten Rechte und die Gesetzgebung*, 517–803. This is the best overall work as yet available, even though it lacks the perspective of the relationship between *ius proprium* and *ius commune* stressed in the present chapter. Nonetheless it is a highly useful work, valuable for information on the editions of normative and other texts cited here and for its bibliographical information, to which the reader is referred.

sources,[25] one of which is particularly interesting for our purposes because it touches directly on custom and on the ways in which customary norms were preserved and passed on in everyday legal practice. This meaning was thus the result of a process of selection that included consideration of the number and the frequency of the cases in which certain customary norms needed to be used in a trial (not to be confused with the "mode" of procedure—the *stylus*—in reaching judicial decisions).

During the eleventh century, many Spanish cities had judges who, for professional purposes, owned brief summaries of customary norms known as *fueros breves*. These collections grew and were consolidated, and between the eleventh and the twelfth centuries more complete versions appeared—the *fueros extensos*—which for two centuries continued to be added to, modified, and at times translated from Latin into Romance dialects.

In the demesnial cities and towns these texts were granted a seal of authenticity and validity through appropriate recognition by the monarchy. Since it was the king who "conceded" to the demesnial cities the free use of local customary norms, town and city councils could present the *fueros extensos*, endowed with the royal "privilege," to the urban population as significant conquests over the monarchical authority. In feudal cities and towns the *fueros* were validated by a pact, called *concordia*, drawn up with the lord of the land. In both cases, finally, some *fueros* originated from dispositions registered by being inserted into a "population charter" or *licentia populandi* granted by a feudal lord or the king for the settlement of a relatively uninhabited area or a city that he had just conquered.

Among the *fueros extensos*, those of Madrid, Toledo, Alcalá de Henares, Avila, and Cuenca in Castile (New Castile), Jaca and Saragossa in Aragón and Navarra, León and Salamanca in Asturias and León all deserve mention. Some of these *fueros* were known and applied far beyond the localities whose names they bear. One such was the *fuero* of León in Asturias and Galicia; another, the *fuero* of Toledo in much of Old Castile.

---

25. See Enrique Gacto Fernández, *Derecho medieval*, Temas de Historia del Derecho (Seville: Universidad, 1979), 61–62. One of the Iberian compilations has been translated into English by Donald J. Kagay, *The Usatges of Barcelona: The Fundamental Law of Catalonia* (Philadelphia: University of Pennsylvania Press, 1995).

Besides the *fueros* (*breves* or *extensos*), there were *usatges* or *usanciae* in circulation, as well as *costums* or *consuetudines*, the contents of which (unlike those of the *fueros*) were not selected according to the needs of courtroom use. Such texts were typical of Catalonia, where their most striking examples were the *Consuetudines Ilerdenses* of Lérida, widely used from the thirteenth to the fifteenth centuries, the *Usatges* of Tortosa, the *Consuetudines gerundenses* of Gerona, and above all two sets of laws from Barcelona confirmed by royal privilege, the *Usatici Barchinoniae* of 1251 and the *Consuetuts de Barcelona vulgarmente dites lo "Recognoverunt Proceres"* of 1284.

As in the *Regnum Siciliae* and in other large territorial entities in Europe during the later Middle Ages, Spain had kings who were particularly keen on claiming and enjoying royal prerogatives. Such kings also manifested their monarchical power in the legislative sphere by conceiving projects for unified bodies of law that often remained a dead letter but that nonetheless encouraged both the idea and the reality of a dual level of the *ius proprium*. The minimal or lower level was the one of the free cities and the feudal territories and the laws that pertained in them and that the crown attached to itself by acts of privilege. The higher level, which offered a greater potential for territorial expansion, was occupied by the legislative provisions of the sovereign. These were often isolated acts promulgated to cover limited instances, but they might also be ample, carefully articulated documents that on occasion even imitated ancient and time-tested models in their external form.

Like its classical model, Justinian's *Code*, the *Fuero Juzgo* (*Forum Iudiciorum*), a translation into Castilian of the seventh- century *Lex Visigothorum*, was divided into twelve books. The translation was made in the thirteenth century by command of Ferdinand III, who in 1230 became king of León and Castile, in practical terms the largest portion of the Iberian Peninsula and an area that stretched from the Atlantic to the north to the Mediterranean in the south. The sovereign's aim was to unify the laws of his new and larger realm under the sign of a glorious common tradition; in reality the *Fuero Juzgo* met with mixed fortunes and was accepted as city law only in some parts of the land (in León, Murcia, and Andalusia).

Under King Alfonso X (the Wise; d. 1284), more ambitious and more significant attempts were made both to bring order to the laws of the various cities and towns and to create a royal law for the entire

kingdom of Castile and León. The first of these aims led to the promulgation, in 1252–55, of a *Fuero Real* in the Castilian language. This
was a royal legislative text that compared the principal municipal legal
systems and that brought together and consolidated identical dispositions, simplifying and amalgamating similar ones, and attempting by
this means to offer a homogeneous and uniform local law and impose
it on the royal cities. The *Fuero Real* was conceded, by "privilege,"
to a number of demesnial cities—Burgos (1256), Madrid (1262), and
Valladolid (1265)—but it was never applied as broadly or as firmly as
the sovereign had hoped.

The second aim led to the emergence in the thirteenth century of a
Libro de las Leyes, also in Castilian, conceived of as a general law for
the entire realm. Formed over several decades by successive additions,
it grew from an original nucleus or first draft known as the *Libro del
Fuero* or *Especulo* (1256–58), but its definitive redaction is known as
Siete Partidas from its division into seven books. This was a cultivated
work that used passages from ancient philosophers (Aristotle, Sen-
eca, and Boethius) and theologians (Thomas Aquinas), fragments of
the *Libri feudorum*, and, above all, many extracts from Justinian's *Corpus iuris civilis* and from the laws of the church. It was above all a legislative text, conceived and promulgated by King Alfonso the Wise as
the general law of the kingdom.

Beyond the problem of their specific application in judicial decisions, the *Siete Partidas* constituted one of the most important legislative initiatives at the royal (and highest) level of the *ius proprium*. The
reasons for the partial failure in practice of this compilation were also
the reasons for its special significance in the overall fortunes of the *ius
commune* in Europe. The *Siete Partidas* attempted to transfer to a royal
compilation the qualities and functions that had been inherent in Roman law and canon law throughout Europe for more than a century—an attempt that is all the more obvious for its perhaps vain
hope of extrapolating from those highest laws and selecting the fragments that were thought the best, seeming almost to want to go one
step further and integrate and harmonize provisions that came from
the two quite different normative corpora of the Roman law and the
canon law. Neither the challenge nor the operation succeeded in the
thirteenth century, because it was the *utrumque ius* (Roman law and
canon law) that had and was to retain the function of *ius commune*,
thanks to its deep-rooted, sacred, and authoritative valence in that po-

litical and cultural world. The ideology of a unified and Christian empire (the ideology of Dante Alighieri) underlay and governed the legal and cultural potential of a complex of norms that were thought of and experienced as "common law" for all the faithful in Christ within the confines of the empire. Thus, in spite of all efforts, the "royal law" proposed as a "general law" for a *regnum* was and remained *ius proprium* in relation to the *utrumque ius*. Decisive critical reappraisal would be needed—from juridical humanism, the "Secunda Scholastica," and natural law theories—before the validity and the role of Roman and canon *ius commune* could be shaken. When that happened it was in an age (the fifteenth to seventeenth centuries) in which national states were reinforcing their unifying structures in order to encourage the breakdown of certain relationships and the emergence of the highest level of *iura propria*, the royal laws. It was also an age in which the common law was changing.

For the thirteenth and fourteenth centuries, the historiographical problem is thus to grasp the relationships between the royal law and the *ius commune* and to understand how the latter was the reference point for all that was vital in the law. It is a problem that also crops up if the royal law of Castile and León is taken as positive law and if one tries to ascertain what gradations in the normative resources were imposed on the judges. According to the *Ordenamiento* of Alcalá de Henares, near Madrid (1348, 1351), of Peter the Cruel of Castile and León, judges were to apply the royal laws of the *Ordenamiento* first, then local customary laws (provided they were long-standing and still in force), and the *Siete Partidas* as a last resort. Comparison with what was happening elsewhere in Europe—in particular in Italy, in the *Regnum Siciliae* and the communes—shows parallels that make it tempting to identify the *Siete Partidas* with what was elsewhere Roman and canon *ius commune*, hence to substitute its laws for Roman and canon law and to understand it as "common law," assigning to it a value, dignity, and function equal to those of the *ius commune*.

5. France: *Pays de droit coutumier*; Local Laws and Royal Law; The Great *Coutumiers*

In the Middle Ages, there were a number of political entities of various sorts and sizes in the vast area of Europe that centered on what is today France and that projected into Switzerland to the southeast and Flanders (Belgium) to the northeast. France (much smaller than the modern nation) and Paris, its capital, were surrounded by large territorial units: to the north, Normandy; to the west, Maine, Anjou, and, on the Atlantic coast, Brittany; to the south, Gascony on the Atlantic coast and Languedoc and Provence on the Mediterranean; plus the land-locked territories of the Dauphiné, Savoy, Burgundy, and Franche Comté.

There are details in the overall situation in French lands that are difficult to follow and reconstruct, but the general lines of development can readily be summarized. Above all, there was a distinction between northern and southern lands, which were divided, with some deviation, by a sinuous line following the forty-eighth parallel. As early as the twelfth and thirteenth centuries (clearly so from the mid-thirteenth century), northern French lands were *pays de droit coutumier* and the lands of the south *pays de droit écrit*. In the north, Roman law was not the "law" that had the force of positive law but was valid only if a judge wanted to take it into account as *ratio scripta* for its power of suggestion and as a "reasonable" aid in making a difficult judicial decision when the law was in doubt; in the south, Roman law was positive law and the "written law" to be taken into account in all circumstances, although in its practical application certain specific priorities pertained.

The split between the two parts of France was accentuated by the famous decretal, *Super speculam*, published by Pope Honorius III. This decretal stipulated that Roman law was no longer to be taught in Paris, which provided the king of France with a way to depreciate the law of the empire (whose prominent opponent he was), evoking a principle of full sovereignty later expressed as "rex superiorem non recognoscens in regno suo est imperator" (a king who recognizes no superior is emperor in his own kingdom). It provided the pope with an opportunity to further that same policy in the context of the opposition and rivalry between the two universal social orders, the church and the empire.

The two portions of France and the independent lands contiguous with them thus came to have dissimilar experiences: custom played a fundamental role in the northern regions (the *pays de droit coutumier*) but a more modest role in southern lands (the *pays de droit écrit*). Wherever they were located, major cities always had their own laws as a projection and proof of their autonomy.

In the *pays de droit coutumier*, municipal law came in two forms, either as a written version of customary norms (*coutumes*) or as normative orders of a different sort (*chartes de franchises*) added to local customary norms for the purpose of integrating or correcting custom, but always distinct from it.

Independent of the *coutumes* there were a great many normative initiatives that, because they regarded the internal life of the urban community, furnished a *ius proprium* of the first (or lower) level. The legislation willed and promulgated by the cities—in general, *chartes de franchises*—was designated as *chartes de communes*, *chartes de consulats*, and *privilèges urbains*, according to the origin and particular juridical title of each document. For example, we find *chartes de communes* in Beauvais in 1182, in Laon between 1189 and 1190, in Amiens in 1190, and somewhat later in Lille (1286) and Rouen (1382); Nîmes (1254) and Bordeaux (1261) had *privilèges*. One demesnial city after another had its charter. In Flanders, city charters were often backed by particularly strong efforts on the part of the municipal governments to claim and guarantee the city's autonomy.

The situation was radically different in the vast territories subjected to seigniory, feudal and nonfeudal. There the initiative for providing a local legal system to the inhabitants of a land came not from the local communities but from the lord, who from time to time made provisions, according to need, his own overriding interests, and his spirit of Christian charity (if he had any). Significant examples are the dispositions emanating from lay lords such as the dukes of Burgundy or the dukes of Brittany, from ecclesiastical lords of such famous abbeys as Sainte-Geneviève and Saint-Germain-des-Prés, or from the bishops of major dioceses such as the bishop of Metz (whose provisions were called *atours*).

The local *coutumes*, the *chartes de franchises*, the *privilèges*, and the *atours* might on occasion be included within or fused with the great regional and multiregional *coutumes*. Thus, by the phenomenon of the "regionalization" of customary norms, the most important *coutumes* were disseminated throughout broad geographical zones much larger than any one city's territory. This is what happened with the *Coutumes* of Normandy, Brittany, Touraine, Anjou, and Burgundy.

These sets of local norms stood in contrast to the sovereign's *ordonnances*, which at times limited and constrained local law but at other times supplemented and enriched it. In France as in the *Regnum Sici-*

liae, the kings were active legislators in certain specific sectors, according to circumstance, need, and opportunity. Witchcraft and heresy, for example, were targeted in the *Ordonnances* of Paris of 1228; Jews figured in an *Ordonnance* of 1230 "pensata ad hoc utilitate totius regni" (considered for the utility of the entire kingdom);[26] the life of local communities was regulated by a *Réformation de moeurs dans la Languedoc et la Languedoil* of 1254; dueling and court testimony were the subject of an *ordonnance* of 1258; relations between the crown and the municipal administrations and the reorganization of the latter were the object of such measures as the *Ordonnance de l'administration municipale de bonnes villes* of 1256–61; the sphere of action guaranteed to craft and trade corporations was treated in measures such as the later *Ordonnance de Chartres* of 1467.

In the interest of putting order into the great variety of measures from different times and places, the contents of the great regional *coutumes* and the royal *ordonnances* were collected and reelaborated in compilations usually known as *coutumiers*. In Normandy there were two important *coutumiers*: the twelfth-century *Très ancien Coutumier*, given both in Latin and in French translation, and the *Grand Coutumier* of between 1254 and 1258, written in Latin, whose title, *Summa de legibus Normandie*, indicates the semi-doctrinaire nature of the work.

The most important compilation and reelaboration, however, was the *coutumier* known as the *Coutumes de Clermont en Beauvaisis*. Its author was a cultivated judge who, in his youth, had also been a poet and a writer and who was active in the court of the count of Clermont, brother to the king of France, Louis IX. The judge's name was Philippe de Beaumanoir, and the work, composed in 1283, was also known as the *Coutumes de Beaumanoir*.[27] Philippe did more than simply write down customary norms: as he reworked and noted down local norms and principles, he made selections of their contents and, inevitably, he reshaped them, making broad use of a cultural background based in a knowledge and study of Roman law and canon law.

The *Coutumes de Beaumanoir* were broadly enforced in the *pays de*

26. *Ordonnances*, I, 35, quoted from François Olivier-Martin, *Histoire du droit Français des origines à la Révolution* (Paris: Donat-Montchrestien, 1948; reprint, Paris: CNRS, 1984), 120.

27. Available in English as *The Coutumes de Beauvaisis of Philippe de Beaumanoir*, trans. F. R. P. Akehurst (Philadelphia: University of Pennsylvania Press, 1992).

droit coutumier of northern France. Hence, even in those lands, the *ius commune* had a significant impact, and full use was made of its cultural valences, its reasoning mechanisms, and its general principles, as well as many of its specific solutions.

Another compilation, the *Etablissement de Saint-Louis* (1272–73), was a reworking and a condensation both of large portions of important *coutumes* (those of Orléans, Touraine, and Anjou) and of two sets of royal *ordonnances*. Thus, once again, an initiative was launched to put order into a congeries of multiple and discordant normative sources, but with the further aim of contributing to the legislative unity and the sovereignty of the kingdom—not so much in the name and under the sign of a Roman and canon *ius commune* (thrust aside because it was the positive law of the empire) as in the name of a national law that came out of the fusion of ancient traditions, popular and local customary norms, and more recent provisions willed by the sovereign and marked with his supreme authority.

This was a tendency that spread geographically and continued in time. Among the other great *coutumiers*, we should recall at least the *Ancien coutumier de Champagne* (late thirteenth century), the *Très ancienne coutume de Bretagne* (1312–ca. 1325), the *Stylus curie Parlamenti* of Guillaume Du Breuil (ca. 1330), the *Grand coutumier de France* of Jacques d'Ableiges (ca. 1388), and the *Vieux coutumier de Poitou* (ca. 1417).

The *Pays de droit écrit*: Municipal Laws, Intermediate Laws, Royal Law

In the *pays de droit écrit* of the south of France, cities actively compiled their laws in ways that made the resulting documents resemble the *statuta* of the Italian communes. Many cities were prominent in this movement: besides Montpellier, there were the *Consuetudines* of Toulouse confirmed by Philip III in 1283 and the *Franchises et coutumes* of Besançon of 1290; Lyons had its *Libertates* of 1320; Avignon had *Statuta proborum virorum* in 1243; Arles added to its older *Carta consultatus* of the twelfth century a later *Statuta et leges municipales* (1162–1202); Aix-en-Provence had its *Constitutiones* of 1234–45 and the later *Statuta facta post pacem*, drawn up in 1268 and enlarged and revised until 1480.

On the second level the *ius proprium* was made up either of regional *ordonnances* in force within a single county or duchy or of royal *ordon-*

nances promulgated for the entire realm of France, as in the case of the 1230 *ordonnance* concerning Jews. Among the *ordonnances* of counties and duchies, we might note those of Franche Comté (the capital of which was Dôle) on the organization of justice and legal procedures (1386) and on the "burghers' rights" (1393); those of Savoy (capital Chambéry) and part of Piedmont, discussed above, which ranged from the *Statuta* of Count Pietro II of 1264–65 to the *Decreta* or *Statuta Sabaudie* of Duke Amedeo VIII of 1430; those of the county of Provence (capital Arles), the *Statuta* "Super officialibus" of Charles I of Anjou of 1245 and after.

Unlike the *pays de droit coutumier*, these territories maintained the principle that the Roman and canon law must also be held valid as positive law to which a judge could and should have recourse when he could find no applicable norm in the royal law, the local *statuta*, or the city or regional *coutumes*. They also differed in that the normative contents of the customary laws derived from a tradition of acquaintance with and use of Roman law that could be traced back to the fifth and sixth centuries—thus, in part, to Roman law of the Theodosian Code. For this reason, the dispositions in the statutes were often similar in content to Roman and canon law.

Finally, famous schools of Roman law were concentrated in the *pays de droit écrit*. Montpellier, from the twelfth century, and Toulouse were highly famed as learned cities, and in their schools, as in Italy, only the laws of Justinian and of the church were studied. Cultural exchanges with Italy were extremely frequent, thanks both to Italian professors who taught in Montpellier (as did Placentinus, d. 1194) and to French students who studied in Italy—especially in Bologna, where there was a sizable contingent of students from Provence, as attested by one of the few *collegia* for students, founded in 1257 by a Bolognese professor of canon law, Zoën Tencararius, after he had become bishop of Avignon.

6. Germany: Municipal Laws; Counts, Dukes, and Princes; The Emperor's Laws; The *Sachsenspiegel*

In central Europe north of the Alps, the Holy Roman Empire—which had become "Germanic" through its ruling dynasties and as a result of the mechanisms for electing the emperor—was divided and fragmented into a number of political entities: Austria, which centered on Vienna; to the south, Styria, Carinthia, and the Tyrol; toward the west, Bavaria, Baden-Württemberg, and Hesse; returning east then north, Saxony, Bohemia, Moravia, Poland, East Prussia; to the north, the lands of Jutland (Denmark) that faced the great Scandinavian Peninsula.

The sources use the synthetic name of *Alamannia* for this conglomeration of lands and political systems. In this central area of continental Europe there were prosperous cities with a well-developed civic life; cities that lived by their ancient customary laws and were governed by city councils that had played a vital role in urban development since the twelfth century. Furthermore, the cities' customary laws were enriched by and intertwined with the corporate rules of a variety of powerful professional, trade, and other associations. At times the trade corporations (*Zünfte*) created conflict, but in general they contributed much to the richness of urban life.

The dynamics of the relations of the German cities and their surrounding territories were different from those of the Italian and Provençal cities. In Italy every city commanded a surrounding agrarian and economic space, great or small, that was articulated into a *suburbium* and *suburbia*, smaller dependent cites and towns, and modest villages; in *Alamannia* municipal jurisdiction reached no further than the city limits. Beyond the city walls there was the countryside, and the countryside was ruled by feudal and nonfeudal seigniory. Hence German lands gave rise to the proverb, "City air makes man free," since it was only within the city's walls that one could shake off submission to a feudal, territorial, or landed lord.

Another difference between German and north-central Italian lands was the relationship between the cities and the highest authority. In Germany, as in most of Europe (southern Italy included), local norms had to be recognized or obtain a title of validity from the emperor or from a lord (prince, count, or whatever). Thus, to cite a few examples, Frederick I Barbarossa conceded the "privilege" of recognition to Augsburg in 1156, to Bremen in 1186, to Lübeck in 1188, and to Hamburg in 1189. Frederick II granted similar "recognition" to Nuremberg in 1219, Lübeck (again) in 1226, and Vienna in 1237 and 1247. Prince Berthold of Zähringen gave an analogous privilege to Freiburg im Breisgau before 1180, as did Duke Henry I of Brabant to Brussels in 1229 and Duke Otto of Merano to Innsbruck in 1239.

Here as elsewhere the municipal law, validated by privileges, might be transferred and transplanted to other cities. Thus in 1261 and 1295 Breslau adopted the law of Magdeburg. This situation was not peculiar to *Alamannia*; analogous cases can be found in other regions of Europe—for example, in Sicily, where, as we have seen, the entire "Ancient Text" of the *Consuetudines* of Messina passed to Trapani to become that city's law.

In *Alamannia* as elsewhere, there were two levels of local law. Apart from the city *statuta* and superior to them was a territorial law of broader application. In certain times and places this occurred within a single political entity; on other occasions (in France, for instance) it involved an entire territory and a variety of political entities within that territory. In the first case such provisions emanated from a count, duke, or prince, as with the *Pfahlbürgergesetze* of Frankfurt am Main promulgated in 1333 and 1341. In the second case, the emperor established a law for the lords and the cities of Germany. There were many of these, some of them of great importance. Frederick II was responsible for two famous measures, the *Confoederatio cum principibus ecclesiasticis* of 1220 and the *Statutum in favorem principum* (German "princes," of course) of 1231–32. These laws were aimed at organizing, defining, shaping, and limiting the power of the lords, ecclesiastical and lay, over the lands under their *dominium*.

An even more famous example is the so-called "Golden Bull" (a name that dates from the fifteenth century), the technical title of which, *Omnem regnum*, came from its first words. The bull was promulgated in 1356 by Charles IV after he had been crowned emperor by the pope in Rome and had returned to German lands. The measure established the procedures for the election of the emperor and granted particular powers, by privilege, to certain princes, seven of whom became the "great electors" of the emperor and the only persons entitled to participate in imperial elections. These seven were the ecclesiastical princes (archbishops) of Mainz, Trier, and Cologne and the lay princes of the Rheinpfalz (the Rheinland and the Palatinate), Saxony, Brandenburg, and Bohemia.

As in French lands under customary law, there were private jurists in Germany who collected and elaborated customary legal materials. We have seen in the *pays de droit coutumier* anonymous works such as the *Grand Coutumier* or the *Summa de legibus Normandie* (1254-ca. 1258) and collections written by jurists of solid learning and high local renown such as the famous *Coutumes de Beaumanoir* (1283) written by

Philippe de Beaumanoir. A similar work in *Alamannia*, the *Sachsenspiegel*, or "Saxon Mirror," of Eike von Repgow, enjoyed such extraordinary success that its author was taken to be a more important jurist than he in fact was.

Eike von Repgow's *Sachsenspiegel* (Saxon Mirror), which was dedicated to Count Hoyer von Falkenstein, followed the structure of the *Decretals* to organize laws of various provenance, some of which were regional or municipal and others feudal or seigniorial. The original nucleus of the work probably dates from the years around 1235. Between 1265 and 1270 the work was translated into German, and it circulated well beyond the borders of Saxony to become the "law" on which all the judges of Germany based their decisions. It also attracted annotations (*glossae*) to clarify its contents. The "Saxon Mirror" became a model for other compilations in the German language, and it inspired a number of lesser works, among which one should mention at least the *Deutschenspiegel* (Augsburg, 1274–75) and the *Schwabenspiegel* (Swabia, 1275–76).

To move beyond municipal and territorial law, except for the few imperial provisions that specifically regarded the structures of the empire or the relations between the imperial crown and the cities or the local lords (or, exceptionally, other limited matters such as river navigation or notaries), the *ius commune*, civil and canon, was not recognized as having the force and authority of "positive law" in German lands. At least this was the case until the late fifteenth century, when Roman law was received with a formal act in 1495. After that act, Roman law became the "law" whose use was obligatory in the imperial supreme court, the *Reichskammergericht*. This means that for centuries—until 1495—the situation in *Alamannia* was similar to that in the French *pays de droit coutumier*.

This is not to say that Roman law was not known and studied intently by young Germans who subsequently made use of it in the activities of their office. We know it to be a fact that as early as the twelfth century German students were always present in sufficient numbers in Bologna to warrant the formation (in the thirteenth century) of a large corporation of students from German lands, the "German Nation" (*natio teutonica*). In the following century this *natio* grew so large that it became the *membrum precipuum* of the entire *universitas* of students from north of the Alps, and it had its own lengthy and detailed *statuta*, written in the mid-fourteenth century.

We also know that toward the late twelfth and early thirteenth centuries some clerics who had come to Bologna from Germany to study law (which meant the *ius commune*, civil and canon) took such an interest in the legislative texts of Justinian and of the church that they acquired excellent copies of them, which they took home with them when they returned to Germany. We know this occurred in Bamberg, where codices from the twelfth and thirteenth centuries (some containing the *apparatus* of Azo) can be seen in a perfect state of conservation. One emperor, Charles IV, stands out for an act that would be incomprehensible if both the crown and legal practitioners had not had a marked interest in the *ius commune*, Roman and canon. It was in fact Charles IV who founded the *Studium Generale* of Prague in 1348. Other institutions followed: the University of Cracow was founded by Casimir the Great in 1364; Rudolf IV, the archduke of Austria, founded the University of Vienna in 1365; the University of Pécs was founded in 1367, the University of Heidelberg in 1386, and so forth.

Everywhere university curricula included the *lectura* of Justinian's *Corpus iuris civilis* and of the great legislative compilations of the church, the *Corpus iuris canonici*. Furthermore, although it is true that at times these universities were ephemeral (the University of Cracow disappeared in the fourteenth and fifteenth centuries, for example), that fact should be evaluated in the general framework of the university schools of the time. A comparison with other universities, Italian and French, shows that they too did not always last.

There is another point: when someone returned to his homeland after years of a difficult separation, after having spent notable sums to study the *ius commune in terra aliena* (in Bologna, Padua, Perugia, and elsewhere), and perhaps after having escaped perils, even mortal ones, he found it an obvious and natural course to put to use what he had learned. Thus we need to think that the costly and hazardous adventure of law school studies was preordained to be a preparation for a professional activity that relied on valuable acquisitions that could be made only in a specialized school. There are many examples of just this. Among them there is one example—albeit a late one— that has particular relevance because it gives concrete evidence of how the *ius commune* contributed to a typical experience of *ius proprium*. In the late fifteenth century, the burgomaster of Hamburg, Hermann Langenbeke, was a *doctor in utroque iure* who had studied civil and canon law and had taken a degree in both disciplines (*in utroque iure*) at Perugia. When he returned to Hamburg he turned his hand to reorganizing and reshaping the customary laws and the *statuta* of his city. The unifying text that he compiled, in German, followed an outline that made use of the ways of focusing theory and the methodological techniques for the distribution of subject matter that he had learned from his schooling. He then enriched his text with marginal annotations in the fashion of the glossators (the earlier authors of *glossae*) and of the commentators (the more recent authors of *additiones*). This was the origin of the *Hamburger Stadtreformation* of 1497, a reorganization of the city laws of Hamburg and a typical example of local law shaped by a jurist formed in the schools of the *ius commune*.[28]

28. The episode is recounted in Wolf, "Die Gesetzgebung der entstehended Territorialstaaten," 611, but without the interpretation given here.

5

The University in Europe
and the *Ius commune*

The School of Irnerius and the Myth of Bologna

During the eleventh century and at the start of the twelfth century, there were still few schools. Monasteries and episcopal seats were active in providing elementary and secondary schooling, but it is very unclear whether or not further instruction on a private basis was given in the house of a *magister* to small groups of zealous young men eager to improve their store of juridical knowledge after their basic course of studies in the "liberal arts," in particular, in the "trivium" of grammar, rhetoric, and dialectic.

One thing is clear: one school soon stood out from the rest for its importance and its reputation. It emerged as the best because it alone concentrated exclusively on the study of law and on reading the legislative texts of Justinian. These texts, which had been rediscovered and recomposed and had become the *libri legales* par excellence, enabled students to regard the law as a new science distinct from (though not separate from) the arts of the trivium, on the one hand, and theology and ethics, on the other.

This school was Irnerius's. We know little about Irnerius's pupils. There may have been many of them, but only four have left abundant and reliable traces, either as a "group" that historians call the "Four Doctors" (although the title of "doctor" is surely inaccurate) or as individuals. Two of the Four Doctors founded prominent schools with a methodology of their own and a unique personality; two seem simply to have been lost to memory in later tradition. The two more important jurists were Bulgarus and Martinus, men to whom later writers credit bitterly opposed positions;[1] the other two were Jacobus (legend tells us that the dying Irnerius indicated him as his true spiritual heir and principal successor)[2] and Hugo.

This first and fundamental development, which gave autonomy not only to the *scientia* of the law but also to the places—the *scholae*—in which that "science" was cultivated and transmitted, took place in Bologna. Furthermore, the names of Irnerius and Bologna were intertwined: the man immediately became a myth; the city won immediate fame through him, even though the city had already become known as a center of studies and was called *docta* before Irnerius's death in 1130.[3]

1. On this point, see Manlio Bellomo, *Saggio sull'Università dell'età del diritto comune* (Catania: Giannotta, 1979; 2d ed. Rome: Il Cigno Galileo Galilei, 1992), 48–49, and the literature cited therein.

2. The Turin MS, Biblioteca Nazionale, E.I.15, fol. 7rb, related a different legend, as discovered and reported by Giacomo Pace, " 'Garnerius Theutonicus': Nuove fonti su Irnerio e i 'quattro dottori,' " *Rivista Internazionale di Diritto Comune* 2 (1991): 123–33, esp. 125: "Set isti quattuor de pari contendebant, et cum recedere vellet dominus Garnerius de Bon[onia] et ire ad domum suam, et quilibet istorum quattuor dicebat domino Garnerio quod dimitteret ei scolas. Ipse vero, cavens ne vinceretur aliquis eorum, ultima die quo legitur dixit: 'Burgarus hos aureum, Martinus copia legum, Hug[o] mens legum, Jacobus id quod ego.' Et hoc dixit volens innuere quod quilibet faceret scolas suas, et ipsi ita fecerunt." Evidently, Irnerius attempted to avoid designating an intellectual successor, and his four most famous students fought among themselves to replace him in his school—unsuccessfully, however, as Irnerius's school closed definitively, and its place was taken by the four schools of his students.

3. I have made ample use of my own previous writings in this chapter, and I refer the reader to them for both the topics treated here and sources and bibliography not specifically given here: Manlio Bellomo, *Aspetti dell'insegnamento giuridico nelle Università medievali*, vol. 1, *Le "quaestiones disputatae": Saggi* (Reggio Calabria: Parallelo 38, 1974); Bellomo, *Saggio sull'Università nell'età del diritto comune*; Bellomo, "Legere, repetere, disputare: I tre impegni del giurista nelle scuole universitarie medievali (secoli XII-XV)," in *XVe Congrès International des Sciences Historiques*, Bucharest 10–17 August 1980, *Rapports*, 3 vols. (Bucharest: 1980), 3:325–26; Bellomo, "Il Medioevo e l'origine dell'Università," in *L'Università e la sua storia*, ed. Livia Stracca (Turin: Nuova ERI, 1980), 13–25; Bellomo, "Studenti e 'populus' nelle città universitarie italiane dal secolo XII al XIV," in *Università e società nei secoli XII-XVI*, Atti del Nono Convegno Internazionale, Centro Italiano di studi di storia e d'arte, Pistoia 20–25 September 1979 (Pistoia: Centro Italiano di studi di storia e d'arte, 1982), 61–78; Bellomo, "Scuole giuridiche e università studentesche in Italia," in *Luoghi e metodi di insegnamento nell'Italia Medioevale (secoli XII-XIV)*, Atti del Convegno internazionale di studi, Lecce-Otranto, 6–8 October 1986, ed. Luciano Gargan and Oronzo Limone (Galatina: Congedo, 1989), 121–40; Bellomo, "Federico II, lo 'Studium' a Napoli e il diritto comune nel 'Regnum,' " *Rivista Internazionale di Diritto Comune* 2 (1991): 135–51; Bellomo, " 'Tenemos por bien de fazire estudio de escuelas generales': Tra Italia e Spagna nel secolo XIII," *Atti del Curso de Verano* "Sancho IV y los estudios generales de Alcalá:

2. Studying Jurisprudence *in terra aliena*

Young men from all parts of Italy and from all countries of Christian Europe flocked to Bologna. They came from Sicily and Campania, from Latium and Lombardy; they came across the Alps from France and Germany, the British Isles, and the Iberian Peninsula. They came because they were attracted by the new science, whether by the image that contemporary preachers gave of it in their harsh and bitter condemnations or by the approval, concealed or open, of both cultivated poets and versifying pedants.

Popular wisdom knew and said that jurisprudence was an art that led to power and wealth. The ironic fable of the ass Brunellus,[4] whose credulity led him to lose his tail and who, tailless, became a student, was symbolic of all those who eagerly strove to win honors and wealth through the study of the law, learned to use "words six feet long," and committed to memory, with immense effort, all of Justinian's *Corpus iuris*.[5] "We do not study vain things," the young men of the twelfth century scornfully declared when they compared rhetoric and philosophy to the greater worth of jurisprudence.[6]

The young were not discouraged by fiery preachers' bitter accusations or by somber predictions of misfortune from bishops (who had their own interests in mind) and timid country parish priests. They did not fear St. Bernard's condemnation of people "who long for knowledge in order to sell its fruits for money or honors."[7] Nor were they shaken by the words of Maurice of Saint-Victor, who declared that jurists "seek knowledge not to become wise but to prostitute

Poder y universidad en el siglo XIII," El Escorial 2–7 August 1993 (forthcoming). This paper will also be published in the *Rivista Internazionale di Diritto Comune* 5 (1994).

4. The fable, which dates from the twelfth century, is told in Nigellus Wireker, "Speculum stultorum": see Thomas Wright, ed., *The Anglo-Latin Satirical Poets and Epigrammatists of the Twelfth Century*, Rerum britannicarum medii aevi scriptores, Rolls series, no. 59, 2 vols. (London: Longman, 1872; Wiesbaden: Kraus Reprint, 1964), 1:1–145, esp. 52–54.

5. Nigellus Wireker, "Contra curiales," in *The Anglo-Latin Satirical Poets*, ed. Wright, 1:164.

6. Oxford, Bodleian Library, *Rawl.C.427*, fol. 70ra, in Hermann Kantorowicz, "An English Theologian's View of Roman Law: Pepo, Irnerius, Ralph Niger," *Mediaeval and Renaissance Studies* 1 (1941- 43), now in Kantorowicz, *Rechtshistorische Schriften*, ed. Helmut Coing and Gerhard Immel (Karlsruhe: C. F. Müller, 1970), 238 n. 37.

7. St. Bernard of Clairvaux, *In Canticum, Sermo XXXVI* (PL 183, col. 968D): "... et sunt ... qui scire volunt ut scientiam suam vendant: verbi causa, pro pecunia, pro honoribus," quoted in the text from the Kilian Walsh translation.

themselves venally for men's praise or for money. Thus, being unworthy of knowledge, they never truly attain it."[8]

The danger of losing one's soul for all eternity was an insufficient threat. The young failed to be terrorized by the thought that Paris in the twelfth century was "hell's lightning bolt,"[9] that it was the chosen residence of all the vices, or that its paved streets, frequented by prostitutes and illuminated by the lights of brothels, led straight to hell.[10] Instead, the young developed a surprising curiosity and an interest nourished by fantastic representations of scenes of a life lived intensely. The lapidary goliardic "Gaudeamus igitur, juvenes dum sumus" (let us then rejoice while we are young) began to be heeded, and such widely shared sentiments became a lifestyle: "Time slips by, and I have done nothing; time returns, and I do nothing."[11]

Raymond de Rocosel, the bishop of Lodève and a mediocre poet, warned students that the threat of losing their lives in the slow voyage that took them, day by day, farther from their paternal house was not worth the risk: "Per mare, per terras, quasi pauper inutilis erras" (like a beggar, good for nothing, will you wander on land and sea).[12] It

---

8. Mauritius, magister (of Saint-Victor), *Sermo Communis* IV, "Quid est bonum Dei?", 3, *Galteri a Sancto Victore et quorumdam aliorum Sermones ineditos triginta sex*, recensuit Jean Châtillon, in *Corpus Christianorum Continuatio Mediaevalis* (Turnhout: Typographi Brepols Editores Pontificii, 1975), 218: "Mali namque legunt ut linguas ornent, non vitam componant; sapientiam quaerunt non propter sapientiam, sed ut venalem prostituant, vel pro laude humana, vel pro pecunia. Unde sapientia indigni, ipsam in veritate non inveniunt."

9. The opinion of Peter of Celle: Petrus Cellensis, *Epistolae*, 73 (PL 202, col. 509).

10. Jacques de Vitry so describes Paris, remembering his student days and writing in 1216 and 1221. See *The Historia occidentalis of Jacques de Vitry*, ed. John Frederick Hinnenbusch (Fribourg: The University Press, 1972), chap. 7, "De statu parisiensis civitatis," 90–91: "The city of Paris, like many others, drifted in the shadows enveloped in many crimes and perverted by innumerable abject [acts]. . . . Like a scabious she- goat and like a soft ewe, it corrupted many of the newcomers who flowed in from all parts with its ruinous example. . . . Simple fornication was held to be no sin. Everywhere, publicly, close to their brothels, prostitutes attracted the students who were walking by on the streets and the squares of the city with immodest and aggressive invitations. And if there were some who refused to go in [with them], they called them sodomites, loudly and behind their backs."

11. Charles Homer Haskins, *The Rise of the Universities* (1923) (New York: Peter Smith, 1940, 84): "Li tems s'en veit, / Et je n'ei riens fait; / Li tens revient, / Et je ne fais riens."

12. Raymond de Rocosel, "De certamine animae. Invectio contra goliardos," in Johannes Werner, "Nachtrag zum Certamen anime des Raymundus de Rocosello," *Neues Archiv* 36 (1911): 550–56. The passage cited can also be found in Olga Dobiache-Rojdesvensky, *Les poésies des goliards* (Paris: Rieder, 1931), 184.

was common knowledge that brigands infested the highroads. They might easily rob a traveler and take everything he had—books, money, horses, sword, and clothes—and leave him "naked, beaten, and wounded, miserable, discomfited, [and] alone,"[13] to be brought, if he was lucky, to a monastery. It was also known that in the cities general indifference could lead to a miserable life as a beggar. In spite of all this the young abandoned the paternal house and "maternal kisses"[14] and became "pilgrims for love of learning"[15]—the new learning. On the road the student met other students from Sicily or from the far-off British Isles, and they might join forces with chance traveling companions or with experienced and cautious merchants. Such encounters accustomed students to life in common and encouraged a sense of solidarity; as the students talked, they compared habits and customs, and their various "vulgar" tongues were harmonized by the lexical and grammatical vehicle of Latin, a simple, ductile, living language. Thus they helped to forge a cultural unity that was already finding its typical habitat in the cities.

3. The Growth of Schools in European Cities

There were private schools in the "learned" cities, first in Bologna, then in Montpellier, Toulouse, and Orléans in France, in Palencia and Lérida in Spain, and in Padua, Reggio, and Vercelli in Italy. These schools might have a very long life, as in Bologna, Padua, Naples, Rome, and Perugia, or a short one, as in Vicenza, Arezzo, and Vercelli. Such schools might be recognized by the public authorities or not; they could be set up and organized as part of a *studium*, or their precarious existence could be left to chance.

A student chose which school he wanted to join. Originally (in the twelfth century) his choice might be determined by streams of relatives, friends, or fellow countrymen; on the other hand, it might be

13. Charles Homer Haskins, *Studies in Mediaeval Culture* (Oxford: Clarendon Press, 1929), 18 n. 3: "Me nudum, verberatum, et vulneratum, lugubrem et abiectum in solitudinem dimettentes."
14. Raymond de Rocosel, "De certamine animae," in Werner, "Nachtrag zum Certamen anime," 550–56.
15. Frederick I Barbarossa, *Constitutio* "Habita", in Winfried Stelzer, "Zum Scholarenprivileg Friedrich Barbarossas (Authentica 'Habita')," *Deutsches Archiv für Erforschung des Mittelalters* 34, 1 (1978): 123–65, quotation 165.

an individual decision influenced by the ill-advised faith he placed in the advice of tavernkeepers, merchants, or prostitutes. In a later period (the thirteenth century and after), the choice was more predetermined—as was the case in Paris—or at least partially inevitable thanks to decisions made within the powerful student corporations that applied to all students.

The general pattern of post-secondary academic life was already set by the turn of the thirteenth century. In the early decades of the twelfth century, competition was restricted to the famous and well-frequented private schools of Bologna; by the end of the twelfth century and the beginning of the thirteenth, many cities were eager to attract schools and welcome students, and they did so: Modena by around 1180; Vicenza for some years between 1204 and 1208; Arezzo by around 1215; Padua from 1222 on (with phases of inactivity and silence); Naples after 1224 (with frequent interruptions and new beginnings); Vercelli, for a short time after 1228, thanks to an organized migration of students from Padua; then Rome, in the pontifical curia (*Studium Curiae*) and in the city (*Studium Urbis*), Reggio Emilia, San Gimignano, Siena, Perugia, and others.

4. The Organization of the Academic World

Courses of study were not organized in the same manner throughout Europe. Two distinct forms emerged, hence two types or models for a university. The first and the oldest was the Bolognese model. Although we can speak of its various elements separately, in reality they were of course contemporaneous and solidly mingled in one overall context.

The first element is the *schola*. A *schola* was usually set up in the same house as the master's living quarters, hence the *dominus* of the house was both *dominus* and *doctor* or *magister*, the school's professor. One of his servants, whose tasks became specialized to serve the needs of the school, served as its *bidellus*. In one variant of this model, a professor did not own the house and the school lodged in it but was simply responsible for instruction. This was the case of Placentinus, a jurist whose very name is unknown and who is always given in the sources by the toponym "of Piacenza." He and his students were lodged in the houses of the Castelli (or Da Castello) family; Alberico of Porta Ravegnana was lodged in buildings of the *commune civitatis*.

The second element in the Bolognese model comprised the *scholares* and their associations. The first of the two ways in which students who frequented a school in the twelfth century were organized was by *consortia, fraternitates,* or *communitates.*

Students banded together to form a *consortium* in order to resolve such specific practical problems as finding lodgings or getting access to a book, or else in order to increase their leverage in negotiations with the professor, the city's merchants, the book merchants and copyists, and so forth. When these or analogous and larger associations emphasized mutual assistance they were also called *fraternitates*; when they emphasized pleasure and sociability they were called *communitates.*

The second mode of student association was the *comitiva.* All the students of any given *schola* were associated with their master, who called them *socii mei*; with the *dominus* of their school the students formed a *comitiva* that defined their participation in all phases of daily life, in the school as they sat at their benches in the classroom, in the city as they took part in religious functions, popular holidays, and saint's day processions, or when they went gaming or visited the taverns and other places for dissolute living.

A third element in student life in the Bologna model was the *natio.* Toward the end of the twelfth century, although the *comitiva* did not disappear, it began to loose its central position in the organization of student life, largely because there were some essential needs that it failed to satisfy, such as providing lodging and meals, ways to borrow money (with attendant guarantees), access to books, and judicial guidance in civil and criminal matters. Instead, students who belonged to different schools in the same city began to associate with one another and band together to pursue common ends. The selection process that led to the creation of a group (or to co-opting the members of an existent group) operated by common language, shared habits and customs, and a collective mind-set arising from a common national origin or from a similarity of views among people born in the same place or the same territory (*natio*). Thus students from the various schools and the various *comitivae* began to gather together in these new organizations, all the while continuing to be part of the old *comitivae.* For some years the new associations were called indifferently *nationes* or *universitates*, but as early as the second or third decade of the thirteenth century the term *nationes* prevailed.

At the same time, the relationship between the students and the professor of a school changed because the *comitiva* lost its significance and its functions in daily life. The individual professor still did not have relations with students from other schools.

A fourth part of the Bologna model was the *universitas* (an English translation would be guild or corporation) of the students and the *collegium* of the "doctors." The students' interests and the professors' interests began to diverge. On the students' side, the *nationes* soon grew and took the form of broader associations that came to be called *universitates*. In Bologna there were two such *universitates*, that of the *ultramontani*, which included the *nationes* of students from north of the Alps, and that of the *citramontani*, which included the four Italian *nationes* of the Lombards, the Tuscans, the Romans, and the Campanians. On the other side, teachers' associations developed toward the mid-thirteenth century, when the *domini* of the various city schools joined together in a corporation similar to and on the model of the other craft and trade corporations. Their association took the name of *collegium*, and there were *collegia* for professors of civil law, canon law, medicine, and the arts.

The student *collegia* formed a fifth element. These were organizations for students but not founded by the students themselves nor wholly run by them. In general these were institutions founded by popes, cardinals, bishops, or wealthy lords with the aim of providing a *hospitium*—a place of residence—for a number of young people from one particular city, region, or larger geographical area. This sort of institution was neither common nor particularly important in Italy, but north of the Alps there were many such *collegia*.

Sixth and last, there was the role of the bishop or the archdeacon. In Bologna the archdeacon (elsewhere the bishop)—a person external to the world of studies but not extraneous to it—had tasks that were set and described (somewhat ambiguously) in a famous decretal of Honorius III in 1219. In this decretal, *Super speculam*, the archdeacon of Bologna, a high ecclesiastical dignitary, was charged with granting the insignia of the doctorate to candidates who proved themselves worthy of that honor in their doctoral examination. Since it was unsure whether the certification of that worthiness was a duty of these ecclesiastical dignitaries or a privilege of the professors, a mixed system was set up. Two final examinations were instituted, a private examination (called *privata*) given in the sacristy, for which the professors (and only those professors who were members of a *collegium*) were responsible; and a subsequent public examination (called *publica, conventus,* or *laurea*), which took place in the cathedral and was in essence a solemn (and extremely costly) ceremony.

5. External and Internal Pressures: From the Emperor to the *Universitates scholarium*

The tangled relations within the world of studies were further complicated when emperors such as Frederick I Barbarossa (with the *Constitutio* "Habita" of 1155) or kings such as Frederick II (with the "foundation" of the *Studium* in Naples in 1224) projected their own strategic moves onto them. Popes—Innocent III and, above all, Honorius III during the early decades of the 1200s—did the same, as did communal city governments (Modena around 1180 and Reggio Emilia in 1242) and the papal curia in the 1230s and 1240s.

In some cases the intervention was by happenstance, as in 1155 with the constitution of Frederick Barbarossa. More commonly, however, it was motivated by a desire to put some order into the world of studies and students. One clear example of the latter case is Reggio Emilia, where the *commune civitatis,* in an attempt to organize the school (*ordinare studium*), established procedures for assigning individual students and professors to schools that already lined both sides of the city's main street.[16] *Ordinare studium* or *reformare studium* therefore did not always and in every case mean founding a *studium* (a university); often, and especially at first, it meant, more simply, establishing rules for avoiding confusion and conflict and for subjecting to "order" an already operational and fluid reality.

The students also wanted a hand in shaping the multifaceted world of schools, professors, and would-be professors. Their basic associations, the *nationes* and the *universitates,* moved in just that direction: the *nationes* had the principal aim of gathering together all the students from other regions or from foreign lands and of helping to satisfy elementary everyday needs and study requirements; the *universi-*

---

16. Reggio Emilia, *Consuetudines,* 1242, "Quod fiat distributio scolarum a strata tam superius quam inferius," in *Consuetudini e Statuti Reggiani del secolo XIII,* ed. Aldo Cerlini (Milan: Hoepli, 1933), 36: "Item statuimus quod fiat distributio scolariorum dominorum maistrorum tam a strata superius quam a strata inferius, arbitrio bonorum hominum qui fuerint ad studium ordinandum."

tates worked both to reinforce and defend the functions of the *nationes* and to guarantee students from other regions or lands living space and rules for peaceful cohabitation within the city and scholarly discipline within the schools. These organizations struggled incessantly (and victoriously): first against the communal government under the podestà, then against the people's commune, and eventually against the lord of the city. In their daily operations the *rectores* of the *universitates*—leaders who were older, more experienced students—put the contractual power of the *universitas* to the test as they dealt with professors (particularly regarding the "choice" [*electio*] of a school a student might want to frequent or to avoid) and with such specialized economic operators as the *stationarii* (booksellers).

The *stationarii* were entrepreneurs and merchants. Some of them, the *stationarii exempla tenentes* or *stationarii peciarum*, specialized in keeping exemplars—*exemplaria*—of works containing laws or statements of doctrine and in lending out such originals (or copies authenticated as originals) to be copied or to serve as models for the correction of other texts. Such works could be borrowed whole or, more commonly, divided into sections known as *peciae*. Other stationers known as *stationarii librorum* produced books (*codices*) and sold new or used copies of books. Certain *stationarii* became *stationarii universitatis* by swearing to obey the *rectores* and to respect the rules given in the statutes of the student *universitates*.

There were various sets of dispositions, emanating from a variety of institutions, that laid down rules for the schools. There were imperial norms such as the "Habita" of 1155, pontifical measures such as the famous decretal of Honorius III of 1219, royal decrees such as those of Frederick II on the schools of Naples. There were also laws passed by city communal governments, either included in or scattered through the local statutes (as in Bologna in measures of the Comune del podestà promulgated between 1245 and 1267) or incorporated as a "book" of statutes (as in Bologna with the statutes of the people's commune of 1288). Finally, there were measures decided by the colleges of jurist doctors and, above all, the statutes of the *universitates scholarium* such as the Bologna student statutes of 1252, of 1272–74, and the longer and more fully articulated statutes of 1317, which were then revised and updated every ten years. In Padua student statutes were drawn up in 1262 (the so-called *Pacta vetera*) and in 1321, following the Bologna text of 1317. The *nationes* also had statutes—for example, those of the *natio teutonica* in Bologna in the mid-fourteenth century.

6. A Different Organizational Model: The University of Paris

The other major model for the organization of university studies was more common in France.[17] It existed in Italy as well, however, and it gradually became the rule there as the *universitas scholarium* (the "university" as an organization of students, professors excluded) shifted to the *universitas scholarum* (a "university" that included both students and professors).

The chief characteristic of this second model was the participation, at the same time and in one organization, of three elements that seemed to be and in practice were separate and distinct in the "Bolognese model": students, professors, and a chancellor endowed with governing powers (who was the bishop of the university city). In this model, if there were student organizations they were attached to the student *collegia* or the *nationes* connected with the colleges, or they were completely extraneous to the official structure of the *studium*.

Within the university, activities, spheres of competence, and powers became specifically defined, and "magistracies" were formed that were entrusted with (or recognized to have) power to choose the professors, establish their teaching responsibilities and their stipends, provide for financial administration, guarantee the quality of instruction, establish the curriculum and the program, and safeguard the freedom and set the limits of teaching.

In the 1400s this was the most common university structure, and, although in preceding centuries it had been typical of Paris alone, by that date it was common to universities new and old throughout Europe. We can find the same structures, with certain variants, in Italy in Perugia, Florence, Pavia, and Catania, and outside Italy in Prague, Pécs, Heidelberg, Toulouse, Salamanca, and a large number of other universities.

---

17. The distinction between the two types of university organization is particularly well presented in Alan B. Cobban, *The Medieval Universities: Their Development and Organization* (London: Methuen; New York, distrib. Harper & Row, Barnes & Noble Import, 1975).

7. The Spread of Universities in Europe

One glance at a map of Europe in the mid-fifteenth century shows that every region proclaimed its vocation for university teaching. From Bohemia (Prague, 1348) to Austria (Vienna, 1365) and Germany (Heidelberg, 1386; Cologne, 1388); from the British Isles (Cambridge and Oxford) to France (Paris, Montpellier, Toulouse, Orléans); from Spain (Palencia, Lérida, Huesca, Salamanca) to Italy (from Bologna, eleventh and twelfth centuries, to Catania, 1434–44), there were everywhere tens of universities in which the original *libertas scholarium* was entangled in and governed by the apparatus of the *studium* and student associations (the *universitates*, the *nationes*) and professors's associations (the *collegia*) and had less and less room for action. At the same time, universities tended to have a political and cultural bent strongly linked to the fortunes of the principalities or the *regna* and determined by the will of the lord (prince or sovereign) or the acquiescent or competing will of the bishop or the pope. The cities and the patricians who ruled them could also have a part in university affairs, proof positive that the problems of university teaching had become just as important as problems and views connected with the intellectual disciplines that the universities cultivated and transmitted from one generation to another.

8. Why Were Universities So Successful?

Although the universities faced an impressive number of problems and although it is striking to observe how deeply they were rooted in the city and its neighboring territory and how greatly they contributed to the prosperity of vast segments of society, we cannot ignore other possible reasons for the schools' success—other situations and events that encouraged them and made their multiplication and dissemination inevitable.

Why should Irnerius's law school have become immediately legendary? Why should tens, even hundreds, of other schools open and draw crowds of students from near and far? Why should so many young people have committed and consumed part of their fathers' fortunes and so many fathers have accepted or desired their sons' departure for the university city, even when they both knew that it would bring personal sacrifices and often mortal risks? Why should so many cities and so many kings, emperors, and popes have founded new *studia* and guided their destinies, embellished them, and endowed them with privileges?

The only explanation is that they did so because the law that was taught in those institutions was of vital importance for individuals, families, and kinship groups; for the cities and for the *regna*, for the emperor, and for the church. They did so because the law had to be known in all its aspects; it required full mastery if it was to be used not only on occasions for learned theoretical reflection and for demanding scholastic debates but also in the courts, in notarial practice, in arbitration to avoid lawsuits, and in the peaceful acts of any person who enjoyed a *res* (property) and wanted to dispose of it to his own profit or that of his heirs. Because it was a law essential for acts of public governance, for the legitimation of power, conquered or inherited, for tutelage of the interests of groups or segments of society. Because it was a law indispensable for nourishing the hopes of people engaged in administrative careers who populated the emerging structures of local bureaucracies, lay and ecclesiastical. Thus it is not only reasonable but necessary to see these as the reasons for the universities' development: otherwise we would have to credit the rise and the success of the European universities to collective folly.

There is a problem, however: the law curricula for the university instruction imparted from the twelfth to the eighteenth centuries in Europe was exclusively based on the laws of Justinian, the *Corpus iuris civilis*, and the great normative collections of the church, the *Corpus iuris canonici*, but judges and notaries did not usually apply these laws. Furthermore, as is known, the contents of these bodies of laws gave no guidance and provided no norms for those who had responsibilities for governance or administration on the local level, in the *commune civitatis* or the *regnum*, in the seigniory or the principality, in the hierarchy of the church or in the monastic orders.

Conversely, the programs of the European universities never covered the local law—that is, the laws of the particular governing structure, be it the kingdom, the *commune civitatis*, the seigniory, or the principality. These were the laws that the judges were bound to apply in the first instance, as we have seen, when they contained a precept pointing to a decision in the case at hand; laws that the administrators were obliged to respect as they carried out their duties.

It is obvious that such perspectives are foreign to the thinking of anyone who sees the *ius commune*, civil and canon, only as a complex of norms necessary for judicial decisions or for the redaction of legal acts, or who understands the *ius commune* only in its dimension of positive law and relegates it to the rank of a supplementary or subsidiary law. This approach is a dead end because it fails to explain how the programs of study of European schools of jurisprudence—both the schools originally chosen or later recognized (*electae*) by the *universitates scholarium* and the schools incorporated into the *studia* of royal, imperial, or papal foundation—came to concentrate uniquely on the civil and canon *ius commune*.

We need to take a closer look at these matters.

6

Legal Science

Forms of Exposition and Techniques
of Diffusion

The Orality of Knowledge

Throughout the later Middle Ages both the formation and the transmission of knowledge were typically oral. The obverse of this coin is that an extremely small number of written texts were recognized as speaking with authority. At the head of this list were the Gospels, which, as both "Scripture" and "scripture," were writing par excellence. "Holy Writ" was placed on the altar as an expression and confirmation of the idea that those writings were the books of the faith, sacred for their stamp of divine authority and for the precious truths they contained and preserved. Next to the books of the Truth were the books of Justice. In both cases, these works merited their place out of the conviction that those books, those "scriptures," gave at least a glimpse of the eternal dimensions of the Truth and Justice whose full understanding and total admiration would be the reward in Heaven of only the best of humankind.

The jurist's books were those of the *Corpus iuris civilis*. Soon, however (around the mid-twelfth century), the list began to grow, because Gratian's *Decretum* was awarded the same dignity. It was followed, somewhat later, by some of the church codifications that eventually went into the *Corpus iuris canonici*.

Thus an *utrumque ius* ("the one" and "the other" law, civil and canon) was enclosed within a limited number of volumes, while all around them there was an irrepressible, rampant, and necessarily oral interpretation.

On the one hand, there were the authoritative sacred books, works worthy of a place on the altar. Legend even has it that one famous jurist, Jacopo Baldovini (Jacobus Balduini), intent on understanding a passage in Justinian's compilation, placed the book of human laws beside the divine book on the altar and spent the entire night before them on his knees praying to God for guidance and comfort.[1]

On the other hand, there was the spoken word, free or guided by schemes of argumentation, by "forms," and by molds, but always unmediated and always essential for the construction and diffusion of knowledge. As Roffredus Beneventanus put it,[2] the spoken word had something magical about it because it permitted an immediate, ready communication, whereas an inert and cold written text might act as a resistant, difficult screen between the person thinking and attempting to communicate and the person reflecting and attempting to understand.

This conviction was no less widespread than the habit itself: "From what one hears," Humbert de Romans stated as early as the thirteenth century, "one obtains an excellent result, which is *sapientia*. In no other way, in fact, can man make himself more wise than by what he listens to."[3]

An acute sensitivity to oral communication inspired brilliant investigations. Reading, Hugo of Saint Victor wrote, is of three sorts: it is one thing for the person who is teaching, another for the person who is listening, and yet another for someone who meditates on the writings. None of these three moments was independent of the others, because each one adjusted to and was shaped by their three-way relationship. The person speaking addressed the person listening, the listener selected what he could apprehend, and anyone reflecting on

1. The episode is related in Friedrich Carl von Savigny, *Geschichte des römischen Rechts im Mittelalter*, 2d ed., 7 vols. (Heidelberg: J. C. B. Mohr, 1834–51; reprint Bad Homburg: Hermann Gentner, 1961), 5:105. The anecdote is also given, in the same sense as here, in Francesco Calasso, "Il diritto comune come fatto spirituale" (1946), available in Calasso, *Introduzione al diritto comune* (Milan: Giuffrè, 1951), 177. See also Manlio Bellomo, *Società e istituzioni dal medioevo agli inizi dell'età moderna*, 6th ed. (Rome: Il Cigno Galileo Galilei, 1993), 455.

2. See Sven Stelling-Michaud, *L'Université de Bologne et la pénétration des droits romain et canonique en Suisse aux XIIIe et XIVe siècles* (Geneva: E. Droz, 1955), 74.

3. Humbert de Romans, *Opera de vita regulari*, ed. Joachim Joseph Berthier, 2 vols. (Rome: A. Beffani, 1888–89), 1:256.

the few authoritative written texts available knew that both his read-ing and his reaction to what he read would correlate with those of others.[4]

2. The *Lectura* of Authoritative Texts

From the start, the academic lesson for students of civil law was a *lectura* (reading) of one of the *codices* (books) in which Justinian's legislative texts had been collected, following an organization into the five parts, or *volumina* (volumes), that had become traditional from the twelfth century.

Although all the sections of the *Corpus iuris civilis* were considered of an equal importance, they nonetheless came to be used in quite different ways. The *Institutes* and the first nine books of the *Code* were used intensively in the early twelfth century, but toward the end of that century the *Institutes* became less central (until the fifteenth and sixteenth centuries, when they regained a part of their former impor-tance).

The first of the three *volumina* into which the *Digest* was divided emerged as a major text, usually to accompany the first nine books of the *Code*. This meant that students in the schools had an opportunity to follow *lecturae* on the *Digestum vetus* and the *Code* but were less likely to have occasion to attend *lecturae* on the *Infortiatum*, the *Di-gestum novum*, the *Institutes*, the *Tres libri* (the last three books of the *Code*), or the *Novels*. In the manuscript *volumina* (which were *codices* in the modern sense of "books"), Justinian's laws were usually written in a large hand and arranged in two columns that occupied only the central part of the page. This not only made them easier to read but also left ample space in all the margins—side, top, and bottom—for annotations.

In the classroom the students crowded around the professor, who sat (at least until the last years of the twelfth century) at the center of the room. The professor had before him a lectern or table on which the book of the laws was placed, a position that in theory enabled all

4. Hugo of Saint Victor, *Didascalion: De studio legendi*, PL 176, cols. 741–838. For the passage cited, see also the edition of Charles Henry Buttimer (Washington D.C.: The Catholic University of America Press, 1939), 57–58. For a more recent English translation, see *Didascalicon: A Medieval Guide to the Arts*, ed. and trans. Jerome Taylor (New York: Columbia University Press, 1961).

the students (but in reality, given their number, only a few of them) to read the text along with their master.

For many decades both professor and students spoke in the classroom: the professor posed the problems, at times following an outline, and the students responded, debating among themselves or with the master or offering objections to the way in which the problems were put or to the solutions proposed.

The "degree program" had no time limit. Anyone who wanted to do so could continue his studies for years until he felt he had learned enough. He would start again from the beginning year after year, studying the same book, each time finding some of his old companions in the classroom but also younger, newly arrived, timid, and inexperienced *novelli auditores*.

Some students ended their *curriculum* with an examination in the cathedral, though that exercise was not yet subject to specific regulation. Others managed to grasp little and attended a school for only a short time. John of Salisbury said that they stayed no longer than it took a chick to sprout feathers.[5]

3. The *Glossae*

From the time of Irnerius, jurists expressed their thoughts above all in a literary form determined by untouchable, authoritative legislative texts and by an exegetic technique aimed at furthering understanding of the content of those texts. That literary form was the gloss, and the jurists who made use of it are called glossators.

If over the years some professors and a good many students had not noted down their *glossae* on parchment as a way of documenting and remembering the *lecturae*, we would know little or nothing of that world of ideas, beliefs, and values today. Thanks to them, we can manage to know something—on the condition that we keep in mind that the *glossae* were only an extremely feeble projection of a much fuller investment of both individual and collective reflection, and that we remember that they are a fragmentary and highly reductive expres-

5. John of Salisbury, *Metalogicon*, I.3 (ed. C. C. I. Webb, *Joannis Saresberiensis . . . Metalogicon libri IIII* (Oxford: 1929), 11, available in English as *The Metalogicon of John of Salisbury: A Twelfth-Century Defense of the Verbal and Logical Arts of the Trivium*, trans., intro, and notes, Daniel D. McGarry (Berkeley and Los Angeles: University of California Press, 1955), 15.

sion of the oral activities that revolved around a central nucleus of the few certain, authoritative, and sacred texts.

The gloss is a brief annotation composed and written to explain a text and addressing either its terminology and its exterior trappings or its animating spirit and its underlying principles. The more usual position for a gloss was beside a legislative text on one margin of the page or the other. At times a word, a very few words, or even an entire passage in explanation of a term used in the text was written between one line of the text and another. The technical term for the first is a "marginal gloss"; for the second, an "interlinear gloss."

The jurists of the twelfth century and the first half of the thirteenth century made wide use of this literary form and of the technique it involved. The gloss continued to be used widely until at least the first decades of the fifteenth century, but its significance changed as the elaboration of theory and didactic methods for the transmission of legal knowledge evolved.

The glosses of innumerable masters remain in the hundreds of extant manuscripts of Justinian's *Corpus iuris civilis*, or the *libri legales*. Innumerable masters composed them: Martinus, Bulgarus, Rogerius, Albericus de Porta Ravennata, Henricus de Bayla, Placentinus, Pillius Medicinensis, Johannes Bassianus, Guillelmus de Cabriano, Azo, Hugolinus de Presbyteris, Jacobus Balduini, Carlo of Tocco, Benedetto of Isernia, Roffredus Beneventanus, and many others. Each one of these jurists composed glosses in the school and for the school, and in particular for that central exercise of official pedagogy that was the "lesson."

Glosses were short and synthetic; they strove for clarity and an efficacious use of few words. The text of a gloss might be written by the professor himself, before or after the lesson, or it might come from notes taken by one or more of the particularly gifted pupils. A professor's note is termed a *glossa redacta*; a student's note a *glossa reportata*.

A *glossa redacta* normally closes with a sign or "siglum" made up of one or more of the letters in the professor's name: for example, we have "y." or "w." for Irnerius, "m." for Martinus, "b." for Bulgarus, "r.", "ro.", or "rog." for Rogerius, "Sy." for Simon Vicentinus, "Ro." or "Rof." for Roffredus, and so forth. The *glossa reportata* can be distinguished from the *glossa redacta* because at its end the *reportator* (the person who had listened to the lesson and then written the gloss) attested that he was not the author of the thought expressed but only the author of its formal redaction by noting "secundum m[artinum]" or "secundum b[ulgarum]" and the like. We need to take care, however, to distinguish between the "secundum . . ." of the *glossae reportatae* and a "secundum . . ." followed by a name, which introduced the opinion of another jurist, perhaps even from another generation, within the body of a *glossa redacta* or a *glossa reportata*.

4. Tradition and the Circulation of Glosses: Graphic and Didactic Networks, the *Apparatus*, *Lecturae redactae*, and *Lecturae reportatae*

No annotations written by the hand of twelfth-century jurists have yet been found. It is possible, however, and even probable that there are some autograph additions in the many extant copies of portions of the *Corpus iuris civilis*.

The copies available to us are all derived from lost originals. It often happened that as he was copying the text the copyist (usually a professional scribe) modified something in the original or in the copy before him. This might have happened for a number of reasons: the scribe might have been distracted; a word or a letter might have been difficult to decipher; the scribe's changes might have been made out of ignorance; he might have deliberately chosen to make them. Often a text used as a model for copying had already been used by a number of professors who had made additions to the original gloss, either to confirm its point of view by enriching or explicating its contents or to challenge its explanation (at times with a simple *contra*). In this case the glossator's sign, for example "m.", would be followed by a word or a phrase marked with someone else's siglum. Should the older sign be dropped—the one, that is, identifying the author of the original gloss and placed between it and the more recent text—the authorship of the older opinions would be lost. Furthermore, when one copyist transcribed both the older and the more recent parts of a composite gloss at one time and in one hand, it became more difficult to identify its component strata.

It is less of a chore to grasp the mechanisms of collection and transmission at work in the glosses. A series of successive additions gave rise to "strata" or layers within a single gloss; such strata can be reconstructed along with the gloss, but they can also be traced within a network composed of many glosses. We can in fact demonstrate that some types of addition were recurrent, which means that for every text within the same grid we can identify the individual strata, date them, and locate them geographically.

This "network" was something quite distinct from the "stratum." A "network" was a set of glosses that had not yet been cast in a definitive order, which means that their organization might have been fortuitous, or it might have resulted from a natural process when a professor made annotations to express either his own thoughts or his reactions to previous networks. These networks, like the individual glosses, may have been *redacti* (by the professor) or *reportati* (by a student).

Thus a single *lectura* may have given rise to two or more "graphic networks" of glosses, one of which may have been redacted by the teacher and others "reported" by two or more students. Although the contents of the various glosses may display identical or similar elements, nonetheless the individual glosses may easily differ in their handwriting, their number, and their sequence simply because different minds and hands recorded them, selected among them, and documented them by writing them down. I use the term "didactic network" to refer to a set of oral fragments of a course of lessons that were documented, hence have survived. This means that the only possible documentation of a didactic network is through one or more graphic networks.

Something more complicated may have happened, however: a number of didactic networks (for example, fragments of *lecturae* from different years) that originally had been documented in various graphic networks may later have been reduced to a unified text, thus creating a new "book" (*codex*), when a professor or a student copied them or had a scribe copy them. When this occurred the individuality of the original multiple didactic networks may have been lost since the recopied networks, now documented as a whole, formed a single new graphic network.[6]

The *apparatus* was something quite different. Logically it was just

6. For further discussion of the groups of glosses that I have proposed calling "networks" (*reticoli*), in contrast to the *apparatus* and the *lecturae*, see Manlio Bellomo, "Sulle tracce d'uso dei 'libri legales,' " in *Civiltà Comunale: Libro, scrittura, documento*, Atti del Convegno, Genoa 8–11 November 1988 (Genoa: Società Ligure di Storia Patria, 1989), 33–51, esp. 50–51.

the same thing as a "stratum." In fact, it could reach back to preceding "strata," absorb them, and reduce them to homogeneity, and then become itself a "stratum" in a later *apparatus*. It differed from the "network" in that it resulted from the order that a jurist had assigned to specific glosses, either written *ex novo* for the occasion or selected from among preexistent interlinear or marginal glosses in manuscripts already being used in the schools or for private study. It is dubious whether the earliest professors (Irnerius, the Four Doctors, and so forth) wrote *apparatus*, but it is certain that scattered examples of their *glossae* remain, as well as networks of glosses, simple or stratified. It is also certain that Azo and Hugolinus de Presbyteris experimented with the idea and the basic outline of the *apparatus*. Azo in particular has left impressive examples in his *apparatus* to the *Code*, to the three parts of the *Digest*, and to the *Institutes*. The most complete and authoritative examples of the *apparatus* were those of Accursius, as we shall see.

The *apparatus* was thus a deliberate sequence of annotations commenting on the *libri legales*. In the *apparatus* each gloss had a fixed place, and their sequence was determined by the order and the number of the *glossae*.

We have more direct evidence of a professor's lesson in the network of glosses and more indirect evidence from the *apparatus*, whose nature as a composite work remote from direct and unmediated use in the schools is clear in the crystallization (or canonization) of the order, the number, and the form of the glosses that it gathered together. At times there is also evidence of the lesson in a *lectura redacta* (written down by the professor himself) or a *lectura reportata* (noted by a student). In both of these the *lectura* presents a set of annotations arising out of the school, created for the school, and reflecting the orality of the school lesson, as was also true of the "network." The *lectura* differed from the network in having a completeness and a continuity that were lacking in the "network," but the *lectura* lacked the personal and more thorough elaboration that became possible when a work— albeit based on teaching and done for the purposes of teaching—was composed outside of the school, as was true of the *apparatus*.

5. *Summae*

The *summa* was a work of a quite different sort. Even though it too was linked to the school, it was not as fortuitous and fluid as the fragmentary written documentation of the school lessons. Unlike the glosses and their exegesis in brief, disconnected annotations, the *summa* became a precisely defined literary type; a personal, continuous, and fully elaborated exposition constructed according to a specific logical and formal architecture that at times owed much to Cicero.[7]

Before the appearance of the *summa*, its way was prepared by treatises, some of which dealt with a specific subject (one example is a *tractatus* of Martinus Gosia on dowries),[8] and others of which were more like exceptionally full glosses. In general, however, the *summa* matured soon after the mid-twelfth century. One of the first hesitant attempts was Rogerius's interweaving of a *Summa Codicis* with the *Summa Trecensis*;[9] the genre later became clearer with the *Summa Codicis* and the *Summa Institutionum* of Placentinus and, above all, with Azo's weighty and thorough *Summa Codicis*.

Thus, with the *summae*, theoretical elaboration of the law and the circulation of ideas were condensed in works that could be defined in literary terms, that were written in a homogeneous manner, and that reflected an original thinking process the development and expression of which were controlled by the author.

The great legal collections of the church also came to have important works of interpretation, but these were only in part comparable to the works of the civilians. In the twelfth century, the text that for decades had served as a base for annotations explicating and supplementing its thought was Gratian's *Decretum*—the work of an individual, thus less constraining and less inflexible than the *libri legales*. Although glosses and supplementary networks to the *Decretum* did exist, it inspired *summae* almost immediately. These *summae* differed from their civil-law counterparts, however, in that they did not follow a preordained logical structure. They were more similar to the civil-

7. See Bellomo, *Società e istituzioni in Italia*, 456–59 and n. 44; Bellomo, "Der Text erklärt den Text: Über die Anfänge der mittelalterlichen Jurisprudenz," *Rivista Internazionale di Diritto Comune* 4 (1993): 51–64, esp. 59–60.

8. Martinus Gosia, *De iure dotium tractatus*, in *Studies in the Glossators of the Roman Law: Newly Discovered Writings of the Twelfth Century*, ed. Hermann Kantorowicz with William Warwick Buckland (Cambridge: Cambridge University Press, 1938, reprinted with additions and corrections by Peter Weimar, Aalen: Scientia Verlag, 1969), 255–66.

9. See André Gouron, "L'élaboration de la 'Summa Trecensis,'" in *Sodalitas: Scritti in onore di Antonio Guarino* (Naples: Jovene, 1985), 3682–96; Gouron, "L'auteur et la patrie de la Summa Trecensis," *Ius Commune* 12 (1984): 1–38.

ians' *apparatus* in that they included minute notations in the form of glosses arranged to follow one after the other rather than being absorbed into a continuous, flowing prose. Some canon-law *summae* that stand out for their techniques of composition and their form are those of Rolandus, Rufinus, and John of Faenza (Johannes Faventinus), all twelfth-century jurists, and Stephen of Tournai (Stephanus Tornacensis) and Huguccio, who lived into the early thirteenth century.

6. The *Punctatio librorum* and the Three Phases of Instruction

Toward the middle of the thirteenth century we can begin to see signs of a phenomenon that marked university teaching for a very long time. The student corporations, the *universitates*, put pressure on the professors to present their lessons in a more orderly fashion and to distribute them better throughout the academic year. We do not know with certainty whether or not such demands were met, but a number of indications suggest that, for some decades at least, the university statutes were respected and reflected in practice.

Instruction was divided into three distinct activities. Beginning in some schools in the mid-twelfth century, the *lectura* was accompanied by two other exercises, solemn disputation on particular *quaestiones ex facto emergentes* and special sessions in which the topics of the lesson were treated in more detail than was possible in the official lesson. Thus there came to be three distinct forms of instruction: the traditional *lectura*, now (as we shall see) revitalized, the *quaestio publice disputata*, and the *repetitio*.

Students had begun to show signs of concern and dissatisfaction with the *lectura*. Some scrupulous professors (and some who made a show of their rectitude) declared their intention to read the whole of Justinian's compilation: in the mid-thirteenth century Odofredus tells us as much of himself, comparing his deportment to that of colleagues past and present, with the clear intent of discrediting their fame or their success.[10] Other professors followed the easier path,

10. Odofredus, Proemium to the *Digestum vetus* (MS Paris, lat. 4489, fol. 102), in Savigny, *Geschichte des römischen Rechts*, 3:541–42, note d. Savigny reiterates the attribution of the Proemium to Odofredus in *Geschichte*, 5:380. His opinion was originally shared by Peter Weimar, "Argumenta brocardica," *Studia Gratiana*, 14, *Collectanea Ste-*

however, and read only random selections from the *Code* or the *Digestum vetus*, beginning over every year and yielding to the temptation to treat the easier passages at length and ignore the obscure or difficult ones. Bartolus of Saxoferrato remarked that such professors passed over the hard passages *sicco pede*—without getting their feet wet.[11]

The students' solution to their ongoing dissatisfaction was to subject their professors to discipline and to write precise professorial obligations into the statutes of the student universities (in Bologna in 1252 and the years following). This discipline was known as the *punctatio librorum*.[12]

Through their *universitates*, the students declared that the passages to be read and explicated in the lesson must be determined in advance by an analytic selection process entrusted to a student commission working with professorial assistance. This commission drew up lists

phan Kuttner, 4 (Bologna: Institutum Gratianum, 1967), 104 n. 52. Other historians, including Peter Weimar at a later date, held the Proemium to have been written by Pietro Peregrossi of Milan (d. 1295) for his school in Orléans. Among these scholars, see E. M. Meijers, "L'Université d'Orléans au XIIIe siècle" (1918–19), now in his *Etudes d'histoire du droit*, 3 vols. (Leiden: Universitaire Pers, 1959), 3:3–148, esp. 50–51. This line of thought was followed, with no further proofs, by Frederick Maurice Powicke and Alfred Brotherston Emden, the editors of Hastings Rashdall, *The Universities of Europe in the Middle Ages*, 3 vols. (Oxford: Clarendon Press, 1936), 1:218 n. 3, and by Peter Weimar, "Die legistische Literatur und die Methode des Rechtsunterrichts der Glossatoren," *Ius Commune* 2 (1969): 43–83, esp. 47 n. 13. In my opinion, Meijers's reasons for decisive attribution to Pietro Peregrossi need careful reconsideration, particularly in light of more recent methodological lines of thought concerning the evaluation of the "forms" (fluid or definite) of many of the extant juridical writings. Thanks to its nature (an introductory academic discourse, like other similar pieces, largely ceremonial and repetitive), its style, and its broad correspondence with the actual situations and the university regulations in Bologna, the Proemium's paternity cannot be taken away from Odofredus. What is probable, however, is that Pietro Peregrossi brought back to Orléans a copy of Odofredus's work and, as was customary, used the Proemium in Orléans, retouching it to fit its new environment.

11. Bartolus of Saxoferrato, *Commentaria* in Dig.28.2.11, *de liberis et posthumis.l.In suis*, no. 1 (Venetiis, 1615), fol. 90va: "et Accursius, doctores et scribae sicco pede eam transeunt."

12. On the *punctatio*, see Manlio Bellomo, *Saggio sull'Università nell'età del diritto comune* (Catania: Giannotta, 1979; 2d ed., Rome: Il Cigno Galileo Galilei, 1992), 203, 205–8. On the dating of the oldest university statute in Bologna that contained a registration of *puncta*, see Domenico Maffei, "Un trattato di Bonaccorso degli Elisei e i più antichi statuti dello Studio di Bologna nel manoscritto M 22 della Robbins Collection," *Bulletin of Medieval Canon Law* 5 (1975): 73–101; Miroslav Boháček, "Puncta Codicis v rukopisu XVII.A.10 Národnítho Musea v Praze (Puncta Codicis der Handschrift XVII.A.10 des Prager National-Museums)," *Studies o rukopisech* 20 (1981): 3–22.

of the texts selected and divided them into a number of groups, or *puncta*. For each *punctum* it set a period of time, called a *terminus*, that it considered sufficient, and it obliged the professor to read the text or texts in the *punctum* within that time limit. The *terminus* varied seasonally from a maximum of fifteen days in the winter to a minimum of twelve days in the summer, following the ecclesiastical computation of time that divided each of the two parts of the day, light and dark, into a fixed number of hours, thus shortening the "hour" in the winter and lengthening it in the summer, as opposed to the Roman system of telling time, which divided the day—daylight and nighttime hours alike—into twenty-four equal hourly units.

The procedure specified in the *punctatio librorum* and the resulting lists subjected the professors to fairly rigid constraints. The professor who failed to read the texts of a given *punctum* within the allotted time had to pay a sizable fine (according to complex mechanisms involving denunciation of the violation and guarantees for the payment of the fine). Now that he was accountable for his time, the professor forbade the students from speaking during the *lectura*, since when prolonged discussion got out of hand it exposed him to the risk of failing to fulfill his obligations and having to pay the fine.

Thus the *lectura* became wholly *magistralis*, and the *quaestiones* that the professor felt obliged to treat during the lesson, carefully gauging the time he had available for elucidation and elaboration, were called *quaestiones magistrales*.

7. The *Repetitio*

Thus the *punctatio librorum* took away the students' right to speak during the *lectura*. Now that the professor risked having to pay a fine if he failed to complete the *punctum* within the allotted number of days, he was no longer willing to give over part of his precious time to general discussion. And when time was no longer available to go more deeply into the topics treated in the lesson and to debate them then and there, room needed to be made within the academic framework for the satisfaction of both these needs. The mechanisms for doing this were the *repetitio* and the *quaestio publice disputata* (a question disputed publicly).

Within the lesson the professor could expound completely only some of the legislative texts included in the *puncta*. What is more, there were other texts that contained problems that needed to be investigated in greater depth, articulated in specific ways, or, when it proved necessary or useful, discussed by being subjected to objections and questions (*cum oppositis et quesitis*). For this reason, some texts were the object of a particular didactic activity known as the *repetitio*, called *necessaria* because every professor was obliged to hold at least one such session per year. In practical terms it was certainly a freer exercise, because ample time was made available to discuss each topic.

The *repetitio* took place only one day a week (in Bologna, for example, on Mondays) in the afternoon and during a time-span shorter than the academic year, from St. Luke's Day (18 October), when teaching activities began, to Christmas, and again from Easter to the Kalends of August.

The *repetitio* seems to have been held both for the students of one school and for students from an entire sector of jurisprudence—all the civilians, for example, or all the canonists—who were invited to attend open sessions outside their school.

In Bologna, in fact, an order of priority was respected that makes sense only if the *repetitio* is understood as a didactic activity that brought together students from various schools. Professors of the schools that were recognized by the student *universitates* were called on to hold *repetitiones* in order of age, from the youngest to the oldest, and each teacher was obliged to give only one *repetitio*. This system meant that only rarely was a *repetitio necessaria* offered by the same professor who had given a formal lesson on the legislative text to which the *repetitio* referred.

Accompanying the *repetitiones necessariae* that the university statutes obliged the professor to offer, there were *repetitiones voluntariae* that every master was free to organize in connection with the needs of his own course of lessons.

There were also other sessions (not to be confused with the official *repetitiones*, either *necessariae* or *voluntariae*) carried on by private *repetitores* not recognized by the *universitates scholarium*. The professional qualifications of these *repetitores* varied greatly and were at times dubious or nonexistent. Such persons served as assistants, offering supplementary didactic support to students in difficulty because of their scanty cultural background, their limited intellectual capacities, or their wavering motivation.

The structure of the official *repetitio* differed little from the formal lesson, the *lectura*. Both involved explication of a legislative text of the *Corpus iuris civilis* or the *Corpus iuris canonici*. The two forms of instruction may have differed in thoroughness and in their procedures, but this is difficult to ascertain from the way the original oral *repetitio* is presented in the remaining documentation. In fact, we have evidence of instances in which the professor himself succinctly noted down the essence of his own oral discourse (in which case we have a *repetitio redacta*) or one of his pupils did so (*repetitio reportata*); in other instances the oral presentation was thoroughly reworked and elaborated when it was transferred to parchment and to definitive written form; in still others an original, more detailed redaction was summarized and abridged to give the nub of the argument for the purposes of a *lectura*.[13]

8. The *Quaestio disputata*

The third form of instructional activity was the *quaestio disputata*.[14] The origins of this exercise go back to around the mid-twelfth century, and the oldest examples take us back to one school and to the extremely concise texts of the *quaestiones in schola Bulgari disputatae*. Very little remains of what was actually said other than a very brief listing of the legal texts discussed. Even less remains of the professor's final solutions, nearly always expressed with one word of assent or refusal, a simple *sic* (yes) or a sharp *non* (no).

13. For significant examples of these various types of *repetitio*, see Federico Martino, *Dottrine di giuristi e realtà cittadine nell'Italia del Trecento: Ranieri Arsendi a Pisa e a Padova* (Catania: Tringale, 1984); Cornelis Huibert Bezemer, *Les répétitions de Jacques de Révigny: Recherches sur la répétition comme forme d'enseignement juridique et comme genre littéraire, suivies d'un inventaire de textes* (Leiden: E. J. Brill, 1987). The latter work has a serious lacuna in its bibliographical information in that it fails to cite the Martino work just cited. Furthermore, generalizations drawn from research concentrating specifically on Jacques de Révigny lend rigidity to both the general opposition expressed in the book's subtitle and to some of its conclusions (see, for example, p. 70, note 202, and pp. 23–25) and lead to some internal contradictions: the point made on p. 70, note 202, is contradicted on pp. 23–24. In spite of these reservations, the book is to be commended as an attempt to focus on some of the principal problems of juridical *repetitiones* during the late Middle Ages. For a more attentive and simpler presentation, see Cornelis Huibert Bezemer, "Style et langage dans les répétitions de quelques romanistes médiévaux, ou sur l'importance de reconnaître les répétitions," in *Langage et droit à travers l'histoire: Réalités et fictions*, ed. Guido van Dievoet, Philippe Godding, D. van den Auweele (Louvain and Paris: Peeters, 1989), 73–79.

14. See Manlio Bellomo, *Aspetti dell'insegnamento giuridico nelle Università medievali*, vol. I, *Le "quaestiones disputatae": Saggi* (Reggio Calabria: Parallelo, 1974), 38.

Later, this activity became more important, more demanding, and more solemn. At this point the *quaestio* began to be disputed publicly before a vast audience of the students from all the city's schools. Such debates were thus known as *quaestiones publice disputatae*.

A talent for disputation—the *liberaliter disputare*—was a trait typical of academic culture and the world of the schools. Debates pitted reason against reason, argument against argument. *Modi arguendi* (methods of debating) were forged and stored like an artisan's tools in the house of the master, taking the master's name, until vast deposits were laid down, one layer on another, of the techniques of disputation contributed by teachers and their pupils. At times disputations turned violent, when a puerile *libido rixandi* (lust for fighting) broke out,[15] passion gained the upper hand over intelligence, and the encounter ended "non ratione, sed stomacho" (not with reason, but with guts).[16]

In any event, the potential inherent in disputation was clear from the outset. Disputation revealed theoretical perspectives that were all the more extraordinarily fertile as the flexibility of the *quaestio* as an instrument for forging a global vision of the system of the *ius commune* became apparent. The disputation usually centered on a question arising out of everyday life. Ideally, the topic should not be covered by either the laws of Justinian, in the civil field, or the codifications of the church, in canon law,[17] or, at a later date, by local customary or statutory law. In such cases the *quaestio* was *ex facto*

15. This expression appears in a fragment from the theological school of Anselm of Laon (1050–1117); it is transmitted in the MS Bamberg, Staatsbibliothek., lat. 10, fol. 69v, and is cited in Odon Lottin, "Nouveaux fragments théologiques de l'école d'Anselme de Laon: Quelques autres manuscrits allemands," *Recherche téologique ancienne et médiévale* 13 (1946): 267.

16. Rabanus Maurus (784–850), *Enarrationes in Epistulas Pauli*, lib.25, tit.III (PL 112, col. 689).

17. Nonetheless, it was possible for the topic of the *quaestio* to refer to a *casus legis*, on the condition that the latter be kept in mind as a presupposition for a debate centering on a practice or a norm analogous to the codified one but that was not included in the "codification." One example of this is a *quaestio* of Riccardo Malombra, the topic for which is based on a decretal in part contained in the *Liber Sextus* (hence based on a *casus legis*) but which wends its way through doubts arising from practice and from the interpretation of the decretal *Ad extirpanda* of Innocent IV (15 May 1252) and other similar measures not included in the *Liber Sextus* or in the *Clementinae*. See Manlio Bellomo, "Giuristi e inquisitori del Trecento: Ricerca su testi di Iacopo Belvisi, Taddeo Pepoli, Riccardo Malombra e Giovanni Calderini," in *Per Francesco Calasso: Studi degli allievi* (Rome: Bulzoni, 1978), 9–57, esp. 36–43 and 22, n. 21.

emergens. If instead the facts to be debated were connected with cases that had already attracted the attention of a local legislator or fell under feudal customary law, the relative *quaestiones* were called *quaestiones statutorum* or *quaestiones feudorum*.

Toward the end of the thirteenth century it became clear that, in principle, a *quaestio* could be set up regarding any topic whatsoever, as long as the situation was not treated in the *Corpus iuris civilis*. When, by command of the emperor, such a case had been made subject to a certain and absolute law, it would be, technically, a *casus legis* and not admissible to question by disputation. In this manner, two realms of legal knowledge came to be defined. One of these was the terrain of the "certain," the terrain of the *ius commune*, civil and canon, which involved normative solutions, technical arguments, and legal concepts and doctrines. The only doubts that the interpreter might entertain in this realm were in the limited perspective of aiming at a better comprehension of what existed and was certain because it was "true." The other realm was the terrain of the "probable," where what is might not be, and where there might be a negation to correspond to every affirmation. This was the terrain of real-life events not subsumed into the norms of the *Corpus iuris civilis* or those of the church; activities and situations that may or may not have been regulated by the *ius proprium* (customary law, statutes, royal laws, and so forth).

The didactic exercise that took shape in the *quaestio publice disputata* was thus tied to (one might say rooted in) a basic conviction that the *ius commune* had both the value and the function of certain and eternal law. Like all debate, it was fundamentally oral.

We would know little about these disputations (perhaps only that they existed) if the students of the Middle Ages had not set rules for them in the statutes of their *universitates* and, in particular, if they had not required written documentation of those statutes. The statutes tell us, first, that the topic of a disputation could not be a *casus legis*, an article of faith, a passage from Holy Writ, or anything that might cause disorder and discord within the student world. Second, they established that the disputation must be open to students of all the schools in the city (although debates were still held within a single school, just as they had been in the twelfth and early thirteenth centuries). When the debate was open to all students the *quaestio* was *publice disputata*.

The debate itself was preceded by a series of obligations: each professor, in turn, was to *disputare* publicly during the period between Ash Wednesday and Pentecost, and toward that end he was to prepare a *cedula* (a small piece of parchment) on which the topic and the problem (*quid juris?*) were written; this *cedula* must be handed in to the general beadle eight days or more before the disputation; the general beadle then was to inform all the schools (of civil law if the *quaestio* was *in iure civili* or of canon law if it was *in iure canonico*). At the disputation itself the *rectores* of the two *universitates scholarium*, who held power over all the students of all schools, played a prominent role, directing the proceedings and granting or refusing students the right to speak. The professor who proposed the topic was responsible, first, for describing the situation and explaining the juridical problem connected with it and, eventually, for giving his solution. The students who asked to speak also played an important role in the proceedings, each one being called on by the *rectores* in an order of precedence that involved noble birth, wealth, and seniority. Each student was permitted to develop only one *argumentum*, either in favor of (*pro*) a hypothetical solution to the problem or against it (*contra*). At the end, the professor, who gave his own solution, had the right to declare either the *pro* or the *contra* faction as the winner, or else he might dissatisfy both sides by proposing a third and compromise solution. In any event, he was obliged to respond to the various *argumenta* that he rejected.

Within eight days of the public debate, the professor was required to complete redaction of a text faithfully and (when possible) briefly documenting what had been said orally. Some professors injected little or none of their own personality into a listing of the arguments put forth by the students; others, as they wrote, put the stamp of their own thought and knowledge on the variety of student contributions, thus creating a more homogeneous written text of marked intellectual originality.

When he had finished writing up his summary, the professor was required to hand in the original of his report to the general beadle, who kept it with other such loose folios that accumulated through time. At some later date, curiosity might move someone—a professor, a merchant, a *stationarius*, the beadle himself, or others—to have the many parchments on deposit copied in the form of a book (*codex*). In this way anthologies were formed by period, by city, or by author that on some occasions were very modest productions indeed but on others had new *massae* incorporated into them that turned them into *libri magni* containing an immense amount of material. A very small number of copies of such *libri magni quaestionum disputatarum* have been preserved, either in whole or in part. Two particularly rich and complete examples are in the Vatican Library.[18]

9. Tradition and Renewal in the Thirteenth Century

The first phase of didactic experimentation in the schools of law came to an end during the course of the thirteenth century with the definition of all the principal forms of exegetic techniques relating to the *Corpus iuris civilis* and to the most authoritative (the *Decretum*) or official church texts (the *Liber Extra* in particular). These forms were the gloss, the network, the *apparatus*, the *lectura redacta* and the *lectura reportata*, the *summa* (in its civil-law and canon-law variants), and, along with the *lectura*, the *repetitio* and the *quaestio disputata* (both *in schola* and *publice*). During the same thirteenth century, however, new perspectives opened up and jurists began to test the extraordinarily expressive possibilities implicit in the many written forms in use. Some of these offered ways to broaden the horizons of jurisprudence, and, recombined to include or exclude certain elements, they led to the creation of new modes of exposition.

To take the first point first, use of the *quaestiones* became so massive and so widespread that by 1274 it was made mandatory even by the statutes of the student organizations. This means that by then jurists wanted to enlarge their investigations to reach beyond the confines of the *libri legales*, civil and canon: they wanted to venture outside the field of the "certain" for a fuller and freer exploration of the field of the "probable."

18. These are the MSS Vaticano, Arch. S. Pietro A.29 and Vaticano, Chigi E.VIII.245. When I had the good fortune to discover them (at a time when it was doubted that *libri magni* had ever existed), I brought them to the attention of scholars and made partial use of them in Manlio Bellomo, "Due 'Libri magni quaestionum disputatarum' e le 'quaestiones' di Riccardo da Saliceto," *Studi Senesi*, ser. 3, 18 (1969): 256–91. For later utilization, see Bellomo, *Aspetti dell'insegnamento giuridico*; Bellomo, "Le istituzioni particolari e i problemi del potere: Dibattiti scolastici dei secoli XIII-XIV," in *Studi in memoria di Giuliana D'Amelio*, 2 vols. (Milan: Giuffrè, 1978), 1:1–40; Bellomo, "Giuristi e inquisitori del Trecento"; Bellomo, "Giuristi cremonesi e scuole padovane: Ricerche su Nicola da Cremona," in *Studi in onore di Ugo Gualazzini*, 3 vols. (Milan: Giuffrè, 1981), 1:81–112.

They turned their attention to an imposing set of cases that were not expressly mentioned in or regulated by the *libri legales* and that were hence new *quaestiones ex facto emergentes*. Since these cases lacked a governing precept, the jurists combed the *libri legales* for all plausible hints and cues that might help them to construct logically correct arguments in view of a reasonable and satisfactory *solutio*.

Garnering plausible hints from the *libri legales* implied calling to memory one or more of the existent texts of the *Corpus iuris civilis* and subjecting them to dialectical reasoning—argument *a maiori*, *a fortiori*, *a simili*, and so forth—in order to extend their normative content beyond the situations originally cited in the various provisions.

In the construction of their *argumentum* the jurists used *modi arguendi* or *propositiones maiores or minores* derived from Aristotelian philosophy, above all from the so-called "Aristotle Major," the major works of Aristotle that dominated all of culture after their rediscovery and dissemination in the thirteenth century. Furthermore, they experimented with those techniques to render them sufficiently flexible to provide solutions ("probable," not "certain" solutions) for each case under consideration. Although the jurists' point of departure was an event taken from everyday experience, the ways in which they sought a "norm" for it—which did not exist in the *ius commune*—were decidedly based in theory. Not only was their procedure theoretical; it denied or strayed from the *ius commune* so little that the logical arguments the jurists constructed in support of the (probable) "norm" could not even have existed if they had not been able to draw upon a text of the *Corpus iuris civilis* or a rule from one of the church codifications. They always needed a "certain" text to give support—even weak support tortuously arrived at—in order to legitimize the entire logical operation. When, at the turn of the thirteenth century, one student who later became famous, Bernardus Dorna, came, ill-prepared and somewhat bewildered, to Azo's school, he attempted to base an argument on a verse of the Latin poet Ovid. The master's reaction was swift: a jurist did not reason outside the orbit of the common law ("Non licet allegare nisi Iustiniani leges"; It is not permitted to cite anything except the laws of Justinian).[19]

There was more. The jurist's everyday activities involved concrete

19. Azo of Bologna, *Quaestiones*, 10, *Scolaris quidam*, in Ernst Landsberg, ed., *Die Quaestiones des Azo* (Freiburg im Breisgau: J. C. B. Mohr, P. Siebeck, 1888), 74.

life experiences that found expression in the *lectura* or the *quaestio disputata* and determined a selection among the legislative texts that could be employed for argumentation, noting those that should be avoided or, at the most, could be used in disputations and *quaestiones*. Selection also involved a choice among laws of the same type, imperial or papal. The only norms that could be used for the reasoning that underlay the arguments or as the kernel of an argument were the imperial laws included in the *Corpus iuris civilis* and the church laws collected in Gratian's *Decretum*, the *Liber Extra* of Gregory IX, the *Liber Sextus* of Boniface VIII, and the few "codifications" that were included in the *Corpus iuris canonici* (the *Clementinae*, the *Extravagantes Johannis XXII*, and the *Extravagantes communes*). All other norms, of which there were many, particularly in the field of canon law, had to be ignored, even if they were the laws most frequently applied in the courts and in legal practice. The judgment that legal thought in the schools of the late thirteenth and the fourteenth centuries showed "practice-oriented tendencies" is clearly unfounded.

10. *Lecturae per viam quaestionum* and *Lecturae per viam additionum*

The experience gained in the public and solemn disputation of *quaestiones*, an exercise that was not formally a part of regular instruction, carried over into the *lectura*, the primary vehicle for teaching. Indeed, that experience gave both matter and form to the lesson, because the professors devoted considerable time to the *quaestiones*, to the problems on which they focused, and to their implications and solutions, to the point of constructing an entire course *per viam quaestionum*.

On certain occasions, when a famous professor gave the *lectura* and reelaborated *quaestiones* in it, his class notes were sought after, copied, and widely circulated, as in the case of the *Supleciones* of Guido of Suzzara.[20] More often, though, we have only bits and pieces to document the fluid thought of the oral lesson; we have only an ephemeral echo (in the didactic networks) or lucid written fragments (in graphic networks) that fixed that orally expressed thought on parchment and

20. Federico Martino, *Ricerche sull'opera di Guido da Suzzara: Le "Supleciones"* (Catania: Tringale, 1981).

made it knowable outside the restricted circle of people who had the good fortune to hear the professor's voice. Historiography calls these fragments "living texts,"[21] not because, as formal logic might indicate, they were texts that were still inherently flexible or open to modification, but because the thought that lay behind them and gave rise to them was vital and fluid. It was also much richer, more variegated, and more complex than it would seem from the dead and fragmentary remaining documentation.

The manuscripts of both the *libri legales* (the *Corpus iuris civilis*) and the great church "codifications" frequently show significant traces of these cultural and didactic processes; we can analyze internal evidence of their use to reconstruct a basic line of legal thought in late-thirteenth-and fourteenth-century Europe.[22]

By that date the text of the civil and canon law was accompanied by a standard, or "ordinary," *apparatus*. Thousands of additions (*additiones*) to these two sets of writings were collected and disseminated, incorporating and in part documenting ongoing juristic thought in continual transformation. Furthermore, the fact that professors in the schools read the texts of Justinian and the ordinary *apparatus* that completed them opened up the way for even more annotations and comparisons, which enriched legal science but eventually invited revision of both problematics and methodology.

This was how the *lecturae per viam additionum* came into being. These were *lecturae* of varying length and importance whose reconstruction always raises problems because only rarely were they *redactae* by the professor who read the books of law and their accompa-

---

21. The first historian who spoke of "living texts" in this connection was Stephan Kuttner: see Kuttner, "Relazione," Acta commemorationis et conventus quae saeculo VIII post Decretum Gratiani compositum facta sunt . . . A. MCMLII, in *Studia Gratiana* (Bologna: Institutum Iuridicum Universitatis Studiorum, 1958), 5:106–12. Kuttner has repeated this notion on several occasions and it is shared by many contemporary historians. For bibliographic information, see Bellomo, "Legere, repetere, disputare: Introduzione ad una ricerca sulle 'quaestiones' civilistiche," in Bellomo, *Aspetti dell'insegnamento giuridico*, vol. 1, *Le "quaestiones disputatae": Saggi*, 55, n. 87.

22. A research team at the Istituto Storico Germanico di Roma working under my direction and with the sponsorship of the Gerda Henkel Stiftung of Düsseldorf is in the process of investigating this topic. For a list of articles already published, see Manlio Bellomo, "Scuole giuridiche e università studentesche in Italia," in *Luoghi e metodi di insegnamento nell'Italia medioevale (secoli XII-XIV)*, ed. Luciano Gargan and Oronzo Limone, Atti del Convegno di Lecce-Otranto, 6–8 October 1986 (Galatina: Congedo, 1989), 121–40.

nying ordinary *apparatus*. They are a rich source of information, however, since they often record and summarize *quaestiones* and *consilia*—that is, everyday cases debated in the classroom or the courts. On occasion they note *repetitiones* in full or in summary. The transcription of *quaestiones* and *repetitiones* in a *lectura per viam additionum* may not reflect the original shape and oral character of the *lectura* itself: this happened when someone who owned a *codex* (a book) was moved (and had enough blank space in the volume) to embellish the document with a *lectura* containing *quaestiones* and *repetitiones* extraneous to the original lesson.

11. From *Lecturae* to *Commentaria*

It was out of this context that the *Lecturae* of Cinus of Pistoia sprang, as well as the *Commentaria* of Giovanni d'Andrea (Johannes Andreae), Bartolus of Saxoferrato, Bartolomeo of Saliceto, and a very few other jurists of the fourteenth and the early fifteenth centuries—Paulus de Castro, for example, among the civilians, and Niccolò dei Tedeschi (Nicolaus de Tudeschis; known as Panormitanus) among the canonists.

Commentaria have at least two characteristics that distinguish them from the other works of the time. From the point of view of their form, they were the product of a personal and meditated reelaboration of a range of heterogeneous materials that had accumulated, layer after layer *per viam additionum*, during the course of *lecturae* on Justinian's laws and on the *Glossa ordinaria* of Accursius. Thus they were works in a particular "form" that the author had chosen deliberately for a definitive expression of his thought. From the point of view of their substance, they were works of homogeneous content covering one complete part of the *libri legales*—the *Code*, for example, or the *Digestum vetus*.

Because the *commentarium* was a new literary genre and, above all, because of the fame and the authority of the *Commentaria* of Bartolus of Saxoferrato, historiography calls all fourteenth-century jurists "commentators," a term that is decidedly inappropriate or inadequate for a good many of these men.

The differences between the *commentum* and the *lectura* (in its various documented forms and even in its written fragments) had a number of consequences. First, only the *commentum* was made up of a definite text that circulated in the written form conceived by its author. For this reason, we find it in the same form in a variety of manuscripts.

Second, both the *lectura per viam additionum* and the *lectura per viam quaestionum* showed variations in their documentation, because even one course of lessons could appear in different formal guises that reflected the talents or the interests of the person who captured in one or more written phrases thoughts that the professor had exposed orally. When this happened, the circulation of that thought was not linked to the stability or the unity of one written "form," precisely because the original means of expression was oral. Hence manuscripts seldom correspond literally, even when they document the same thought and the same lesson.

Third, a partial reelaboration of this varied documentation led to reworking the material (that is, the *additiones*) that had accumulated on the margins of the *libri legales* and Accursius's *Glossa*. At times it was the professor himself who selected *additiones* written or rewritten by himself or by others and who arranged them in a stable order; at other times this task was done by someone else who made use of the texts—a student, another professor, or a practicing jurist or judge sensitive to the use of the *ius commune*. These two procedures alternate in the *Supleciones* of Guido of Suzzara and the *Casus* of Riccardo of Saliceto.

7

The System of the *Ius commune*

Ius commune and *Ius proprium* as Positive Law: Hierarchy in the Sources

In the long age that began in the twelfth century and continued until the eighteenth century, the many and varied norms of a city, a feudal territory, or a kingdom, which covered the entire population or specific groups, social levels, corporations, or confraternities within the population, gradually came to be clarified, delimited, and consolidated.

All of Europe was honeycombed with a thick network of thriving particular law, giving a first impression of confusion, uncertainty, and precariousness. Anyone who traveled a long distance and went from one country to another might easily change status within the day; he might be of age in one place in the morning and that evening find himself accounted a minor in another place.[1] At least this was the case until the fourteenth century, when radical corrections were introduced into the *ius commune* to define and give concrete form to personal *status* and basic, stable personal rights.

Historians have responded to this panorama in a variety of ways that can barely be touched on here. Some scholars have seen the "ethnic" origins of certain social phenomena as all-important and have supposed that they were perpetuated at the start of the second millennium out of nostalgia for a remote past. Thus "Roman" or "Germanic" descent has been praised from opposed and conflicting points of view. Or else particular events or figures have been picked out and

---

1. This observation is borrowed from Emile Chénon, *Histoire générale de droit français public et privé des origines à 1815*, 2 vols. (Paris: Société anonyme du Recueil Sirey, 1926), 1:488ff.

charged with symbolizing an epoch or a land as the historian follows the conflict between classes or interests as they rush headlong toward open and bloody revolt or resolve their differences in a social compact or *concordia*. Another approach has been to concentrate on life's more mundane moments and the rhythms of everyday living in an attempt to reconstruct a global microhistory.[2] In all cases diversity has been either exploited (moving from a basic conviction that has attempted to document its own past by stressing its difference) or ignored, either in favor of contemplation of the isolated datum or out of an indifference toward comparison that denies it all feasibility or usefulness.

In the circumscribed world of microhistory, an insistent analysis of all the data present in one particular set of historical circumstances led that historiographical school into dealing with problems, concepts, ideologies, languages, and styles of reasoning that it has been unable to comprehend because it isolated the phenomena on which its investigation focused from the broader context out of which they arose and by which they were shaped.

This is what happened concerning the problem of the relationship between particular law, the *ius proprium*, and the common law, the *utrumque ius* or *ius commune*. We have in fact seen little or nothing of the *ius commune* in historiography because either it has been considered completely extraneous to the *ius proprium* or we have been shown only that portion of the *ius commune* that particular law has allowed us to see and appreciate, which means that we have had only a reduced and distorted image of it, or else its various aspects have been reconstructed according to the viewpoint of those who acted within the order of particular law. Obviously, this angle of vision is not only partial but marked by the political interests of the social and political order in question or by the disinterest and sense of irritation of dreamers unable to see beyond their own small provincial world, who imagined that it provided answers to all the demands of their own daily lives in the realms of the law and of values and principles.

---

2. See Bruno Paradisi, "Gli studi di storia del diritto italiano dal 1896 al 1946" (1946–47) and "Indirizzi e problemi della più recente storiografia giuridica," both of which are now available in Paradisi, *Apologia della storia giuridica* (Bologna: Il Mulino, 1973). For a more recent and better organized summary, see Ennio Cortese, "Storia del diritto italiano," in *Cinquanta anni di esperienza giuridica in Italia*, Proceedings of the Congresso nazionale organized by the Università di Messina and Casa Editrice Giuffrè, Messina-Taormina 3–8 November 1981 (Milan: Giuffrè, 1982), 787–858.

The favorite terrain for this sort of reductive historiography is the set of notions that make up the so-called "hierarchy of the sources."

We have seen how—in the *Regnum Siciliae* by means of the *Constitutio* "Puritatem," in a number of municipal normative systems by means of statutes, and elsewhere by royal order—legal sources in Europe came to be organized in order of precedence as a way to provide judges with guidance and a basis for their decisions. We usually find the highest priority given to the law that was the most direct expression of the organs of government: the royal law in various European kingdoms, the statute in the municipal communes, or the feudal law in territories ruled as counties, duchies, and principalities. Customary law had a lower priority: the judge could apply it when he failed to find a disposition that fit his case in the law of the first level of priority. Failing these, the judge was either invited to adjudicate according to justice—that is, according to an equity that he was to determine in the specific case before him—or permitted to search for an appropriate norm in the corpus of civil and canon laws of the *ius commune*.

One episode has on occasion been taken as emblematic of this search for a norm. Andrea Bonello da Barletta (d. 1291) relates that a prominent lawyer (he may have been speaking of himself) was attempting to argue a case for a client in Puglia, within the *Regnum Siciliae* (Kingdom of Sicily), on the basis of the laws of Justinian. The lawyer for the opposing side, whom Andrea scornfully describes as an *advocatellus quidam* (a certain little lawyer), knew nothing of Roman law, but he had a copy of a summary of Lombard law that he kept carefully hidden under his robe, producing it in a surprise move to win his case. The judge decided in favor of the "little lawyer" because Lombard law was taken to be of a higher rank of positive law that took precedence over Roman law.[3]

In both the general problem of "hierarchies" and in this example taken as a model and a basis for historiographic evaluation, there are recurrent terms and concepts that we have already encountered: *ius regium, statutum, consuetudo, ius commune*. These terms are all placed on the same plane, in the sense that they are always understood within the context of "positive law" and with the meaning they have in that

---

3. This episode is noted in Francesco Calasso, *Medio Evo del diritto* (Milan: Giuffrè, 1954), vol. 1, *Le fonti*, 553.

context.[4] "Hierarchy" is conceivable only by doing so; otherwise, there would be no lowest common denominator that could make an operation of the sort feasible or useful for such purposes.

2. The *Ius commune* without Hierarchy

The problem is that a modest reconstruction of a portion of historical reality of that sort neglects at least two fundamental aspects of that reality. First, the *ius proprium* was not merely a "positive law" that exhausted its reasons for being by offering precepts to judges and opportunities for arriving at judicial solutions in a situation of conflict of interest. Second, even less was the *ius commune* merely a "positive law" deprived of all connection with ideas and all ideal roots or stripped of all theoretical, practical, and operational capacities.

We need to seek to understand what the *ius proprium* contained that the *ius commune* did not, and vice versa, and how they differed. We also need to grasp why neither of these complex normative systems can be reduced to or understood uniquely as positive law.

Anyone redacting a norm as a way to fix a fluid custom in writing or to flesh out the will of a citizen assembly or a prince used the Latin language and, within that language, the lexical paraphernalia specific to the Roman jurists. Thus, such a person knew, and had to know, Justinian's *Corpus iuris civilis*, because the technical terms of juridical science were set out in that corpus and transmitted by it. If he spoke of *dominium* (proprietory right), of *obligatio* (legal obligation), or of *emptio-venditio* (purchase-sale), he necessarily did so in reference to the meanings that those terms bore in the laws of Justinian, whether he wanted to use them in that precise sense or to move away from that meaning.

The notary was in an analogous position with respect to the wishes

4. For this line of historiographic interpretation, see esp. Ugo Niccolini, "Diritto romano e diritti particulari in Italia nell'età comunale," *Rivista di storia del diritto italiano* 59 (1986): 13–172. For a clear example of an erroneous historiography completely indifferent to the problematics of the system of the *ius commune*, see Carlo Guido Mor, "Considerazioni su qualche costituzione di Federico II," *Archivio storico pugliese* 26 (1973): 423–34, now also available in *Il "Liber Augustalis" di Federico II di Svevia nella storiografia*, ed. Anna L. Trombetti (Bologna: Il Mulino, 1987). Mor even claims that every "reading" of the *ius proprium* "must" necessarily and methodically avoid noting any possible relation between *ius proprium* and *ius commune*.

of the private persons who expected him to help them make out a will, make an *inter vivos* (among the living) transfer of a *res* (property), or assume a debt or a credit. The notary had to use a prescribed language (Latin) and a specific technical language (that of the *ius commune*); hence, he too wrote of *testamentum* (will), of *obligatio*, of *emptio-venditio*, and so forth.

In both cases, the increasing precision in the technical language perceptible in the sources beginning in the late eleventh century can be explained only if we keep in mind that knowledge of the *ius commune* was essential for the redactor of a law or for the notary. Consequently, behind the completed act—be it a "law" or a notarial act—there had to have been practical and concrete study of the *ius commune*. Such study was intrinsic to the work at hand, and it served to vitalize that work and to determine its technical value, even when no citations to *ius commune* texts appeared and no texts of the *ius commune* were applied.

The interpreter of the law, be he a judge who had to hand down a decision or a lawyer who needed to construct a defense, was involved in a similar operation. Even if a norm of *ius proprium* (royal, communal, or other) or a clause in a contract that needed to be interpreted was an obligatory point of reference, the judge or the lawyer could not ignore the common and accepted meanings of the technical terms that he found in the law or in the notarial act. In other words, he could not be unaware of the *ius commune*, which established the significance of those terms and which even designated what Gaius called the *variae causarum figurae*—the legal concepts and doctrines that were the inheritance and the wealth of every jurist.

In these mechanisms it was not important whether or not the "content" of the norms or of the clauses being negotiated agreed or disagreed with the precepts of the *ius commune*. Thus it was totally irrelevant whether the *ius commune*, as positive law to be applied, was first or last in the hierarchies of sources of law. What mattered were simply the concepts and doctrines that were the stuff of the *ius commune*, the principles that inspired it, and the values that it expressed.

Furthermore, as we shall see, reference to concepts and rules and knowledge of them was accompanied by a faith that they were eternal and unchanging, because they gave concrete form to a system of values and of superior and absolute principles. They offered a standard of evaluation, a model of representation, and a tool for understanding that surpassed the fortuitous and contingent nature of the *ius proprium*. Thus the *ius commune*, in its objective and metahistorical consistency, also became functional, in and of itself, for safeguarding the interests of the jurists and of their class, whether the jurists were aware of this function or not, and whether they appealed to and stressed the universality of the *ius commune* out of a deep-rooted and reasoned conviction or only out of an ingenuous and unreflecting trust.

If we look at the question in these terms we cannot (and we should not) be surprised that practice reflected just the opposite of what is thought by those who restrict their vision to the norms of the *ius proprium* and who establish a fixed hierarchy of laws and assign the last place to the *ius commune*. It should not seem astonishing that in every important practical act the *ius commune* was the basis of every decision, thanks to a rational mechanism broadly attested in the extant records of court cases, official and ancillary, and in *allegationes* and *consilia*. Not only did the *ius commune* serve to provide concepts and technical language; its norms also served a purpose, even if they were not applied and even if they differed from or even contradicted those of the *ius proprium*. It was the grafting of Aristotelian dialectic onto jurisprudence that made it feasible to utilize the *ius commune* in court cases or arbitration. When the "practical" jurist found an adequate *modus arguendi* in the available logical paraphernalia, he used a disposition included in the *Corpus iuris civilis* or in the universal laws of the church as the linchpin of his argument. Then, reasoning by similarity, *a contrario*, *ex silentio*, or *ab auctoritate* (according to the *modus arguendi* that he chose from among the many available), he used that base to construct an *argumentum* that led to a juridical resolution of a problem not present in the civil or canon laws, but adequate to resolve a problem arising from interpreting a provision of the *ius proprium* or even a contractual clause that lay behind an actual or eventual law suit or extrajudicial quarrel.

One can see at a glance that when the jurists of this middle period were involved in a practical activity (writing *consilia*, for example), they always argued from the norms of the *ius commune*. It occasionally happened that they chose to (or were obliged to) argue only *ex iustitia* rather than *ex lege*, but they never argued from texts other than those of the *ius commune*, and certainly never on the basis of norms from the *ius proprium*. It is thus misleading to think that the *consilia* can be understood historically only as an excellent mirror of practice; the *consilia* provide just as good a reflection of the theoretical potential, used in a concrete situation, of the *ius commune*. Moreover, the jurists of the thirteenth and fourteenth centuries had behind them a long apprenticeship. As we have seen, they learned their craft in the schools when a *quaestio ex facto emergens* or a *quaestio statutorum* was being debated, and they knew perfectly well that arguments on the basis of any text from *ius proprium* or of any sort other than the *ius commune* were inadmissible.[5]

3. *Ius commune* and *Ius proprium* as One System: The Problem of Legality

It soon began to be clear that the *ius commune* and the *ius proprium* shared a system of relations and values that far exceeded the notion of hierarchical sources of law, and at the same time new cultural movements arose that, as we shall see, had little or nothing to do with that hierarchy of precedence. It came to be even less true that the *ius commune*, as a subsidiary law in that hierarchy, was a phenomenon of little practical importance, to be considered at best a model and a product of the abstract theorization of pedantic absent-minded professors.[6]

I might also note one constant, recurrent fact: the contemporaneity of the *ius proprium* in the extraordinary variety of local situations. The various terms for the particular and contemporaneous local norms known in Spain as *fueros* and *usatges*, in France as *coutumes*, in Italy as *statuta* or *consuetudines* often reveal their origins and the reasons for their formation. Thus the *statuta* reflected a desire for free and autonomous municipalities and a need to consolidate the internal processes for the institutionalization of autonomous power; *consuetudines* reflected the traditions of a people; the *usatges* and *laudamenta curiae* showed legal procedures; royal laws and *ordonnances* expressed the will

5. See above, chap. 6, sections 8 and 10.
6. See the bibliographical references in Manlio Bellomo, *Società e istituzioni dal medioevo agli inizi dell'età moderna*, 6th ed. (Rome: Il Cigno Galileo Galilei, 1993), 451–53.

of a king, count, or duke; *concordiae* and *Landfriede* arose out of compromises or agreements reached between a lord and a community.

Everywhere in Europe there was a shift from a regime of oral
norms (custom, Carolingian capitularies) to a regime of written law,
and everywhere, with varying degrees of awareness, people saw the
terms of a new law in the written law. At the risk of schematic simplification, we might say that until the eleventh century people believed
that conflicts within the society in which they lived could be resolved
either *per pugnam* or *per iustitiam*, even if here and there the hope
was expressed of resolving them *per iustitiam* alone; from the twelfth
century on, however, it was thought that all conflicts of interest must
be prevented, avoided, or resolved and settled *per legem*, even if the
sizable problem of *iustitia* was never lost from sight.

In other words, a new value arose, and without separating from the
old faith or from a confident trust in *iustitia*, it manifested itself and
crystallized in the notion of legality. I should stress that this new value
surfaced and took shape both in exegesis of the *ius commune* and in a
concrete affirmation and spread of the *ius proprium*. The ruler, like
any other legislator, had to be not only a just ruler but also a *princeps
legalis*, a lord who respected his own law. To act according to justice
signified acting *secundum ius*.[7]

Two currents coexisted: on the one hand there was the constant
practice of the particular norms—a phenomenon uniform in its methods and its animating ideas even in the immense variety of its concrete
manifestations. On the other hand, reflecting that practice but also
driving it forward, there was the thought of the great jurists of the
Middle Ages, men who expressed original and highly significant ideas
on equity, human justice, and legality.

This was the thread that bound the *ius proprium* and the *ius commune* together in one quintessential relationship, a relationship that
was implicit, unexpressed, but nonetheless evident and sure. Without
the *ius commune*, the *ius proprium* would never have had so much vitality and so much of an impact on people's consciousness; conversely,
without the notable differences and the variety of the *ius proprium*, the
ius commune would have lacked roots and had no field of operations in
which to function.

7. Francesco Calasso, *Gli ordinamenti giuridici del rinascimento medievale*, 2d ed. (Milan: Giuffrè, 1949; reprints, 1953, 1965), 267–70.

4. *Ius commune* and *Ius proprium* as One
System: Sovereignty

Another thread connected the *ius proprium* and the *ius commune*. We can discern it by examining society—each particular society—to analyze institutional trends within it, seeking to understand how these trends were solidified and perpetuated by having the stable forms of a legal structure—an adequate network of laws—shaped to them and applied to them. Thus, if a distinction emerges between what was typical of a society per se, considered as an entity, and what was the part of the private subjects who made up that society, we can distinguish between *imperium* and *dominium*, between public power and individual property, between the *voluntas principis* (will of the prince) that gave society its law and the will of the private individual forging his own laws by juridical negotiation.

It is undeniable that in the extraordinary multiplicity of particular social orders the problems central to all forms of social cohabitation were resolved in multiple ways. The fact remains, however, that those problems arose everywhere, and, while they stimulated and nourished legal thought, they drew from it a paradigm for their own organization.

In the legal thought of those centuries the chief paradigm and the supreme model was dual: both the Holy Roman Empire and the church were universal orders with enormous power inherent in their heads, the emperor and the pope. As is known, earlier (twelfth century) emperors and popes needed to know and jurists wanted to establish the nature and limits of the *iura reservata principi* (rights reserved to the prince), or *regaliae*, and whether the emperor's or the pope's *dominium* over the things of this world was property ownership (*dominium quo ad proprietatem*; right of property) or governing power (*dominium quo ad iurisdictionem et protectionem*; right of jurisdiction and protection). It is clear that the way these complex problems were approached reflected the difficulties that feudal circles experienced in understanding them: they found it difficult to grasp the meaning of the term *dominium*,[8] and they had good reason to balk at conceiving of a public dimension of power and to try to bend public powers to fit the patterns of private law. It is just as clear, however,

8. Ibid., 254–55, 232–34.

that there were pressing reasons on the side of those who were intent on "uprooting the concept of state from feudal terrain."[9] When the latter convictions prevailed, and when the components of the superior model were set (for instance, by lists of the *regaliae* pertaining to the secular or ecclesiastical ruler), an integral and profound change took place in political structures. Even if seigniory (feudal, territorial, or landowning) continued to be the rule in large areas in Europe, it nevertheless had to compete with free cities and great institutionalized aggregations (counties, duchies, principalities, kingdoms—*regna*) that were beginning to lose their original feudal characteristics and to take on the new attributes of sovereignty. From this point of view, the history of the Kingdom of Sicily is exemplary. It was a fief of the church, but it was also an independent and sovereign kingdom.[10]

Thus the characteristics of the imperial powers were reproduced in innumerable smaller entities. More and more, the jurists quoted the lapidary formula, "Rex in regno suo est imperator" (A king is emperor in his own kingdom); they embellished it with the added attributes of exclusivity and independence: "Rex superiorem non recognoscens in regno suo est imperator" (A king recognizing no superior is emperor in his own kingdom);[11] and they applied this notion to the powers of government of particular political orders. These in turn were revitalized by use of this same notion, clarified by theory, with the result that any head or lord of an institutionalized community had public powers modeled on those of the supreme head, the emperor, and differing from the emperor's only in their more limited scope.[12]

In short, the jurists competed with one another to define a political and institutional reality and bring it to the attention of their contemporaries, to the point that the same theory of power was taken over

9. Francesco Calasso, "Jurisdictio nel diritto comune classico," in *Studi in onore di Vincenzo Arangio-Ruiz nel XLV anno del suo insegnamento*, 4 vols. (Naples: Jovene, 1953), 421–43, quote 425, now available in *Annali di storia del diritto* 9 (1965), quote 93.

10. Francesco Calasso, *I glossatori e la teoria della sovranità*, 3d ed. (Milan: Giuffrè, 1957). On the problem of sovereignty in the *ius commune*, see Kenneth Pennington, *The Prince and the Law: Sovereignty and Rights in the Western Legal Tradition* (Berkeley-Los Angeles-London: University of California Press, 1993).

11. Ibid.; Ennio Cortese, *Il problema della sovranità nel pensiero giuridico medievale* (Rome: Bulzoni, 1966).

12. See Bellomo, *Società e istituzioni in Italia*, 377–80. On the problem of normative power and its theoretical justification, see Federico Martino, *Dottrine di giuristi e realtà cittadine nell'Italia del Trecento: Ranieri Arsendi a Pisa e a Padova* (Catania: Tringale, 1984), 102–18.

by feudalism and became the theoretical basis of seigniorial power as expressed, particularly in France and southern Italy, in the formula, "Baro in sua baronia est imperator" (A baron is emperor in his barony). This motto inverted the basic principles of feudal civilization, twisting them by transplanting the political and ideal dimension of the emperor's public power to a feudal terrain that never could have invented it, let alone accepted and practiced it. This opened the way for the formation or the strengthening of the great institutionalized political concentrations, which gave rise, in the fifteenth to the eighteenth centuries, to such regional and multiregional states as the principalities of Italy and elsewhere and to national states such as France and Spain.

None of all this would be comprehensible or could have occurred if the destinies of the *ius proprium* had not become interwoven with those of the *ius commune* and if the latter had not offered a model, propitious terrain, and the raw materials to construct an overall vision of the law. This vision was realized on the level of the *ius proprium* in the multiplicity of the European political orders, which varied according to place and time and according to local traditions and original contributions and to the presence and the inventiveness of single individuals and entire peoples.

Thus the *ius commune* contributed to creating a single juridical civilization in Europe, a civilization that was not feudal but fundamentally urban and solidly built on a number of firm and staunchly defended ideas: *imperium* (which was public) and *dominium* (which was private); the liberty of the prince ("Quod principi placuit legis habet vigorem"; What pleases the prince has the force of law), and the need to observe the precepts to which that liberty led, as a way to guarantee stability to power and to defend the life of the individual—in a word, the new value of sovereignty.

5. Major Figures: Irnerius

Two figures stood out in this movement, dominating the scene: Irnerius and Gratian.

We know these two men. We have encountered them at work constructing the bases of their thought: Irnerius by reorganizing, restoring, and redistributing the texts of Justinian's laws; Gratian by endowing the church with a programmatically homogeneous, abundant, and flexible normative text. We need to look now at the theoretical works of these two men and seek their translation into contemporary terms of a problem considered perennial in a human heart forever torn between yearning for justice and being blinded by private interests.

Historians credit Irnerius with separating the law from ethics and from logic.[13] This is an operation that might not be considered precisely to his "credit" if it did not mean—as indeed it does—that Irnerius viewed justice as an autonomous phenomenon and theorized on it in those terms, although he never rejected the necessary relationship in the substance of what he was distinguishing. Thus a norm that was considered juridical, and that hence was represented as autonomous, could also be considered for its ethical content and in its verbal formulation, including all the associated problems touching on man's inner life and his intellectual and expressive capacities. Indeed, this was so much the case that not only Irnerius but whole generations of jurists after him posed as a vital problem the question of the relationship between a norm that was discerned as juridical—hence complete in itself, rational, and authoritative—and a norm that could clearly be discerned as ethical, hence was necessary intrinsically.

Equity, Irnerius stated, meditating on a fragment of the *Digestum vetus*, although a part of justice, differs from it: it can be perceived in things and in human relations, but it only becomes "justice" (a juridically defined and juridically relevant phenomenon) when there exists the will to give it a "form"—a verbal garb and a cogent value. Only the emperor, "lex animata in terris" (living law on earth), had the power to transform equity into justice, because the Roman people had delegated its own original power to the emperor once and for all. Thus all the Roman laws determined by Emperor Justinian constituted "justice": justice was indeed distinct from equity, but it had emerged out of equity and was still and would forever be connected with equity.[14]

A concrete illustration may help to clarify Irnerius's argument. In the exchange of a thing for the payment of a price, for instance, it was in the nature of things (*in rebus*) that no one deprives himself

13. Calasso, *Medio Evo del diritto*, 1:503ff., 557.
14. Ibid., 477.

of something without some compensation (in a sale or a transfer) or without a reason (in a donation). Hence it was just and equitable that the person who receives a *res* pays a price, provided that the compensation reflects the will of the giver or seller (a determining factor and a specific stage in the transaction). All this was equitable and a concrete, specific exemplification of *aequitas*. But it remained on the level of a *rudis aequitas*—that is, on the level of moral evaluations—until such time as there was a norm that stipulated an obligation to pay a price for a *res* received or to give over a *res* for a price received. The glossators held that the act still remained outside the province of the law if this process of discerning the equity in the concrete relationship was conducted by a private subject, because in that case one would have either a *ius strictum* (strict right)—not yet *scriptum*—if that discernment was reasonable and responded to the *bonum generale* (general good), or an *aequitas bursalis* (personal equity; the equity of one's purse) if it responded to personal or particular interests as a convenient "rule" that anyone might bring forth, at his will and pleasure, from his own *bursa* (purse). According to Irnerius, in order to transform the *aequitas* into *iustitia*, the emperor had to lend his authority to the entire logical operation, a move that would also serve to guarantee absolute certainty to the outcome (as opposed to the tendency of the particular case toward justice). In other words, the norm had to become cogent, the *ius scriptum* had to correspond to the *ius strictum*.

The expressions used by Irnerius and the jurists of the generations of glossators and commentators who followed him are often vivid and picturesque. *Aequitas*, wrote Rogerius in the twelfth century, does not become justice if it is not "in praeceptionem redacta et iuris laqueis innodata"[15]—if it is not set down in legal norms and by that means well knotted into the web of the law. Jacques de Révigny, writing in the thirteenth century, explained that *aequitas* was like a raw material out of which a manufactured product could be made; it was like silver, which exists in nature, is extracted from mines, and can be transformed into a vase, but becomes a vase only thanks to the

15. Rogerius, *Enodationes quaestionum super Codice* (no. 2), in *Studies in the Glossators of the Roman Law*, ed. Hermann Kantorowicz with William Warwick Buckland (Cambridge: Cambridge University Press, 1938), reprinted with additions and corrections by Peter Weimar (Aalen: Scientia-Verlag, 1969), 282.

craftsman's skill. *Aequitas* was a *genus*; *iustitia* was a *species*, and as such equity had its own specific characteristics while retaining those of the *genus*.[16] Similarly, the law was indeed autonomous and distinct from morality, but it retained and actuated moral precepts.

In this conception, *aequitas* had a vast meaning because it was the source of justice (*fons iustitiae*) and the source from which all positive law flowed. There was a different meaning of the term, however, that brought it down to more limited dimensions: *aequitas* could be understood as a way to temper the *rigor iuris* (rigor of the law), as *benignitas* (mercy), but always within a specific order of relations and subject to clearly defined logical operations. This occurred when the first step in the process—the emergence of justice out of equity— came to an end and a cogent norm came into existence. At that point what was needed was only to interpret and apply the norm, which could be done in the most human and merciful way.[17]

6. Gratian

Gratian achieved a similar result, further affirming and heightening the new value of legality—that is, of the role assigned to the "law" in assuring order in society. That "law" was not to be conceived as detached or isolated from justice and divine precepts, yet it had to be distinct from them in its form and function in order to establish and broadcast its own autonomous value.

Gratian deserves our admiration for the audacity of his innovative positions identifying a canon law autonomous of theology. This was a burning problem, difficult to resolve in any clear-cut manner, and in fact Gratian treated it with great prudence and expressed a variety of reservations.[18]

Every human action and every human thought could lead the human soul to perdition or salvation; it could be a sign of virtue or vice, of heavenly destination or condemnation to hell. The repentant Christian was expected to tell his sins, in deed and in thought, to his

16. See Calasso, *Medio Evo del diritto*, 478–79.
17. Ennio Cortese, *La norma giuridica: Spunti teorici nel diritto comune classico*, 2 vols. (Milan: Giuffrè, 1962–64), 1:68; 2:347ff.
18. See Calasso, *Medio Evo del diritto*, 394–96.

or her confessor because God sees everything and judges everyone. But what of the earthly judge? How was he to judge thoughts not transmuted into deeds, accomplished or initiated? How were thoughts to be proven? And why should they be proven if unexpressed thoughts had harmed no one, damaged nothing, and did not disturb civil cohabitation, but had offended only an order that God had imprinted into the human conscience?

Gratian's position had a revolutionary impact. It assigned to the jurist (and thus to human law) only the task of evaluating and judging acts, not hidden thoughts. This position had several important consequences. It removed from the clergy, as clergy, the power to control the entire range of human activities in view of practical ends, because it was not the task of the clergy to restore a violated social order. The church was recognized to have and to retain control over actions, and even over thoughts, insofar as they concerned the dictates of Christian doctrine and related to the goal of the soul's salvation. The earthly judge (who might on occasion wear ecclesiastical vestments) was entrusted with judgment of earthly acts relevant to the social context, as expressed in the new *ordo* of Roman and canon trial procedure of the last decades of the twelfth century.

Although in Dante's eyes Gratian had earned his place in paradise for having separated "l'uno e l'altro foro," the inner "forum" of conscience and the outer one of acts (*Paradiso*, X, 104–105), for many people of his time Gratian must have seemed a nettlesome personage who was working hard to take power and social functions away from the church hierarchy. Quite the opposite was true: following in the footsteps of a long line of reformers in the pre-Gregorian reforms, the Gregorian reforms, and the reforms of monastic culture instituted by the Camaldolese order, he was using the law to regenerate the church as a universal order.

7. The New Science of Law

A *scientia*, and indeed a new *scientia*, was emerging from a vague *sapientia*. This new "science" was a system of relationships within the "laws" of the *ius commune*; it involved identification of the general principles of its own existence and development: "Habet quaelibet scientia principia et radices, super quibus regulariter constituitur fundamentum" (Every science has principles and roots on which the foundations of the science are regularly established).[19] It cast its light on the *ius proprium*, became incorporated into the *ius proprium*, and soon proved a stiletto-sharp weapon in the hands of practitioners—judges, arbitrators, lawyers, legal advisors, and notaries.

This new *scientia*, once it had been clearly defined and was completely elaborated in all its complexity, constituted one "form" of the broader culture from the twelfth to the sixteenth centuries. From the twelfth century on, people's overall vision began to include a fundamental relationship between *esse* (being) and *existentia* (existence)—between what is perfect and eternal and realizes the idea of God and what is imperfect, transient, and consumed in this world in the human life-span.[20] The imperfect tended toward the perfect: it could not reach its goal short of the celestial beatitude of Heaven, which only the few would deserve. The only other choice for imperfection was to rebel against perfection and be lost to the torments of Hell. All of human life was beset by error, injustice, and imperfection, but it was also illuminated by an aspiration toward perfection and toward symmetry in forms, order in thoughts, justice, and the good. Thus all the sciences, each discipline in its own way, were imbued with a profound religious tension: geometry was the earthly projection of the divine symmetry of forms and spaces, arithmetic a projection of divine calculation, music of harmony, astrology of immense but finite distances, ethics of the eternal good to be realized on earth, logic of the immutable order of thought, rhetoric and grammar of the perfection of the expressive forms and the properties of language. Last but not least, human law was the projection of divine justice in its new, hard-won and avidly defended autonomy.

In the field of the law as elsewhere, there reigned an aspiration toward order, symmetry, and coherence in thought and a yearning for absolute justice. All that humankind constructed must correspond, within the limits of human capacities, to the eternal and transcendent models. This was imperative when the legislator established a legal

19. Azo of Bologna, *Summa Institutionum*, Proemium, no. 1 (Venetiis, 1584), col. 1043.

20. For bibliographic information on this question and for a view of the problem as it matured in fourteenth-century doctrine, see Manlio Bellomo, "Per un profilo della personalità scientifica di Riccardo da Saliceto," in *Studi in onore di Edoardo Volterra*, 6 vols. (Milan: Giuffrè, 1971), 5:251–84, esp. 266 n. 34.

system, and it was just as necessary when the interpreter modeled the concepts and doctrines of the law or the judge resolved a drama in civil litigation or in a criminal case.

Because they were the outcome of human operations, all terrestrial acts were condemned to imperfection. Nonetheless, what the emperor had decided was the best one could do and the nearest one could come to God's designs, because the emperor was conceived as a *divina sacrata maiestas* (divine, consecrated majesty) who had descended to earth among humankind. In the Byzantine world, the emperor was conceived as himself a divine being living out his earthly career, but the Roman Christian tradition saw him as God's representative on earth. The emperor shared this privilege with the pope; hence, Roman and canon law served as the linchpin for all reflection on human law, almost as if it were a providential mediation between a severe and immutable divine justice and an unreasoning human will that groped for justice, often with personal and particular cases as a point of departure, and that on occasion lost its way out of earthly blindness and fell into a squalid and degrading *aequitas bursalis*.

In this perspective, the jurist's first responsibility—a responsibility that was felt with full religious impact but that was also bent, within only a few decades, to serve the interests of the consortium, the corporation, or a social class—was to study Justinian Roman law and canon law, to consider them as the most direct reflection of the *veritas divina* (divine truth), hence as law common to all Christians, and to think that only on the basis of these two laws were the practice of the law and a didactic, technical, and professional apprenticeship in the law possible. Only these two bodies of law offered a legitimate basis for the formation of a juridical mentality, a juridical methodology, and a specifically legal culture.

Imperial and pontifical law needed to be studied analytically, in minute detail, and with care if their unity and order was to be discovered. Above all, jurists needed to grasp the splendor of God's unity and of divine order, which were present with the greatest intensity in Roman and canon law. For this reason the *ius commune* began to be thought of as a corpus. The first great work of the new times, Gratian's *Decretum*, was born of a declared intent to bring discordant canons into harmony. The intellectual efforts of entire generations were singlemindedly and profoundly committed to pointing out concordances, identifying antinomies, and interpreting the meanings of dis-

cordant passages. Jurists put all their intellectual energies into eliminating disagreement.

Step by step, Roman and canon law were consolidated into one
corpus by both intent jurists who cared little for the interests of their
kin and their corporations and cold jurists lucidly and astutely pursuing their political calculations and the accumulation of immense
wealth. It continued to be thought of as a corpus for centuries to come.

Within a narrower scope, the movement toward coordination was
led by glossators and commentators persuaded that it was possible to
describe some juridical concepts theoretically and to conceive of each
of them as an entity. They held that with the help of Justinian's laws
and an ongoing, evolving canon law, one could distinguish a *natura*
in part extraneous to the laws and that preceded the laws and existed
independent of them, even though nature lived again in the laws because it was part and parcel of them and found a terrestrial and comprehensible *forma* in them.

The author of the *Summa Trecensis* warned his readers that the
treatment of a concept (in this instance the *donatio propter nuptias*)
must be carried on in such a way that the essential *natura* of the concept could be contemplated, but also in such a way that the same essential *natura*, now reconstructed and understood, could serve as a
base to which whatever novelties the imperial laws may have established could be added.[21] Other jurists followed the same line of
thought to decide on the validity of specific agreements according to
whether or not they conformed to the "nature" of an institution (the
dowry, for instance).[22] In this view, it was the duty of the legislator
to translate the theoretical *natura* of legal institutions into workable
practical terms, while it was the interpreter's task to reconstruct the
reasoning processes of the legislator and compose the resulting materials in a unified framework. In perfect coherence with the culture of
the age, "essential" lines were distinguished from "accidental" ones
within this framework, following a division between the *proprium*
(inherent) and the *accidens* (nonessential) that paralleled the basic dis-
crimination between *esse* and *existentia*.

---

21. *Summa Trecensis*, C.5.3, *De donationibus inter sponsum et sponsam*, no. 2, in *Summa Codicis des Irnerius*, ed. Hermann Fitting (Berlin: J. Guttentag, 1894), 138–39.

22. Martinus, *De iure dotium*, 21, *Studies in the Glossators of the Roman Law*, ed. Kantorowicz, 261: "Pactum inutile est, quod contra dotis naturam sit."

8. Great Jurists of the New Age

After Irnerius and Gratian, new actors appeared on the juridical scene. The next generation was dominated by the "Four Doctors," Martinus, Bulgarus, Jacobus, and Hugo. Although legend states that the dying Irnerius chose Jacobus as his heir,[23] the men who most truly continued the work of the great master were Martinus Gosia (d. before 1166) and Bulgarus (d. 1166). Martinus and his followers (called *gosiani*) and Bulgarus and his followers pursued distinct and at times conflicting approaches. Martinus and his school were more interested in testing the equitable possibilities of the *ius commune*; Bulgarus and his pupils sought a more rigorous method for analysis of the formal logic of Justinian law.

During the course of the twelfth century, other jurists were prominent teachers. One of these was Rogerius, who flourished in the mid-twelfth century (around 1162); another was Placentinus, who was active in his native Italy but also in the south of France, where he died in Montpellier in 1192; still another was Pillius Medicinensis (d. after 1207), who was prominent for a number of reasons in the last decades of the twelfth century. Pillius was the first of the Bolognese professors to leave that city (he went to Modena some time after 1180 to open a school of law); he was also the most important jurist of his time to give close consideration to feudal law, and he compiled an *apparatus* to the *Consuetudines feudorum* (or *Libri feudorum*). Toward the end of the century Johannes Bassianus (d. 1197), a man with an extremely acute intelligence but who lived a disorderly life, taught in Bologna. Famous and much appreciated in his own right, Bassianus was the master of one of the most talented jurists of the age, Azo of Bologna (d. 1220, perhaps after 1230).[24]

Azo gave a new theoretical dimension to jurisprudence in Europe of the Middle Ages when he parted ways with an earlier doctrinal tendency to emphasize everyday happenings, use them as exemplary, or reinterpret them for the purposes of legal discussion. Azo instead took great care not to trespass beyond the limits of the Justinian com-

23. See above, chap. 5 n. 2.
24. The date of Azo's death is uncertain: on this question, see Piero Fiorelli, "Azzone," in *Dizionario Biografico degli Italiani* (Rome: Istituto della Enciclopedia Italiana, 1960–), 4:775; Johannes Fried, *Die Entstehung des Juristenstandes im 12. Jahrhundert* (Cologne: Böhlau, 1974), 72 n. 22 and 98 n. 71.

pilation; rather than muddle his discourse with references to events from his own time, he decanted to their maximum purity the legal concepts embodied in and handed on by the laws of Justinian. This aspect of his method and his thought is particularly clear in the various *apparatus* that he composed on passages from the Justinian texts, the *Code* in particular.[25] In his famous *Summa Codicis* Azo used schemes of classification borrowed from Ciceronian philosophy, which gave the materials he elaborated in his exegesis of the *Corpus iuris civilis* a firm and consistent architectonic structure.[26] Azo's *Summa Codicis* was a work basic to both theoretical study and practical use of the *ius commune*. The enormous importance of the *Summa* for legal practice is clear in the somewhat disrespectful goliardic motto that circulated in scholastic and juridical circles: "Chi non ha Azzo non vada in palazzo" (If you don't have Azo, don't go to court).[27]

Like Azo, his contemporary Hugolinus de Presbyteris (d. after 1233) was a pupil of Johannes Bassianus. Also like Azo, Hugolinus composed profuse, extensive *apparatus* to the *Corpus iuris civilis*, to the *Code* in particular. He went his own way, however, which meant that the two jurists' *apparatus* were in competition with one another as the two men contended for supremacy. Their rivalry developed into differing schools of thought, a question to which I shall return. Legend soon intervened concerning the life and personal behavior of these two heads of schools. Odofredus, a pupil and follower of Hugolinus, later stated with undisguised hostility that Azo was so busy teaching that he took sick only on holidays, which made it inevitable that he would die on a day when he was on vacation.[28]

25. See Manlio Bellomo, "La scienza del diritto al tempo di Federico II," in *Frédéric II et les savoirs*, Atti del II Seminario Internazionale su Federico II, Erice 16–23 September 1990 (Palermo: Sellerio Editore, 1994), also available, with some modification, in *Rivista internazionale di diritto comune* 3 (1992): 173–96.

26. Manlio Bellomo, "Der Text erklärt den Text: Über die Anfänge der mittelalterlichen Jurisprudenz," *Rivista Internazionale di Diritto Comune* 4 (1993): 51–63, esp. 59–60.

27. See Thomas Diplovatatius, *Liber de claris iuris consultis*, ed. [Fritz Schulz, Hermann Kantorowicz], Giuseppe Rabotti, *Studia Gratiana* 10 (Bologna: Institutum Gratianum, 1968), 68.

28. See Friedrich Carl von Savigny, *Geschichte des römischen Rechts im Mittelalter*, 2d ed., 7 vols. (Heidelberg: J. C. B. Mohr, 1834–51; reprint Bad Homburg: Hermann Gentner, 1961), vol. 5 (1850), 9 n. g, which quotes Odofredus: "Et audivi . . . quod non infirmabatur nisi in diebus vacationis, et ita tempore vacationis mortuus est."

Their rivalry and intellectual dissent led to fantastic tales: Hugolinus and Azo quarreled regularly with one another on their way to court in the palace of the podestà, and one fine day, "instigante diabolo" (at the instigation of the devil), Azo was said to have killed Hugolinus when they met on the stairway.[29] Another legendary anecdote states that Azo's most prominent and most loyal student, Accursius, detested Hugolinus because Accursius had discovered that his wife had had an affair with Hugolinus, and in a move to send his rival packing, Accursius pulled political strings to have Hugolinus banished from Bologna.[30]

Legend aside, there are some elements in the situation that can be documented. It is certain that Accursius, who followed Azo's approach but was not above picking out the best features of Hugolinus's teaching, completed the more challenging work, an *apparatus* so vast that it was commonly called the *Magna glossa*. Throughout the Middle Ages, Accursius's *Magna glossa* surpassed all other *apparatus* in importance, authority, and diffusion.

9. Accursius and Odofredus

Accursius was a jurist endowed with extraordinary capacities of analysis and synthesis. Between the second and the third decades of the thirteenth century, when he was no longer a very young man, he left the territory of Florence to attend the law schools of Bologna.[31] He is reported to have responded curtly to companions who teased him about his age that, since he had arrived after them, he would finish before them. In 1229 he was already a *doctor iuris*, but we do not

29. Diplovatatius, *Liber de claris iuris consultis*, ed. Rabotti, 71: "Azo fuit de principalioribus illuminatoribus iuris et ipse Ugolinus glossator; et regulariter in palatio discordabant in tantum, quod tandem instigante diabolo semel Azo Ugolinum dum descenderent de palatio potestatis interfecit." See also Savigny, *Geschichte des römischen Rechts*, 5:9.

30. Diplovatatius, *Liber de claris iuris consultis*, ed. Rabotti, 93: "Item dicebat dominus Bartolus, quod ita Accursius glossator reprehendit in glossis sepe Ugolinum, quod eius inimicus erat, immo, quia eius uxorem supponebat; scivit tantum tractare, quod fecit eum bannire de Bononia." See also Savigny, *Geschichte des römischen Rechts*, 5:50. For other stories about rivalries among the jurists, see Pennington, *The Prince and the Law*, chap. 1.

31. On Accursius's place of birth, see Giuseppe Speciale, " 'Accursius fuit de Certaldo . . . ,' " *Rivista Internazionale di Diritto Comune* 1 (1990): 111–20, and the literature cited therein.

know how many years earlier he received his doctorate.[32] He died in
1263.[33]

We know from the sure evidence of some annotations in manuscripts that have come down to us—a few scattered observations
among the glosses he was studying—that Accursius first concentrated
on an attentive and impassioned study of the *apparatus* of Azo, his
master, and Hugolinus.[34] At first Accursius was keenly attuned to
contemporary happenings and to episodes that could be used to illus-
trate or clarify the laws of Justinian. This was already a custom that
had given rise, in some of the schools (that of Jacobus Balduini for
instance), to a current of thought and a methodological option that
developed further in the following decades in both the official lessons
(the *lecturae*) and the afternoon "exercises" (the *quaestiones disputatae*,
quaestiones ex facto emergentes, *quaestiones statutorum*, and so forth).
Around 1230, however, Accursius started to devote full time to the
work that was to guarantee him immense fame throughout the centuries.

Once again, legend masks the truth and mixes fact and fantasy. The
idea of composing a text so complete and so polished that it could
serve as an automatic exegetic accompaniment to the texts of Justinian's laws and merit a place beside them is supposed to have occurred,
simultaneously, to Odofredus Denariis and to Accursius. Legend tells
us that Accursius let it be known that he was sick, and he retired to a
villa that he owned near Bologna, thus fooling Odofredus into thinking that he himself had a great deal of time to finish his own project.
Accursius beat him to it, however, suddenly returning to Bologna
with a completed work in the form of an *apparatus*.[35]

As is always the case, there is a kernel of truth behind the legend.
Odofredus was indeed writing a major work, but he followed a different methodology from Accursius's, and he became the leading expo-

32. The documentation has been published recently in Paolo Colliva, "Documenti
per la biografia di Accursio," in *Atti del Convegno internazionale di studi accursiani*, Bologna 21–26 October 1963, ed. Guido Rossi, 3 vols. (Milan: Giuffrè, 1968), 2:403.

33. For discussion of Accursius's date of death, see ibid., 395–402.

34. Such annotations are well documented in MS Prague, Knihovna Národního
Musea, XVII.A.10, on which, see Manlio Bellomo, "Consulenze professionali e dottrine di professori: Un inedito 'consilium domini Accursii,'" *Quaderni Catanesi* 7
(1982): 199–219, esp. 200–202.

35. The episode is told by Benvenuto Rambaldi of Imola in a passage of commentary
on Dante; see Savigny, *Geschichte des römischen Rechts*, 5:275–76.

nent of a current of thought that not only resisted the overwhelming success of Accursius's *apparatus* for decades but also was supported and carried on by great jurists up to the early years of the fourteenth century. Hence, from roughly 1230 on, there were two principal but divergent currents of thought: the first and dominant current was that of Accursius (and before him, Azo); the other, a persistent alternative, that of Odofredus (derived from Hugolinus).[36]

Odofredus's work, known under the title of *Lectura*, was a vast commentary on the laws of Justinian. It was an expository work made up of lengthy passages elaborated and written by Odofredus, to which brief glosses supplementing them in one way or another were added.

The work that Accursius composed was more traditional in its approach, because it was modeled on the *apparatus* of Azo (and, in part, on that of Hugolinus); it differed little either in its expository techniques or in its interpretive methodology from the models that it imitated. It was an outstanding and valuable work, however, full of valuable materials. Unlike Odofredus's work—and unlike the work of Accursius himself in the first phase of his study of the *apparatus* of Azo and Hugolinus—all reference to actual events disappeared from it, even major events in living memory. The dross of the occasional and the contingent was perfectly eliminated; what remained were the concepts and doctrines in all their purity, principles and legal problems, unadorned and thought through anew in their full abstraction but, at the same time, with full capacity and potential for serving the practical jurist and being replicated an infinite number of times in his practical activities, when he needed to define a legal case submitted to him for decision or a legal problem entrusted to his tutelage and defense.

Accursius finished this magnificent work because of his extraordinary command of the entire *Corpus iuris civilis* and thanks to the respect he showed to his models and his fidelity to them. He was in

36. On this "alternative line of thought," see Bellomo, "Consulenze professionali," 189–201; Bellomo "Intorno a Roffredo Beneventano: Professore a Roma?" in *Scuole diritto e società nel Mezzogiorno medievale d'Italia*, ed. Manlio Bellomo, 2 vols. (Studi e ricerche dei "Quaderni Catanesi," 7; Catania: Tringale, 1985–87), 1:135–81, esp. 147–48; Bellomo, "La scienza del diritto al tempo di Federico II"; Federico Martino, "Testimonianze sull'insegnamento del diritto a Napoli nei secoli XIII-XIV: Il manoscritto ambrosiano E.29.inf.," in *Scuole diritto e società*, 2:25–38, esp. 32–33.

fact so faithful to Azo that his work has been criticized for lacking originality. In reality, however, it was not the novelty of their content that distinguished Accursius's *glossae* and his *apparatus*; it was his formidable achievement in selecting and integrating his materials. The work was made up for the most part of glosses—extrapolated from the *apparatus* of Azo and Hugolinus—which Accursius often reproduced in their entirety, including the siglum at the foot of the comment that identified its author, or which on occasion he edited slightly by making cuts or additions. Into this basic outline Accursius inserted other glosses taken from various other jurists' manuscripts, notably Johannes Bassianus (Azo's master), Pillius, Placentinus, and, going further back in time, Rogerius, Martinus, Bulgarus, and Irnerius. Selecting from among tens of thousands of annotations, Accursius found a place in his *apparatus* for more than ninety thousand glosses. They touch on all parts of the *Corpus iuris civilis*: the *Digest* (*Digestum vetus*, *Infortiatum*, and *Digestum novum*), the *Code*, the *Institutes*, the *Tres libri*, and the *Novels*. The enormous size of Accursius's work gave it the title by which it has been known ever since: *Magna glossa*.

The *Magna glossa* contains all the principle themes of the jurisprudence of the age—problems of equity, of worldly justice, and of the interpretation for which the jurist is responsible (within and outside the limits of the given law). It by and large neglects the problem of the *ius proprium* and its relationship, by its very existence and in its administration, to the *ius commune*. When used from this point of view, the *Magna glossa* offers excellent evidence of the most pressing topics of its time. As we have seen, however, the principal attraction of this work lay on the theoretical plane, where its analyses of legal doctrine and principles were of constant use to practice. The *Magna glossa* brought together a theoretical patrimony of truly inestimable value. For centuries it has offered that treasure to any jurist who might want to look beyond blind practice for ways to orient and improve the quality of his everyday activities and sharpen his technical skills.

10. The *Magna glossa*: Authoritative Text and Sure Guide

Toward the mid-thirteenth century, the *Magna glossa* was universally accepted as an essential and standard accompaniment to the texts of Justinian.

Some manuscripts that contained only the laws of Justinian (and had sufficiently empty margins) were used to copy the glosses of Accursius's *apparatus* next to the laws to which they pertained. On occasion *apparatus* of Azo or Hugolinus or anonymous networks of glosses were erased by the usual technique of scraping the margins of the parchment leaf, and the freed space was used to transcribe portions of the *Magna glossa* instead (which is why such reworked manuscripts are called palimpsests, from the Greek for "rescraped"). When new *codices* were made, Justinian's laws were always accompanied by the *Magna glossa*, often copied in the same hand. In this manner the laws lent some of their sacrality to the *apparatus*, and in their reflected glory Accursius's *Glossa* became as untouchable as the laws themselves.

The *libri legales* and the *Magna glossa* were surrounded by something like a sea of orality that highlighted and increased the permanence and the sacred aura of the legal writings. We would have no knowledge of this vast amount of thought expressed verbally if it were not for the few traces—some more fully elaborated and better thought out than others—that it has left in writing.[37]

From the mid-thirteenth century on, the diffusion of the *Magna glossa* in Europe reached impressive proportions. It became such a common custom of the schools to accompany the *libri legales* with Accursius's *Magna glossa* that it came to be called *Glossa ordinaria*.

We can find copies of Accursius's *Glossa ordinaria* in all regions of Christian Europe—on the Iberian Peninsula, where one of Accursius's sons, Guglielmo (Guillelmus Accursii), went to teach civil law,[38] in France, especially in the *pays de droit écrit*, where we find the same Guillelmus Accursii,[39] in Germany in monasteries and the libraries of cathedral chapters and collegial churches, in what is now Switzerland,[40] and in many other European lands.[41]

37. See above, chap. 6.

38. See Frank Soetermeer, "Un professeur de l'Université de Salamanque au XIIIe siècle, Guillaume d'Accurse," *Anuario de Historia del Derecho Español* 55 (1985): 753–65.

39. Henri Gilles, "Accurse et les Universités du Midi de la France," in *Atti del Convegno internazionale di studi accursiani*, 3:1042–43.

40. See Sven Stelling-Michaud, *L'Université de Bologne et la pénétration des droits romain et canonique en Suisse aux XIIIe et XIVe siècles* (Geneva: E. Droz, 1955).

41. For a useful overview, see the papers in vol. 3 of *Atti del Convegno internazionale di studi accursiani*.

On occasion the statutes of Italian cities (Padua, for one)[42] required the judges to own a copy of the *libri legales*—further proof, should it still be necessary, that not only was the *ius commune* used as the third degree of positive law (after *statuta* and *consuetudines*) but it had validity beyond the hierarchy of norms and independent of that hierarchy.[43]

11. An Alternative Line of Thought in the Thirteenth Century

The current that provided an alternative to the *Glossa ordinaria* continued for several decades, lasting at least into the early fourteenth century. It is attested in the use, well after Accursius's lifetime, of the *apparatus* of Hugolinus, continued and supplemented by Jacobus Balduini, Benedetto of Isernia, and Roffredus Beneventanus. It also persisted in several Bolognese schools in the tradition of Odofredus, in Naples, where Odofredus was studied with particular intensity,[44] and in such smaller cities as Reggio Emilia.[45]

In other instances it was the work of Azo that survived, not because a current of thought different and distinct from that of Accursius developed from it, but rather because the *apparatus* of Azo remained, buried and forgotten, in a few ecclesiastical libraries, where they had been put during the early thirteenth century by a monk or a canon who had studied jurisprudence in Bologna, had commissioned the local *stationarii* to copy some works in a fine hand, and had later brought them back with him when he returned to his homeland.

Thus Hugolinus's *apparatus* were in use and continued to be studied with lively interest. The legal thought that derived from them had its own unique characteristics reflecting the intellectual personality of Odofredus—a personality that should be seen in the context of a thought that had developed even before Odofredus began to teach and that continued in his day.

The annotations that came from this current of thought included

---

42. On this point, see Federico Martino, "Giuristi di scuola e 'pratici' del diritto a Reggio e a Padova: Il ms. Olomouc C.O.40," *Quaderni Catanesi* 16 (1986): 443 and n. 134. The Padua statute is dated 1265.

43. Martino, "Giuristi di scuola e 'pratici' del diritto," 423–45.

44. Martino, "Testimonianze sull'insegnamento del diritto."

45. For example, MS St Gall, 746 (a *Codex*).

frequent references to everyday events. Although these may have detracted from the limpidity of the juridical discourse, they gave it such concreteness and anchored it so firmly in the real world that the theoretical potential of the many legal concepts was enhanced—concepts that juridical doctrine controlled and used with masterful skill.

Among the scholars in this second line of thought, one man soon stood out: Roffredus Beneventanus, who was active during the first half of the thirteenth century and came from the prominent Epifani family. Although the documents are still in part lost or have not been studied adequately, we can see that Roffredus's thought bore the stamp of Odofredus, particularly in his examples and the tone of "festiveness" that made his writing particularly attractive. They also reveal interests unusual in a civilian of those years, however, because Roffredus made frequent, cultivated and relevant use of canon law.[46]

Roffredus also showed a tendency (which became explicit in some sectors of jurisprudence in the latter half of the thirteenth century) to take account of the needs of practice and to offer practical remarks in which the theory of the *ius commune* was translated into concrete institutional applications, particularly in regard to court procedures. Roffredus left two works on *libelli*, one on civil law and the other on canon law, containing examples of legal documents useful as models for practical jurists.

12. The Great Canonists

The thirteenth century in Italy was a time of extraordinary creativity. If we also consider the jurists who read and interpreted canon law, the panorama becomes crowded with great figures.

The canonists' exegetic activities were fully as intense and their results just as polished as those of the civilians. The canonists concentrated on the great legal collections of the church, the *Decretum*, the *Liber Extra*, and, in the fourteenth century, the *Liber Sextus* and the *Clementinae*, but they also worked on such texts as the *Quinque compilationes antiquae*. Just as Accursius had selected and crowded into the *Glossa ordinaria* a complete *apparatus* of glosses to supplement all the

46. On Roffredus, see Bellomo, "Intorno a Roffredo Beneventano"; Stephan Kuttner, "Canonisti nel Mezzogiorno: Alcuni profili e riflessioni," in *Scuole diritto e società*, ed. Bellomo, 2:16–19.

laws of Justinian, so a number of canonists composed thick *apparatus* on the laws of the church.

Summae on Gratian's *Decretum* began to appear around the mid-twelfth century. There were *summae* by Rolandus, Rufinus, John of Faenza (all twelfth-century jurists) and by Stephen of Tournai and Huguccio, who lived into the early thirteenth century.

Aside from the *summae*, networks of *glossae* formed around the laws of the church, in particular around the texts officially promulgated by the popes. These glosses were similar to those of the civilians, but in canon law the phenomenon seemed to have arrived later—in part for reasons we have already seen, such as the nature of Gratian's *Decretum* as a private work. They became more the rule after the church's pro-mulgation of its own first official body of laws in 1209–10 with the *Compilatio* of Innocent III (the third of the so-called *Quinque compi-lationes antiquae*).

The term "summa" and the methodology for exposition connected with it remained in the canonistic tradition, and weighty *summae* were composed in the thirteenth century on the *Liber Extra* (*Decre-tales*) of Gregory IX. The most important of these were the *summae* of Goffredo of Trani (Goffredus de Trano, d. 1245), Sinibaldo dei Fieschi (Sinibaldus de Fieschis, later Pope Innocent IV, d. 1254), and Enrico of Susa (Henricus de Segusio), called Hostiensis (d. 1271). For its concision, its completeness, and its "golden" eloquence, the *Summa* of Hostiensis became commonly known as the *Summa aurea* in the late fifteenth century.

One jurist from German lands, Johannes Teutonicus (d. 1245) brought together *glossae* to the *Decretum*, added his own comments, and wrote a comprehensive *apparatus* (ca. 1217). Another jurist, Bar-tolomeo of Brescia (Bartolomeus Brixiensis, d. ca. 1258), lightly re-vised Johannes Teutonicus's *apparatus*. This work became a *glossa or-dinaria* to the *Decretum*.

Intense exegetical activity also centered on the *Liber Extra*. An Emilian jurist, Bernardo Bottoni of Parma (Bernardus Parmensis, d. 1266) was the author of an *apparatus* of glosses that was accepted as the *glossa ordinaria* for that work.

Apparatus were compiled for the *Liber Sextus* of Boniface VIII of 1298 as well. Giovanni d'Andrea (Johannes Andreae, d. 1348) com-posed a *glossa ordinaria* for the *Liber Sextus* out of excerpts and exeget-ical passages from various works to which he added his own annotations and, in his later years, a series of *additiones*. He wrote other works in a similar format on the *Clementinae*, both in the form of networks—*apostillae*—and as an ordinary *apparatus* (the *Glossa ordinaria* on the *Clementinae*).

Following the tradition begun in the twelfth century with the oldest *summae* and developed in the thirteenth-century *summae*, Giovanni d'Andrea also wrote lengthy *commentaria* on the *Decretales* (*Liber Extra*) of Gregory IX and on the *Liber Sextus* of Boniface VIII. These *commentaria* also appeared in manuscripts under the titles *Novella in Decretales* and *Novella in Sextum*. According to legend, these titles recall the name of one of Giovanni d'Andrea's daughters, Novella, whom the same legend claimed was such an expert jurist that she was capable of replacing her father in the lecture hall.[47]

The *commentaria* of other fourteenth- and fifteenth-century canonists followed. By far the most important of them, for both the wealth of doctrine it offered and for its reputation, was the *Commentaria* of another great jurist, Niccolò dei Tedeschi (Nicolaus de Tudeschis, d. 1453). A native of Catania but active in a number of cities of northern Italy, Siena in particular, Niccolò dei Tedeschi played a prominent role in the famous Council of Basel (1431–48), where he worked to define his own position on the various theses proposed and debated at the council for limiting the absolute powers of the papacy.[48] He has passed into history as "Abbas Panormitanus" or simply "Panormitanus" because he spent the last years of his life as abbot of Maniace (near Bronte, on the northwest slopes of Mount Etna, in the province of Catania) and as cardinal archbishop of Palermo.

13. Late Thirteenth-Century Civilization in Europe

The latter half of the thirteenth century was a crucial period in European legal history, as it was in many other domains of civilization

---

47. See Guido Rossi, "Contributo alla biografia del canonista Giovanni d'Andrea: L'insegnamento di Novella e Bettina, sue figlie, ed i presunti *responsa* di Milancia, sua moglie," *Rivista trimestrale di diritto e procedura civile* 11 (1957): 1451–1502.

48. See Knut Wolfgang Nörr, *Kirche und Konzil bei Nicolaus de Tudeschis (Panormitanus)* (Cologne: Böhlau Verlag, 1964). See also Charles Lefebvre, "Panormitain," in *Dictionnaire de Droit Canonique*, 7 vols. (Paris: Letouzey et Ané, 1935–65), vol. 6, cols. 1195–1215; Stephan Kuttner, "Canonisti nel Mezzogiorno," 22–23; Pennington, *The Prince and the Law*, chap. 6.

on the continent of Europe. The empire put down roots in German lands with the establishment of the long-lasting Hapsburg dynasty by Rudolf I, king of Germany from 1273 to 1291. The French monarchy was put on a more solid footing by Louis IX (d. 1270) and Philip the Fair (d. 1314), while on the Iberian Peninsula the aristocracy grew in power in the great kingdoms of Castile and Aragon.

In the cities of north-central Italy the *arti*—the Italian word for guilds—celebrated their triumph in the formation of the Comune del popolo after bloody struggles with the nobles in the mid-century. In southern Italy the unity of the Kingdom of Sicily was shattered in 1282, when the Sicilian Vespers detached Tinacria (the island of Sicily) from the continent and from Naples.

In 1265 Thomas Aquinas began writing his *Summa Theologica*. Around the same time, acquaintance with the major works of Aristotle, in particular, the *Metaphysics* (known as "Aristotle major"), was spreading throughout Europe. Aristotle's works, which arrived in Europe through the Arabs in Spain and the Greeks in Sicily, were translated into Latin beginning around 1230 and soon were introduced into high culture throughout the continent. Dante Alighieri was born in Florence in 1265. In 1270 Cino Sighibuldi—a poet, but principally a jurist of genius, known as Cinus of Pistoia—was born in Pistoia.

The works that provided the bulwarks of European culture were the Gospels, the *libri legales* of civil and canon law, Aristotle's *Metaphysics*, the *Summa Theologica* of Thomas Aquinas, and, somewhat later, Dante's *Divine Comedy*. It was a truly and intensely European culture, a culture that overrode frontiers, knew no linguistic barriers, and had no other difficulties linked to the idea of "nation" that was just beginning to surface. New languages—national languages—were indeed becoming defined, but although they were in current use in everyday life they were no substitute for Latin, which was and continued to be the linguistic vehicle for the circulation of ideas throughout Europe. Almost all the books of the *ius commune* were written in Latin. It was a living language: it gave the Romance languages their base and even influenced the national languages in Germanic and Slavic lands.

The parallel between the vicissitudes of the Latin language and those of the law is striking. As the Latin language offered a unified basis for national languages and provided them with useful theoretical and practical notions, so did the *ius commune*, civil and canon. As the national or regional languages were many, so were local laws (the *iura propria*). And as the national languages not only recognized the Latin language but accepted it and intermingled with it, so the various *iura propria* intertwined with the *ius commune*, from which they might also diverge profoundly, however, just as the Romance languages split off from Latin.

Thus an understanding of the unity of legal life in Europe requires a grasp of the necessarily dialectical relationship that existed between the unity of a *ius commune* and the plurality of the *iura propria*. The latter could not have existed without the one *ius commune*, and today we cannot relive their history without taking that dialectical relationship into account.

14. The System of the *Ius commune* and the *Corpus iuris civilis*: Dialectic

Around the 1270s legal theory began to show signs of change, diverging in two main directions. Thus the overall problem of the *ius commune* in Europe can be looked at in two ways, distinct yet not separate, like the two sides of a coin.

The long-standing tradition that considered the laws of Justinian and those of the church as a corpus, hence as unified and as sacred and authoritative, not only persisted but strengthened. From this point of view the *ius commune* was a "system," a system of laws that obligatorily corresponded to a system of rights and that was conceived in programmatic terms as exhaustive.

The second current was more sensitive to the problem of increasingly vast sectors of the law that were emerging everywhere (as we have seen in chapter 4) but that did not correspond to the corpora of the civil law and the canon law and so remained closed as sectors of the *ius proprium*. Some jurists discovered that the norms in the *ius commune*'s "system of laws" lacked full potential to provide for all the acts of everyday life, which meant that the "system of laws" did not coincide with the "system of rights."

We need to follow each of these two evolving lines of thought separately. The first was older and can be documented at least as far back as two passages in Accursius's *Glossa*, one of which referred even farther back to the thought of Jacobus, to whom Accursius attributed the idea of a common law as *corporis universitas*.[49] The other reiterated the widely shared conviction that "omnia in corpore iuris inveniuntur" (all things are found in the body of law [the *ius commune*]).[50] This last phrase, read in its entirety, not only expresses the idea that the civil law must be separate from theology, from morality, and from what was by that time considered extraneous to the *scientia iuris* but also expresses faith in the idea that a discipline for human actions is always and in every instance found in positive norms, taken as a whole, and in the idea of positive law as a *sistema legum* (system of laws).

Jurists in the twelfth century and the first decades of the thirteenth plunged with interest and passion into problems inherent in this vision, and they wondered increasingly frequently whether it was not perhaps the jurist's task to investigate the correspondence between the *sistema legum* and a substantive *sistema iuris* (system of rights). This led them ineluctably to a search for the "justice" intrinsic to every law. The search found its best expression in debate and reflection on *aequitas rudis* and *aequitas constituta*—in short, in the court cases through which equity was transformed into justice and the *ius* (*ius strictum*) into law (*ius scriptum*). In the fourteenth century, when the issue had crystallized, one great southern Italian jurist, Lucas of Penna (before 1345–after 1382), put it succinctly: "Manifestum autem est, quod, cum voluntas principis ab aequitate, iustitia aut ratione deviet, non est lex" (It is clear that when the will of the prince deviates from equity, justice, or reason, it is not law).[51] Thus he drew a distinction between the prince's law, which corresponded to equity, justice, and reason, and the prince's will, which, even when it reached out toward the law, in reality did not become law because it "deviated from equity, from justice, and from reason."

The only way to create and elaborate a *sistema legum* was to discern the internal connections between one precept and another in the Justinian compilation or the laws of the church, and then to bind these

49. Accursius, the *iuri communi* to Dig.1.1.6, *De iustitia et iure*, 1., *ius civile*: "Responditur secundum Iac[obum], non detrahitur iuri communi in sua corporis universitate."

50. Accursius, the *notitia* to Dig.1.1.10, *De iustitia et iure*. 1. *ius civile*: "Sed nunquid . . . oportet, quod quicumque vult iuris prudens vel iurisconsultus esse debet theologiam legere? Responde: non, iam omnia in corpore iuris inveniuntur."

51. Lucas of Penna, *In Tres Libros Comm.*, Cod.10.26.3.

connections together so that the entire mass could be thought of as one unified corpus.

The jurists of the twelfth and the thirteenth centuries at first worked toward this goal with techniques and logical methods of modest scope. For example, they worked to construct their system using the scheme of *sic et non*—whatever is not prohibited is permitted—or they linked one norm to another by assuming a juridical problem centering on a given question and posed increasingly specific alternatives (*aut . . . aut*) in a branching "tree" that brought together in one visual field legal precepts scattered throughout the various books and titles of the *Code* or the *Digest*. To take representation as an example of such problems: if a servant acquired a sick animal, he either was aware that the animal was unhealthy or not; if he was aware of the state of the animal's health, one must ask whether he acquired the animal for himself, out of his own *peculium*, or for his master; in the latter case one must distinguish whether or not the master knew of the acquisition or not, and if not, whether or not he could have known about it. And so forth, following up each alternative until the original alternatives had multiplied and ramified to become an analytical outline of all foreseeable cases, and at each step in the process citing an appropriate provision in the corpus of the *ius commune*.[52]

As time went by the logical process became more refined. The rediscovery of the major works of Aristotle and the study of dialectic helped to consolidate logical experimentation in the aim of constructing a systematic vision of the *ius commune*. Especially after the mid-thirteenth century, the Italian schools produced brief repertories, organized by cumulative strata of contributions, of the essence of the principal *modi arguendi in iure* (modes of arguing in law) and *loci loicales per leges probati* (arguments, in the form of maxims, applicable to the law).[53] The technical modes of argumentation that were classified in this manner had in part already been incorporated into

52. This example is drawn from a *distinctio* constructed, with some differences in form, by Jacobus ("Cum servus emit animal . . .") and by Martinus ("Scientia vel ignorantia servi . . ."). See Manlio Bellomo, "A proposito della rappresentanza: Due inedite 'distinctiones' di Iacopo e Martino," *Annali di storia del diritto* 7 (1963): 115–24.

53. On this question, see Manlio Bellomo, " 'Loci loicales' e forme del pensiero giuridico in alcuni testi inediti dei secoli XIII e XIV," *Rivista di storia del diritto italiano* 47 (1974): 5–18 and the bibliography therein.

the texts of the *Digest*, because they had been used by Roman jurists of the republic or the empire, but now they were rediscovered and retempered for the purposes of Aristotelian dialectic. Such techniques served to argue *in iure* to reinforce a dubious interpretation or lend it certainty. There were tens of these techniques: one could argue *a maiori* (from the greater reason), *a minori* (from the lesser reason), *a toto* (from the whole), *a diffinitione* (from a definition), *a nominis interpretatione* (focusing on the meaning of a term), *a genere* (referring to generic characteristics), *a similitudine* (by analogy), *a contrario* (by opposition), *ex silentio* (holding an activity licit if not expressly prohibited), and so forth.

The use of dialectic could lead to excess, especially in the schools of philosophy. A famous anecdote that circulated concerning the school of Anselm of Laon was often repeated to note and warn of the perils of abstract logical exercises. It begins with a simple and incontestable opposition, "Quod ego sum, tu non es" (What I am, you are not). It then adds, "I am a man," in the circumstances equally incontestible, and concludes, with impeccable logic but against the facts, "Therefore you are not a man."[54]

The study of dialectic was particularly intently pursued in France, where dialectic continued to be used and refined in the field of jurisprudence. During the final decades of the thirteenth century two major jurists, Jacques de Révigny (Jacobus de Ravanis) and Pierre de Belleperche (Petrus de Bellapertica), were particularly active in this area. The intellectual personalities of these two men are typified by a search for all the possible normative solutions implicit in Justinian's laws. In fact, as Justinian's laws were increasingly defined as a corpus, and as dialectic was applied to the law to greater and greater effect, that corpus gave the impression of having no lacunae simply because it was thought there could be none.

We may need to examine at least one example if we want to understand the sort of reasoning that led these jurists to "create" a norm if one was not explicitly given in the corpus but was thought implicit in it and so could be extracted from it by dialectical argumentation.

54. This anecdote from the school of Anselm of Laon (eleventh-twelfth centuries) is reported in Odon Lottin, "Nouveaux fragments théologiques de l'école d'Anselme de Laon: Quelques autres manuscrits allemands," *Recherches théologiques anciennes et médiévales* 13 (1946): 267.

There was no explicit rule in the laws of Justinian that covered the husband's obligation to maintain and provide for his wife if he had received no dowry or if the dowry was deemed insufficient. Jurists called on a range of data to circumscribe this marital obligation. Hugolinus de Presbyteris combined two texts to argue that the wife had a right to maintenance, to foodstuffs, and to medicines because she was in the service of her husband, in support of which he cited a fragment of the *Infortiatum*, Dig.38.1.48, on the labor of freedmen. Another argument used an ecclesiastical example: if an obligation bound a person's conscience, one could argue that the person deserved excommunication for nonfulfillment of this duty.[55]

Jacques de Révigny "constructed" the missing norm with a typical and rigorous *argumentum a fortiori* (for a still stronger reason): "Let us put the case," he states, "that there is no dowry and that the wife dies. The law states that the husband must bury her (at his own expense). It is obvious that alive he owes her something more than dead; thus, if the husband must bury her at his expense when she dies, for even stronger reason must he feed her at his expense when she is alive."[56] Thus by taking an existent disposition and using it as an indisputable base on which to construct a dialectical argument, the jurist expanded the normative capacities of Justinian's laws.

Extending Roman law in this fashion granted power to those capable of bringing off the operation—that is, the interpreters—who inevitably took an active role in the process. It also involved handsome earnings, as the professors pointed out to their students: there were subtle theoretical problems of no immediate use that did nothing to swell one's money purse,[57] but there were also pressing, current, and lucrative problems in search of a solution that met the needs of a broad variety of clients.

The great initial formative phase of the system of the *ius commune* can be said to have ended with the thirteenth century. Examination

55. On this problem, see Manlio Bellomo, *Ricerche sui rapporti patrimoniali tra coniugi: Contributo alla storia della famiglia medievale* (Milan: Giuffrè, 1961), 152–55.

56. Attributed to Pietro Bellapertica (Pierre de Belleperche) but Jacobus de Ravanis (Jacques de Révigny), *Lectura* super Cod.5.12.20, *De iura dotium. l. Pro oneribus* (Parisiis 1519), fol. 229vb.

57. See, for example, Johannes Andreae, add. *De peculio* to Guillielmus Durantis, *Speculum iudiciale*, IV.3, *De peculio clericorum*, no. 2 (Augustae Taurinorum 1578), fol. 158b: "Ioan[nes] de Bla[nosco], licet parum, instet in hac materia, dicens quod ipsa nunquam fecit suam bursam hydropicam."

and experimentation had been pursued, decade after decade, for nearly two centuries. The *ius commune* was a reality, not only as a system of positive law but also as a system of legal thought. That was where it revealed its greatest potential. For one thing, it served as a model for the *ius proprium* when and to the extent that particular social and political communities of Europe wanted to reflect or reproduce its dictates (with modifications or additions). For another, it provided the principles, the concepts, the terminology, and the *modi arguendi* that the jurist could not do without when he turned to practical affairs and needed to write up the articles of a city statute or a sovereign's laws. Finally, it provided an orientation (thus, once again, it served as a model) in the complex practical operation that led to the determination of every norm of *ius proprium* if those provisions were to be as just and rational as those of the *ius commune*.

15. The System of the *Ius commune* and the *Corpus iuris civilis*: The *Ius proprium*

During the final decades of the thirteenth century, the second main current of legal thought reached clearer definition. It stressed the notion that, although the "system of laws" translated and encompassed a large part of the "system of rights," it failed to cover the entire field of the law, which meant that entire sectors of the normative materials in the *ius proprium* were totally irreconcilable with the discipline and the theoretical concepts of the *ius commune*. In their attempt to resolve this formidable problem the leading theorists of juridical doctrine in Italy and southern France (the *pays de droit écrit*) drew up the main outlines of an overall vision of the law that was destined to last for centuries (though in the sixteenth century that vision was challenged and even combated in some countries and certain circles in Europe).

The principal protagonists in this drama were two Italian jurists, Cinus of Pistoia and Bartolus of Saxoferrato. It would be a grave error in historical perspective, however, to isolate these two men from their historical context, the tradition in which they operated, or their generation and those of their students and successors.Concerning their tradition, it is enough to recall Cinus's master, Dinus of Mugello, and some of the jurists active during the latter half of the thirteenth century, including at least Franciscus Accursii, Albertus Odofredi, Guido of Suzzara, and Lambertinus de Ramponibus.

Above all we need to look at a didactic practice that the *doctores moderni*, as the sources call them,[58] reinstated and reinvigorated around 1270 by defining (with the aid of their students and the student statutes) the procedures and the structure of the public disputation of *quaestiones* selected for that purpose.[59]

Because the *quaestio* could not be based on a *casus legis* (that is, on a case provided for and regulated by the *ius commune*, civil or canon), and because it could be based on an actual event or act that might be covered by communal statutes (*quaestiones statutorum*) or feudal customary law (*quaestiones feudorum*), disputation provided an ideal terrain for testing possible theoretical links between the *ius commune* and the *ius proprium* and between the world of the "certain" and that of the "probable." As we have seen, that connection was made was in forging the arguments that were needed to resolve the juridical problem (*quid iuris*) inherent in the event stated as the topic (*id quod accidit*). At every step, each argument had to be linked to legislation in the *ius commune*, by use of a *modus arguendi*, before it could be used as a reasonable and plausible base for the next move.[60]

Norms taken from the *ius commune*—at times only from brief and incidental phrases in the texts or from cases of a totally different nature—thus offered fragments, hints, and principles that could be transplanted into the particular law, the *ius proprium*. There they could support or deny a normative solution that may have been given in the *ius proprium* but that, since its provisions were "probable" rather than "certain," required confirmation (or refutation) from another solution.

In actual practice, disputation served in the great majority of cases not to confirm or deny the validity of a particular law, statute, or custom in the *ius proprium* but to fill in normative gaps when a statute or a customary law was assumed but no specific provision was given.

58. This expression can be found in MS Vatican, Chigi lat.E.VIII.245, fol. 91rb: "Infrascripte questiones disputate sunt per doctores modernos sub anno domini Mᵒ.CCᵒ.sept.secundo . . .". At the same date of 1272 there is an analogous notation in MS Vatican, Arch.S.Pietro A.29, fol. 137va.

59. For the reconstruction of a specific statutory rubric before 1274, see Manlio Bellomo, "Legere, repetere, disputare: Introduzione ad una ricerca sulle 'quaestiones' civilistiche," in Bellomo, *Aspetti dell'insegnamento giuridico nelle università medievali*, vol. 1, *Le 'quaestiones disputatae': Saggi* (Reggio Calabria: Parallelo 38, 1974), 55–56 and n. 88.

60. See above, chap. 6, section 8.

To borrow a phrase from Bartolus of Saxoferrato,[61] the *ius commune* dominated the *ius proprium* because it projected its doctrines and norms into the areas in which the *ius proprium* reigned.

Clearly this was theoretical activity of the highest level. That the constant presence of influences of the *ius commune* owed nothing whatever to the daily practice of the *ius proprium* is equally clear.[62] Nonetheless, it was precisely the theoretical context and the methodological tools of the *ius commune* that the practical jurist used to shape his professional mentality. Here was where he learned to consider contingent events by imagining a theoretical model to which they must correspond, and where he learned to take responsibility for shaping a rule for the case under examination when he gave his solution. The jurist, both theoretical and practical, enhanced his own function and the *ius commune*, which was the legacy of his methodological training and a body of laws containing well-honed instruments for use in theory and practice alike.

This was the context in which Cinus of Pistoia and Bartolus of Saxoferrato wrote and worked.

16. Cinus of Pistoia

Cinus of Pistoia was a contemporary of Dante Alighieri. He was born around 1270 and died in 1336.[63] His thought was fertile, rich in fantasy and wisdom, and he was capable of extremely clear and incisive expression. His soul was imbued with a strong religious tension, expressed as a yearning for an absolute justice that God had impressed in the human heart and that humankind could rediscover and try to realize in everyday activities if men could only keep from falling into vanity and injustice.

Cinus made use of all the most vital experiences of the culture of his twelfth- and thirteenth-century predecessors. He had the soul of a poet and his poetry had met with some success, but he soon devoted himself entirely to the study of jurisprudence, beginning with a criti-

61. Bartolus of Saxoferrato, *Tractatus de procuratoribus*, quaestio VIII, *An in causis criminalibus admittatur procurator*, no. 7 (Venetiis 1585), fol. 205rb.

62. Some historians disagree on this point; see above, n. 4.

63. On salient moments in the life of Cinus of Pistoia and for the historiography of this great jurist, see Pier Luigi Falaschi, *"Ut vidimus in Marchia": Divagazioni su Cino da Pistoia e il suo soggiorno nelle Marche* (Naples: Jovene, 1987).

cal review of the *Corpus iuris civilis* and the *Magna glossa* that supplemented it. Under the guidance of an excellent master, Dinus of Mugello, and at his suggestion, Cinus decided to test the limits of this heritage. The Roman laws were admittedly a corpus, and Justinian's authority was indisputable and Accursius's merits uncontestable, but legislators and interpreters were human—like all humans, their memories were fallible and they might make mistakes or contradict themselves. Even Accursius, who could not be expected to remember everything, had written glosses that contradicted one another. Cinus expressed these thoughts in a brief preface to a short compilation that he wrote as a school exercise during the very first years of his scholastic training, but, because his remarks were extracted from the laws of Justinian, they applied not only to the interpreters (Accursius in this instance) but to the legislators as well.[64]

Thanks to Dinus of Mugello and Lambertinus de Ramponibus (another of his masters), Cinus knew statutory and customary law and knew how to exploit them. In his mature works he continuously records the many *quaestiones* that he heard disputed, that he himself had disputed, or that he had read in the written versions in circulation. He thus had a fund of practical experience in the systematic connections between the *ius proprium* and the *ius commune* that were part of the techniques of argumentation of the *quaestio disputata*.

Cinus had thoroughly absorbed the lessons of two French scholars, Jacques de Révigny and Pierre de Belleperche, whom he had very probably heard in France and seen again in Bologna. Thus it is sure that he had contacts with French circles that may have helped him learn how to apply syllogisms and *modi arguendi* to extract a norm from the *Corpus* with simplicity and clarity.

Cinus's major work was his *Lectura super Codice*, written between 1312 and 1314. He also wrote valuable though lesser and unfortunately fragmentary *lecturae* on the *Digestum vetus*, at least two of which were written some years later.[65]

Several tendencies are visible in the many topics that Cinus treated

64. Cinus of Pistoia, *Glossae contrariae*, Proemium. This work has been identified and in part published in Manlio Bellomo, " 'Glossae contrariae' di Cino da Pistoia," *Tijdschrift voor Rechtsgeschiedenis* 38 (1970): 433–47, Proemium p. 443.

65. An unknown *divina lectura* of Cinus on the *Digestum vetus* has been identified by Domenico Maffei, *La "Lectura super Digesto Veteri" di Cino da Pistoia: Studio sui mss. Savigny 22 e Urb.lat.172* (Milan: Giuffrè, 1963).

in his works. He used dialectic, but he was aware that every *via brocardica* was dubious and dangerous because it might have consequences contrary to good sense, truth, and justice. For that reason Cinus shrewdly avoided letting himself be swayed or misled by the iron grip of an abstract logic or by the canonized forms of expression that logic often implied. Thus at times his argumentation seems quite free, as when he dared to dispute a *quaestio* without the usual opposition of arguments pro and con, or when he suggested somewhat brusquely that his listener use his own head ("Tu cogitabis"). These liberties attracted the criticism of a young and pedantic professor, Jacobus Buttrigarius Junior, who cared more for the proper respect of hallowed techniques and forms of argumentation than for using his own head.[66]

In Cinus's thought, dialectic was simply one instrument that the human mind could make use of, but it must not be allowed to condition, much less dominate, men's minds. The central problem for which dialectic was a means and an instrument was the discovery of truth and justice, which could be accomplished by following a tradition of thought continuously consolidated and enriched over two centuries. In every human relationship, a jurist may discover and evaluate the worldly dimension of an absolute but unknowable divine justice. Even when a principle of equity had been identified, however, *aequitas* (equity) was not a *praeceptum* ("Potest dici quod equitas non est preceptum"; It can be said that equity is not a norm); it required the intervention of someone with the power to formulate and promulgate a cogent norm: "Ius vero est preceptum ab his qui auctoritatem precipiendi habent" (A law is a norm when it is promulgated by those who have the authority of establishing it). Errors might be committed during that intervention out of negligence, ignorance, or interest, and, when they were, the *ius* would not correspond to *aequitas*: "Legislators at times ordain what is iniquitous, because as men they err and will continue to err."[67]

What was new in Cinus was the breadth of his discourse, which no longer kept strictly to the norms of Roman law, as with the glossa-

---

66. Manlio Bellomo, "Un'opera ritrovata: La 'quaestiones' di Iacopo Bottrigari jr.," in *Aspetti dell'insegnamento giuridico*, 86–87.

67. Cinus of Pistoia, *Lectura* in Cod.1.14.1, quoted in Calasso, *Medio Evo del diritto*, 1:479 and n. 32.

tors, but considered all legal norms—those of the highest imperial and pontifical authorities and those of the governing forces of kingdoms, communes, and seigniories. As an interpreter of norms and rules (*praecepta*) Cinus granted himself great liberty and independence, as if he could and must judge whether or not each norm conformed to *aequitas*. In this process of judgment he made use of all the argumentative possibilities offered by the extremely rich range of weapons in dialectic's kit—but he simply made use of them and did not allow himself to be submerged by them.

Cinus was sincerely sensitive to motivation, which he viewed in its full religious dimension, and he frequently accused statutory dispositions of being iniquitous and tyrannical. He thought the field of local law was the most fertile for this sort of abuse, thanks to the variety of its decisions and the fact that many of them regulated personal and particular interests. "A man," he stated, "a Lucchese, captain of the people in Pistoia, stood in the middle of the City Hall and sold himself like a prostitute in the middle of a brothel." This politician was not the object of public scorn, however, but "was reputed *sapiens* [wise] in Lucca, as a skillful thief might be in a band of thieves."[68] Cinus's opinions had a clear and consistent set of moral values, especially those concerning the *ius proprium*. Questions concerning statutes occupy much of the discussion in the *Lectura* and are constantly present in the fifth point of his program.

Cinus's vision of the relationship between *ius commune* and *ius proprium* was marked by this particular aversion to the *ius proprium*, which he saw as normally iniquitous and the product of thieves and sharpers. The decisive factor in this relationship was how well each set of norms reflected equity, and here the *ius commune* always proved superior. In all his discussion of their relationship, the *ius proprium* always came second for Cinus. Following a logical scheme current at the time, the *ius proprium* was an accidental, occasional, hence very changeable law, whereas the *ius commune* was the law par excellence;

68. The episode is recounted in Cinus of Pistoia, *Lectura* in Cod.2.6.5, *De postulando*, 1. *si qui* (Francofurti ad Moenum 1578), reprint (Turin: Bottega d'Erasmo, 1964), fol. 71rb. It is studied in Mario Sbriccoli, *L'interpretazione dello statuto: Contributo allo studio della funzione dei giuristi nell'età comunale* (Milan: Giuffrè, 1969), 409. It is also discussed, with a different view of the problems involved, in Francesco Migliorino, *Fama e infamia: Problemi della società medievale nel pensiero giuridico nei secoli XII e XIII* (Catania: Giannotta, 1985), 9.

it was stable to the point of seeming eternal, and it was just. The *ius proprium* was only an "accessory" law; the *ius commune* was the "principal" law. But the justice intrinsic to that same *ius commune* was just as relative and problematical as it was in every human action and every human work in comparison to the supernatural, to the values of the faith, and to divine Will.

17. Bartolus of Saxoferrato

Bartolus of Saxoferrato was a person of mythical proportions in a golden age. He was born between November 1313 and November 1314 in Venatura, a hamlet in the Marches in the territory of the town of Sassoferrato. He began his legal studies at a very young age and had an extremely short life, since he died in Perugia in 1357 when he was barely forty-three.

Bartolus was a feverishly active man: he was a professor, a lawyer, and a legal advisor; he was involved in public life (as a member of the city council—an *assessore*—in Todi and perhaps in Cagli); he played an active role in religious confraternities. He allowed himself no rest, and during one brief summer vacation, while seated on the banks of a river watching its placid waters, he quickly drew up a summary of all the hypotheses in the legal questions connected with riparian rights and wrote a treatise on the subject.[69] He truly lived for the law.

Bartolus's works were vast and numerous. They included *commentaria* on the three parts of the *Digest* (*Digestum vetus*, *Infortiatum*, *Digestum novum*), on the *Code*, and on the *Novels*; a long list of treatises on particular topics (tyranny, reprisals, city ordinances, riparian rights, and more); *quaestiones disputatae*; and several hundred *consilia*. His knowledge of Roman law, canon law, and statutory and feudal questions was endless and extremely solid. His dialectical formation was rigorous and perfectly fitted to the study of the law.

These were Bartolus's more obvious merits, but they fail to give a sense of the man's personality or to show the goals of his vision of the law, a vision that embodied thoughts so complex it is difficult to put it into focus and to grasp its most significant traits. Indeed, historiog-

---

69. Bartolus of Saxoferrato, *Tractatus Tyberiadis*, or *De fluminibus* (Venetiis 1635), fols. 132v–137r; reprint of Bononiae 1576 with a preface by Guido Astuti (Turin: Bottega d'Erasmo, 1964).

raphy has often picked out either the most generic and obvious facets of this great jurist or has concentrated on highly secondary and irrelevant characteristics.

In the fullest scholarly evaluation, Bartolus has been presented as Cinus's successor in the task of subjecting the law to dialectical rationalization. Bartolus attended Cinus's lessons in Perugia for only a short time, but he acknowledged that his mind had been "modeled" by Cinus. He was a pupil who surpassed his master not only in "refinement of the technique of the commentary," in his "dialectical force," and in his "exceptional skills in excavating the depths of the *littera legis* (letter of the law) to extract its most hidden *mens* (mind) and *ratio*," but also, by shattering the *littera* of the law and by a dialectical recomposition of the contents of the law, he succeeded in bringing to the old fabric of the *ius commune* "the first signs of life of the new *societas iuris* (society of law)."[70]

This portrait is undoubtedly true to life, and it gives some notion of Bartolus and his works, but it is little more than a sketch. It notes some similarities between Bartolus and Cinus, but it fails to do justice to Bartolus's originality as he dealt with the problem, vitally important in the fourteenth century, of the *ius commune* and its relationship with the *ius proprium*.

These problems were hardly new. They were felt on the theoretical plane, since, as we have seen, they had been posed for some time regarding both the relationship of norms within the *Corpus iuris civilis* and the relationship between that entire corpus and the many norms of the *ius proprium*.

Such problems had also been experienced in practice by those who wrote the laws of the kingdoms, the statutes of the communes or the corporations, or the customary laws of the cities; by notaries drawing up acts and by judges in need of concepts, principles, and methods from the *ius commune* in order to decide cases—in short, by people who needed to distinguish between the use, the formal or substantial reproduction (local legislators), and the application (judges) of the *ius commune*.

In Bartolus the two lines of the system of the *ius commune* acquired

70. Francesco Calasso, "Bartolo da Sassoferrato," in *Dizionario biografico degli Italiani*, 6:640–69. The same article appears in *Annali di storia del diritto* 9 (1965): 472–520, quotation 516.

a particular clarity. Theoretical recognition of the *ius proprium* had been definitively achieved, something to which Bartolus himself had made a decisive contribution with his theoretical construct of *iurisdictio*, in which he stated that every ordinance contains, on a reduced scale and in reduced measure, the same powers that the emperor had in the empire—powers that thus become a "model."

Bartolus deepened and modified Cinus's vision. If I may be permitted the image, Cinus's view of the "system" of the *ius commune*, unified by the central problem of *aequitas*, was like the Ptolemaic system in which the earth lay immobile at the center of a horizontal plane while the sun in its heavens moved around it every day, illuminating and warming it. So the question of *aequitas* could be configured as a complex of norms as varied as the various parts of the planetary system, some parts of which were principal, others accessory, but all of which gathered together to make a whole that was integrated but had no life without the light and the warmth of equity, their vitalizing sun.

Bartolus's vision was different. *Ius commune* and *iura propria* were not located on the same plane, and if they must be distinguished from one another the concepts of "principal" and "accessory" were inadequate. They moved instead as if within an immense spherical space in which—to return to the planetary image—the sun was the *ius commune* and the *iura propria* were planets.

Equity lost the definition and the fullness that Cinus had ascribed to it, but it reacquired a full function, since it was the spirit that moved this legal universe. It resembled the divinity, which has no corporeal substance: just as the divine circulated within the human being, *aequitas* was the vital fluid that circulated in both the *ius commune* and the *ius proprium*.

Furthermore, just as the sun had no life but was the prime origin of all possible life, so the *ius commune* was lifeless in the terrestrial sense of the word but was the origin of all possible (legal) life for the *iura propria*. That was where there was tumultuous action, order and disorder, violence and peace; in short, that was the province of man, with all his problems. The *ius commune*, with its concepts and its *principia* (norms), descended to the level of human acts, inspiring them and giving support to their legal organization. The inverse was impossible, however: "The truth of the civil law must not be obscured by the images of the statutory law," Bartolus wrote in one of his treatises.[71] The *ius commune* was central: "All interpretations of the statutes must be made with the authority of the Roman laws."[72]

Legal images came to be formed in the *ius proprium*, and they too had a legitimacy that derived from their orderly placement in the system, just as the earth had its position in respect to the sun and man in respect to God. But the statutory images could no more transcend the limits of their specific legitimacy—limits set by the fact that they were inscribed in the system—than the earth could seek a life of its own outside its habitual orbit and outside its constant relationship with the sun, or than men could renounce God, because only in their relationship with God did their soul have existence.

No one explained the master's thoughts better than did Baldus de Ubaldis, Bartolus's most prominent pupil. Baldus did so first in general terms: "One might say that the *ius commune* inspires the statutes and invests them but is neither inspired nor invested by them: and this is because of the force of attraction [*vis attractiva*] that the *ius commune* has toward the law of the communes. But the contrary does not occur."[73] Baldus continued in even more specific terms and with a clear example: "I wonder whether the statutes are to be interpreted by means of the *ius commune*. Bartolus maintains that the statutes undergo a passive interpretation from the *ius commune*: thus if the statute says that Bartolus is a citizen, all the norms of the *ius commune* relative to citizenship acquire relevance for him," and for that reason become applicable to his person.[74]

This example illustrates the principle that no norm on any level of the *ius proprium* (royal, city, corporative, or other) could be applied without taking the accepted doctrines of the *ius commune* into account—not even an extremely simple norm whose content seemed evident, such as the imposition of taxes on the citizens of a given city. A statute of the *ius proprium* permitted the taxation of a subject who lived in a city insofar as that subject was qualified as a "citizen," but

71. Bartolus of Saxoferrato, *Tractatus de procuratoribus*, q.VIII.7 (Venetiis 1585), fol. 205rb: "Veritas iuris civilis per imaginem iuris statutorum obumbrari non debet."

72. Bartolus of Saxoferrato, *Comm.* in Dig.1.1.9, *De iustitia et iure*. 1. *omnes populi*, no. 65 (Venetiis 1615), fol. 14ra: "Omnes dictae interpretationes fiunt authoritate legis." I might also recall a *dictum* that circulated widely: "Statutum interpretatur secundum ius communem."

73. Baldus de Ubaldis, *Super Decretalibus*, X 1.2.9, *De constitutionibus*, c. *Canonum*, no. 15 (Lugduni 1551), fol. 11va.

74. See Sbriccoli, *L'interpretazione dello statuto*, 440–41.

for all their clarity and precision, the city statutes said nothing about how one became a citizen. Thus one had to turn to the *ius commune* for the concept and doctrine of citizenship and for the provisions pertaining to it, and make use of them to render the statutory norm applicable. Here the distinction between the "use" and the "application" of a norm are clear: the judge (or the interpreter in a theoretical context) "used" the *ius commune* to "apply" the *ius proprium*.

In this context, the use of the *ius commune* was no longer and not only the practice of the judge who only as a last resort looked to the *ius commune* to seek a norm to fit the case before him. As is clear, the situation was quite different. Use of the *ius commune* responded to a need to provide the concepts and doctrines that were indispensable if a precept of the *ius proprium* was to have legal force. It also avoided the problem—or the expectation—of finding in the *ius commune* a precept identical or analogous to one in the *ius proprium*; it even suggested that any contradiction between the specific normative contents of the *ius proprium* and the *ius commune* would be totally irrelevant.

Legality came to be defined as polarized, with the *ius commune* and its energizing wealth of concepts, general principles, and legal doctrines to one side, and, to the other, the *ius proprium*—real, effective, and human. Like a body without warmth, a man without a soul, the soul without God, the one was meaningless and lifeless without the other.

Religious motivation and love for human life were organically merged in Bartolus's vision, and he experienced both the divine and the human with a deep sense of involvement. Scholars have quite rightly stressed Bartolus's profound humanity, comparing him to Dante "not only for chronological reasons."[75] Bartolus has also been presented as the leading figure in a culture working to redeem "the very figure of the jurist, who in the common opinion is no more than a man of law" because people have often forgotten "that those laws all arose *hominum causa* [because of human beings], and that their study is first of all the study of humankind."[76] This culture was working to construct a true humanism that in no way resembled Jakob Burckhardt's definition and that was "the only [humanism] that the

75. Francesco Calasso, "L'eredità di Bartolo" (1959), now in Calasso, *Storicità del diritto*, ed. Piero Fiorelli (Milan: Giuffrè, 1966), 325.
76. Ibid., 322.

jurist can and must feel: not just discovery and exaltation of humankind but defense of them in thought and in action."[77]

This undeniably describes genuine facets of Bartolus's thought and ones that were sincerely felt and experienced. The fact remains, however, that the "system" that Bartolus rigorously constructed and that remained paradigmatic could function in the interest of the jurists' *consortia* and corporations. It was precisely because the jurists were necessary interpreters of the needs of humankind, because they were the depositories and creators of a legal science composed of principles and categories, because they were trained in the arts of proper reasoning and the skillful application of abstract concepts to concrete human acts that they could concentrate (and defend) in their person, their family, their corporation, and their class a power and a political weight proportional to the role they played in society. Even more: thanks to their discourses on the human soul and on divine and terrestrial justice, to the casual observer in the great popular masses (and on occasion in the eyes of their own students) these jurists were intellectuals much like, if not identical to, the moralists and preachers. The jurists found still greater power in being identified with such figures, whose roles they assimilated, and their new cultural attributes consolidated their prestige and increased their ascendancy.

18. *Scientia iuris*: The Role of the Jurist in the Fourteenth Century

The jurist was anchored to the width, breadth, and characteristics of his *scientia*; when jurisprudence reigned supreme over the other disciplines, the jurists who had dominion over it and who stepped forward as leaders achieved a social rank that translated into and was manifested in prestige, power, and wealth. This occurred in two closely related ways.

The *vulgus* (common person), who looked at the professional figure of the jurist from the outside, was struck by the social prestige and the wealth of the man of law. For that reason, jurisprudence itself seemed a science of power and a lucrative discipline. "Jurists," Nigellus Wireker wrote in the twelfth century, "are everywhere where there is money and power, at the king's court and in the dwelling of the

77. Ibid., 336.

pope, in civil society and in the monasteries."[78] They assumed an aspect and a function: "They advance stiff as a ramrod, and they cling to kings."[79] Nigellus is repeating here one of the century's favorite themes, one that other writers—St. Bernard, Maurice of Saint-Victor, and others—treated with burning accusations. Fables and goliardic poetry also treated the theme of a rich and powerful jurisprudence. In spite of his "sensus hebes et cervix praedura" (dull mind and strong neck), the ass Brunellus fully understood that the law was a road to the summits of power.[80]

This was how the common people viewed legal science. Some scholars agreed: Placentinus gave a lively personification of *legalis scientia*, contrasting it to *ignorantia*. Jurisprudence is like a greedy woman looking for prey: she strikes fear in all who behold her; she has black hair streaked with white that glistens like coal and dark, sunken eyes; she is thin and pale, with wrinkles running over her face; her only luminous aspect is a set of gleaming sharp teeth in a dry and bloodless face ("Facies, colore arida, sanguine desolata").[81]

Others, however, knew that the law had inherent values and positive features. Sensing its unity as parallel to the unity of the empire ("Unum est ius cum unum sit Imperium"; The law is one as the empire is one)[82] was a way of transferring to the law the sacrality and the authority of the empire. Devoting one's efforts to studying justice in order to measure the extent to which a law was or was not congruent to justice implied concentrating on the same acts and the same behaviors that concerned the theologian and the churchman, and the parallel between their activities reflected divine authority onto the figure of the jurist. It was true that the legal field remained clearly distinct

---

78. Nigellus Wireker, *Contra curiales*, in *The Anglo-Latin Satirical Poets and Epigrammatists of the Twelfth Century*, ed. Thomas Wright, 2 vols. (London: H.M.S.O./Longman, 1872), 1:187, also available in reprint (Wiesbaden: Kraus Reprint, 1964).

79. Nigellus Wireker, *Contra curiales*, in ibid., 1:164.

80. Nigellus Wireker, *Speculum stultorum*, in ibid., 1:53.

81. On Placentinus, *Sermo de legibus*, and its publishing career, see Hermann Kantorowicz, "The Poetical Sermon of a Mediaeval Jurist: Placentinus and his 'Sermo de Legibus,'" *Journal of the Warburg Institute* 2 (1938): 22–41, now available in Kantorowicz, *Rechtshistorische Schriften*, ed. Helmut Coing and Gerhard Immel (Karlsruhe: C. F. Müller, 1970), 111–35. For Placentinus's text, see 127–35.

82. *Questiones de iuris subtilitatibus*, rub. II, *De iure naturali, gentium et civili*, ed. Ginevra Zanetti (Florence: La Nuova Italia, 1958), 16, lines 176–79: "Horum igitur alterum concedi necesse est: aut unum esse ius, cum unum sit imperium, aut si multa diversaque iura sunt, multa superesse regna."

from those of ethics and theology, but that distinction by no means signified a total separation, among other reasons, because intuition or observation showed them to have a common goal. Thus Placentinus displayed no embarrassment (perhaps a bit of irony) when he taught that jurisprudence was "most true philosophy," reiterated that it was a "most holy thing," and announced that it "chases away vices, supports good mores, and most admirably detests bad ones," or that it taught everyone, young scholars in particular, the three cardinal qualities of character, which were generosity, strength of soul, and (even) chastity.[83] Placentinus explained all this in the cathedral of Bologna, because this discourse was part of his *Sermo de legibus*, read to inaugurate the academic year, and because the school year was always begun in the house of God with the professors normally speaking right along with (although after) the ecclesiastics who carried out the religious part of such functions. This setting inevitably evoked the idea, current at the time, that the law contributed in its own distinct way to the *melioratio ad statum perfectum* (betterment to a perfect state) of humankind that was the focus of all medieval culture.

This perspective lends significance to the internal coordinates of legal culture and the very nature of the law. These coordinates were: the jurists' insistence on justice and equity; their basic conviction that the *ius commune* was a universal law, one as the Holy Roman Empire was one and as the church that brought all the *fideles Christi* into one fold was one; the arduous construction of a "system" to bind together the texts of the Justinian compilation and make them so homogeneous that they could be perceived as one corpus ("Omnia in corpore iuris inveniuntur"); twelfth-century efforts to reduce to unity and concord the discordant normative passages in church law (Gratian's *Concordia discordantium canonum* or *Decretum*) and to promulgate the great "codifications" of the universal church of the thirteenth century (the *Liber Extra* of Gregory IX and the *Liber Sextus* of Boniface VIII) and of the early fourteenth century (the *Clementinae* of Clement V and John XXII); finally, the slow definition of another meaning of "system" as a link between the *ius commune* and the *ius proprium*.

Our next problem is, first, to understand why jurists who took up the topics of the universality and the sacrality of the law and the unity

---

83. Placentinus, *Sermo de legibus*, in Kantorowicz, "The Poetical Sermon," lines 77–78, 150–55, 166–67, 165–66, 176–213.

of a *ius commune*, conceived as a corpus, took such pains to prove their points; and second, to understand why, at the same time and with a related involvement, jurists attempted to discern real-life connections between *ius commune* and *ius proprium* and to theorize on those connections, proposing a different picture of systematic relationships and a different meaning to the "system" of the *ius commune*.

Personal motivations have little importance in the search for such reasons. Principles and values may indeed have passed "from ideals to myths, and from myths to useful instruments in the hands of those whose goal was action."[84] That might have been the case among lawyers, judges, or office-holders in public administration, even among notaries, because all these men had reason to mask the true face of their operational choices behind solemn proclamations of ideals and mythical principles. It is difficult to establish, case by case, whether it actually occurred.

It is certain, on the other hand, that there were connections between the *ius commune* and the *ius proprium*, and that those connections were explicitly described in a clear theoretical position. These were real data that always operated in the same way; in and of themselves they produced effects that were independent of the will or the awareness of the persons involved in the acts, either when they made conscious use of the *ius commune* when setting down a norm of *ius proprium* in writing or when they constructed a systematic vision of the law according to the two currents of thought that I have sought to describe. Whether or not a jurist, practical or theoretical, became aware of the possibilities inherent in the "system," whether or not, out of distraction, ignorance, or innocence, he neglected to consider the features and constructs implicit in the real workings of a "system," the result was the same, because everyone—the pettifogging lawyer, the judge with few scruples and little intellectual inclination, the inexperienced, ingenuous professor enamored of the logical creations of his own imagination—everyone, and in every instance, for his own part and by his own efforts, even when he knew nothing (and hence had no desire to do so), participated actively in this historical process. I might note, incidentally, that something analogous is occurring in our own century and our own times in the field of the economic order of the capitalist "system," where the farmer, the worker, and the retail

---

84. Guido Morselli, *Un dramma borghese* (Milan: Adelphi, 1978), 244.

merchant, even if they know nothing about the capitalistic "system," nonetheless live in the daily reality of that "system" and, no matter how unaware they may be, contribute to constructing and maintaining it.

The universality of the Roman and canon law and of the "system" of the *ius commune*, conceived of in the dual perspectives of coordination within the *ius commune* and coordination between the *ius commune* and the *ius proprium*, had consequences that radiated in all directions. It was objectively impossible for those who cultivated juridical science not to be aware of these consequences. Certainly some jurists engaged in seeking out such real connections and theorizing about them were quite lucidly aware of the effects of their theoretical position and realized how much it contributed to the consolidation, prestige, and power of their class.

First, the jurists' position was strengthened vis-à-vis heads of government but also in relation to the craftsmen and merchants who furthered production and commerce. They also reinforced their ties to the ecclesiastical world, because the two groups displayed common intentions in their insistence on comprehending the things of this world and interpreting them *sub specie aeternitatis* (as a quality of eternity) as an imperfect reflection of divine perfection and of the supernatural and eternal sphere. Furthermore, the jurist exploited these ties, whether he made a show of them, hid them, or was totally unaware of them.

Second, a *ius commune* and a universal "science" permitted, postulated, and by their very nature required an extremely open communication among those who undertook legal studies, because jurists could easily recognize one another, not only when they came from the same city or the same region but throughout Christendom. Differences in local customs, vernacular languages, customary laws and city statutes, and regional or royal laws put no obstacle in the way of their relations and their integration. In short, we have the phenomenon that the sociologists call a "horizontal integration of the elites"—in this case, among the jurists of the various cities of Europe. This is why I believe that the problems heretofore studied and reported only under the inaccurate labels of the "pre-reception" and the "reception" of the Roman law in German lands and elsewhere need to be reconsidered in a new and more profitable perspective. It will not come as a great surprise to find that in Germany as in the Iberian Peninsula or in France, legal culture of the Bolognese type was present as early as the twelfth century and constituted a solid base for establishing robust relations within all of Europe. It should hardly be necessary to emphasize that this formidable process of horizontal integration multiplied its own powers of expansion in direct proportion to the multiplication of centers specialized in the academic formation of jurists, hence in direct proportion to the spread of universities throughout Europe.

Thanks to a universal science and a universal law, a vertical integration was also realized among those city elites, the pope and the emperor, who reigned at the summits of the two universal organizations, and the sovereigns of the various countries of Europe at the summits of the great monarchical organizations. There were in fact thousands of opinions given, letters written, and instances of technical assistance rendered to the pope, the emperor, or the kings on the part of jurist-doctors, who always made use of the *ius commune*, civil and canon.

One episode among the many that might be cited is truly paradigmatic of the dual process of the horizontal and vertical integration of the power of European jurists. In 1328 Riccardo Malombra, a famous professor of law in Padua and a consultant for the Venetian republic, who two years earlier had been suspected of heresy for having had commerce with certain people in Alexandria, was called to Bologna on the order of the pope, John XXII, to be "examined" by the cardinal legate. Certain elements in this story seem to have had a decisive effect. The jurist presented himself, at the place and the hour in which the examination of the solidity of his faith was to take place, accompanied by the entire College of the Jurist-Doctors of Bologna, an organization of which he was not a member, since he taught in Padua, but whose full solidarity he evidently enjoyed. The cardinal legate expressed his astonishment that so many illustrious persons would "dare to take the defense of an impious [person] and a heretic." He spoke "sharp words of reproach" against Riccardo, not so much for his as-yet-unproven heresy as for his imprudent behavior, but he went no further than delivering a generic injunction enjoining Riccardo to remain in Bologna for an unspecified period of time.[85] Riccardo remained in Bologna for several years, still awaiting a judgment

---

85. On this episode, see Enrico Besta, *Riccardo Malombra, professore nello studio di Padova: Consultore di Stato in Venezia: Ricerche* (Venice: Visentini, 1894), 29.

that never came either to sentence him or to exonerate him. He seems to have suffered no harm from the experience, because we know that his intimate knowledge of the *ius commune* earned him generously remunerated *consilia*, to the extent that some relevant theoretical points of one of his opinions merited inclusion in the *commentaria* of Bartolus of Saxoferrato.[86]

This episode illustrates the chief components of legal reality in the fourteenth century: the unity of the law (*ius commune* and *ius proprium*), the universality of legal science, the solidarity of jurists as a group, which the unity and the universality of the *ius commune* helped them to achieve, but which was also aided by their close relations with the local and central political powers. Jurists were guaranteed ample elbow room for at least the entire century.

The political class has always had to deal with jurists, even on the political terrain of power struggles between the jurists' corporations and the constituted governmental powers. The law was repeatedly suggested as a means for setting limits for the actions of the lord or the prince.

Once again, Bartolus gave a clear statement of the question: the lord was not a tyrant if he acted "secundum ius" (according to the law); a lord was a tyrant "qui in communi re publica non iure principatur" (who did not rule his principality legally).[87] Thus the jurist reserved to his own domain an area of specific pertinence that excluded lords and princes: "Quia hodie Ytalia est plena tyrannis, ideo de tyranno aliqua ad iuristas spectancia videamus" (Because today Italy is full of tyrants, we may look to jurists in matters touching tyranny).[88] I cite from a fourteenth-century manuscript in the Vatican Library (Vat.lat. 2289, fol. 73ra) because the phrase does not appear in the humanistic edition of the works of Bartolus.[89] I do not believe

---

86. Bartolus of Saxoferrato, *Comm.* in Auth. *sacramentum* post Cod.5.35.2, *Quando mulier tutele officio.* 1. *matres*, no. 2 (Venetiis 1585), fols. 172rb–172va. See also Manlio Bellomo, "Giuristi cremonesi e scuole padovane: Ricerche su Nicola da Cremona," in *Studi in onore di Ugo Gualazzini*, 3 vols. (Milan: Giuffrè, 1981–86), 1:91–92.

87. Bartolus of Saxoferrato, *Tractatus de tyranno*, II, in *Politica e diritto nel Trecento italiano: Il 'De Tyranno' di Bartolo da Sassoferrato (1314–1357)*, ed. Diego Quaglioni (Florence: L. S. Olschki, 1983), 177.

88. Bartolus of Saxoferrato, *Tractatus de regimine civitatis* (in fine), in *Politica e diritto nel Trecento italiano*, ed. Quaglioni, 170.

89. For other manuscripts of Bartolus's work, see Quaglioni, ed., *Politica e diritto nel Trecento italiano*, 148. For the historiographical reasons expressed here, I do not agree with the proposal to eliminate the final phrase from the text as extraneous to the

the omission to have been due either to chance or to a printer's error, because it is precisely the final portion (". . . ideo de tyranno aliqua ad iuristas spectancia . . .") that refers explicitly and openly to the jurist's power to deliberate on the acts of the lord and render judgment on them. The fourteenth-century "lord" accepted the idea of listening to and even submitting to the jurist's judgment, but the "prince" of the new times was no longer willing to expose himself to that judgment or to respect the confines of an exclusive legal domain.

In the fifteenth century, when relations between the *ius commune* and the *ius proprium* began to change in Europe, it was precisely in this area that they changed. And when the value assigned to legal science shifted in the great currents of humanism, the "Secunda Scholastica," and the *Usus modernus Pandectarum*, the role of the jurist changed along with it. So did the social and political power of jurists as a class when the corporations of both theoretical and practical jurists were attracted, swallowed up, caged, enmeshed, and at times desiccated as they were caught in the institutional trammels of the new principalities, the absolutist monarchies, and the national states.

---

original. Quaglioni's view (ibid., 170) is shared by Paolo Mari, "Problemi di critica bartoliana: Su una recente edizione dei trattati politici di Bartolo," *Studi medievali*, ser. 3, 26, pt. 2 (1985): 907–40, esp. 924–25, n. 45.

8

In Time and Space

Preface

The fifteenth and sixteenth centuries were times thick with events and dominated by several major problems. To the south, in particular on the Iberian Peninsula, the Arabs still pressed at the edges of the continent. In the east, Constantinople fell into the hands of Mohammed II, and as the Byzantine era came to an end the Ottomans, a people hostile to Christianity, loomed and spread terror on the eastern frontiers of Europe.

During those same years the great navigators, in a series of adventurous voyages, pushed ever farther along the west coast of Africa, and between 1497 and 1500 Vasco da Gama circumnavigated the African continent. In 1492 Christopher Columbus (1451–1506) crossed the Atlantic and made landfall on unknown lands that he thought were the Indies.

Over the course of roughly a century, Europe marked out its confines. In 1492, the armies of Isabella of Castile and Ferdinand II of Aragon conquered the Kingdom of Granada, the last Arab outpost on Spanish soil; in 1571, a great fleet collected and armed by Philip II in the name of Christ inflicted a ruinous defeat on the Turks at Lepanto, thus putting a definitive stop to an expansion that had been aimed at the heart of the old continent of Europe.

These events helped Europe to acquire a more lucid self-awareness and an awareness of the value of the faith that it knew and practiced; at the same time, comparison with the "infidel" peoples (Arabs and Turks) and with the "savage" populations first of Africa and then of the Americas (the "Indies") gave Europeans a clearer view of the traits of their own civilization.

Between the fifteenth and the sixteenth centuries, Europe was a world tormented by doubts and questions that at times could be dramatic and extreme. The legal field underwent a frontal attack: for centuries (at least from Irnerius and Gratian) jurisprudence had traditionally been thought of as one and universal, serving the entire human race; now it was discovered that a large proportion of humanity had no knowledge of the *ius commune*, had never had occasion to know it, and was incapable of comprehending either its practice or its spirit.

2. Legal Humanism: An Overview

New currents of thought—legal humanism, the "Secunda Scholastica," the *Usus modernus Pandectarum*—rose to confront the traditional jurisprudence of the fourteenth century (Bartolus and his successors). All these movements, but the first two in particular, threatened an equilibrium that had permitted the *ius commune* and the *iura propria* to coexist within the order of a *sistema iuris*. Furthermore, in many parts of Europe, by casting doubt on the organizational function of the *ius commune*, they helped to redefine the roles of the jurist, the scholar, the philosopher, and the theologian.

Let us take humanism first.[1] Humanism challenged the authority of the *ius commune*, weakening the certainty, universality, and eternity that it advocated and claimed as its own. When humanism proposed mutability and uncertainty as historical perspectives, it crumbled the monolithic structure and the theoretical basis of the *ius commune*. In the process, many of the areas that had been the special province of the jurist were gradually occupied by the historian or the scholar or by early experiments in philology, with the result that the jurists' function shifted and their social image was reduced to more modest dimensions. Not only was the universality and eternity of the *ius commune* contested and criticized; attempts were also made to replace it with a princely or royal legislation of a strongly national cast that viewed such systems of law as a general (hence a common) law.

---

1. For a broad range of specific biographical and bibliographical information, see Hans Erich Troje, "Die Literatur des gemeinen Rechts unter dem Einfluss des Humanismus," in *Handbuch der Quellen und Literatur der neueren europäischen Privatrechtsgeschichte*, ed. Helmut Coing, 3 vols. (Munich: Beck, 1973–87), vol. 1, pt. 2, 615–795.

In short, for the humanists the relationship between the *ius commune* and the *ius proprium* had been broken, and rightly so. They insisted that the law of the kingdom or the principality should no longer be considered *ius proprium* but a general and common law that stood in contrast to the variety of customary laws and local statutes. In this point of view the *ius commune* became either a residual law or a law to be taken into account on a cultural plane, valuable for the store of human reasoning and human reasonableness that it had elaborated and embodied through the ages. Those who had formerly enjoyed (and still claimed) a monopoly on legal knowledge must move out of the spotlight, because their role had shrunk and their prestige and social and political power had declined. Moreover, the humanists (and not only the humanists, as we shall see) insisted on changes in the ways in which Justinian's books and the laws of the church were studied. The *ius commune* was increasingly beset and compressed: relegated to the past, it was to serve as a means for gaining knowledge of ancient times; as a monument that had survived from former ages, it was to help reveal the true ancient world and, in particular, the grandeur of Rome.

Scholars debated the relative excellence of the various branches of knowledge; now they wondered whether or not literature and philosophy had preeminence over jurisprudence and medicine. Even though the scholar who pored over documents from the past to see what value there might be in the extant evidence—narrations, contracts, or other—might easily have appeared to be engaged in an ascetic activity untouched by politics, his place (and those of the philosopher, the historian, and the philologist) in the society of the day and, even more, in the courts of the princes, was not determined by politically disinterested criteria. The scholar's operating space had been taken away from the jurist. Some jurists reacted by recasting their thinking; others only made a show of doing so or more simply adapted to the new method by sharing some of the humanist's tasks, seeking to conform to the trends of the times and to aid the prince or the sovereign in working to construct a "national" order. There were also jurists who fought the new currents with all their might, both on the level of theory and on the level of a practice that remained—and, they insisted, must remain—tied to the traditional methods of jurisprudence. Then there were some jurists who played a starring role, occupied center stage, and had a hand in writing the scenario—although, as has prudently been remarked, the label of "humanist" did not always express a jurist's entire personality, nor did it always represent all the components of his thought.[2]

3. Legal Humanism: France

The new legal humanism had representatives in Italy (as we shall see), in Germany, and in Spain. In German-speaking lands there was Ulrich Zasius (1461–1535), active in Freiburg, who was sensitive to the influence (through Basel) of Erasmus of Rotterdam and Bonifacius Amerbach. Spain had Elio Antonio de Nebrija (Nebrissensis) and Antonio Agustín.

But it was in France, with the so-called *mos gallicus*, that humanism offered the most serious challenge to a still-vital equilibrium that had gradually formed from the thirteenth century on within a system of *iura propria* based in the *ius commune*. Some French jurists were motivated by a "nationalistic" sentiment that they displayed openly. They claimed full and preeminent validity for French law on the two levels of the particular laws (city and seigniorial law; royal law), and they assigned to the royal law the function of a general law in respect to the local laws (*coutumes*, statutes, and so forth). These jurists, however, embodied and documented only one aspect of a more complex phenomenon. Various methodological tendencies competed to reach a common goal of increasing the scope of the national law in force: some jurists accused Justinian of irrationality; others suggested that the reworked legislative materials that they had inherited could be given a new and rational order; still others studied and used Justinian's compilation only as an important witness to the past.

We need to follow all three of these tendencies. The task of discrediting the Justinian compilation fell in particular to François Hotman (1524–90), a jurist of less than outstanding intelligence who nevertheless became famous for the clarity and incisiveness with which he tackled this historically significant task. Hotman lived in the mid-sixteenth century, an age in which the chief themes of legal humanism were fully mature.

Hotman was the author of a diffuse work, the *Antitribonianus*, in

2. Mario Ascheri, "Giuristi, umanisti e istituzioni del Tre-Quattrocento: Qualche problema," *Annali dell'Istituto storico italo-germanico di Trento* 3 (1977): 46–47.

which he attempted to strip bare the peccadillos, the failings, and the errors of the Byzantine compilers. (Tribonian, as is known, headed Justinian's legislative commissions and bore the major responsibility for compiling and editing the *Corpus*.) Hotman's critical judgments were openly aimed at promoting the French national law.[3]

Hotman's work was not isolated from the context in which he moved or from critiques that had preceded it. It was fashionable in some sectors of the humanistic culture of the time to treat all jurists of earlier times as ignorant. Medieval jurists were defamed in long strings of insults: they were "plebei, nocui, inepti, sophistae, barbari [plebs, noxious, inept, sophists, barbarians] . . . imperiti [unlearned] . . . sordide nostram tractantes disciplinam, rixantes de lana caprina [handling our discipline foully, to contend over goats' wool; that is, over trifles] . . . ad aratrum nati, non bene de mente constituti [born to the plough, not well endowed mentally] . . . improbi, ambitiosi, avari [base, ambitious, greedy] . . . exoticae linguae homines [men of exotic, that is, bad, language]" and worse.[4]

The jurists of the second group worked to reformulate the materials and the arguments of the *Corpus iuris civilis* on a more rational level and on the plane of historical relativity and to redistribute them in a new architecture. Such men took care to point out (and they made it abundantly clear by the way they themselves operated) that the various topics and legal institutes were bundled together in no proper order in the Justinian compilation, where they were sometimes juxtaposed and sometimes divided among titles and books that were organized with no logical or systematic arrangement. A new order was needed. Among the many jurists who shared such ideas were Guillaume Budé (Guillelmus Budeus, 1465–1530), François de Connan (Franciscus Connanus, 1508–51), André Tiraqueau (Andreas Tiraquellus, 1488–1558), François Duaren (Franciscus Duarenus, 1509–59), Charles Dumoulin (Carolus Molineus, 1500–66), and, above all, Hugues Doneau (Hugo Donellus, 1527–91) and Antoine Favre (Antonius Faber, 1557–1624), the author of one work, *Rationalia ad Pandectas*, whose title was a clear indication of his program.

Jurists of the third current in French legal humanism were less apt to expose their political motives and less explicit about their polemic

3. Domenico Maffei, *Gli inizi dell'umanesimo giuridico* (Milan: Giuffrè, 1956), 61–63.
4. Ibid., 34.

biases. Some of these were jurists who continued to study the *Corpus iuris civilis* in depth, but with a shift in method and within the context of other sources, which they sought with passion and sometimes found, with good luck. Motivated by a need, a desire, even a yearning to study the past and to appreciate the grandeur of Roman or Greek antiquity, they launched massive scholarly projects. They also inaugurated modern philological studies in the field of law. They approached Roman law with love rather than criticism, reproach, or aversion, but they saw it with new eyes. They used Roman law as testimony to the past; as documentation that made it possible to know an epoch, a civilization, and a culture that, because they belonged to the past, were no longer entirely of the present. At most Roman law could be regarded as the base or the foundation for a present that was completely different because it had and practiced its new national, regional, or local "laws." There was admittedly a connection between the present and the past, and the past generated interest, curiosity, and a need to know, but the present was not the same as the past, hence the laws of the past could not be the laws of the present.

One of the best-known of the jurists in this third current in French legal humanism was Jacques Cujas (1522–90). A contemporary of Hotman, Cujas followed a totally different direction. Avoiding polemics, accusations, and scornful judgments, he worked constructively in a number of powerful works to relegate Roman law to the past. A few decades after Cujas came Denis Godefroy (1549–1622), the author of a painstaking edition of Justinian's *Corpus iuris civilis*, and Jacques Godefroy (1587–1652), who wrote a masterly commentary to the *Codex Theodosianus*.

It should hardly be necessary to note that defining three tendencies in French legal humanism and mentioning the principal figures in each current does not mean that individual humanist jurists were not influenced by tendencies that were not particularly congenial to them, or that they did not to some extent consciously accept that influence.

4. Legal Humanism: Italy

Humanistic jurisprudence was less intense in Italy than in France. After Francesco Petrarca (1304–74), whose groundbreaking and original thought long preceded the new trends, no significant breach was opened in the traditional method.

The scholarly humanism so powerfully represented by such major figures as Flavio Biondo (1392–1463) and Lorenzo Valla (1407–57) had little effect on jurisprudence; nor was it much influenced by the new historiography inaugurated by the genius of Niccolò Machiavelli (1469–1527)—who wrote not only *Il Principe* but also the *Discorsi sopra la prima Deca di Tito Livio* and the *Istorie fiorentine*—and continued by an entire school of Florentine historians, notably by Francesco Guicciardini (1483–1540) in his *Storia d'Italia*.

Legal humanism made sporadic appearances in Milan, Florence, Siena, Bologna, Padua, and Naples. The movement was hesitant, however, and the works it produced were often wishful thinking, than actual projects, as in Bologna with Ludovico Bolognini (1446–1508).[5]

Other jurists allowed themselves to be absorbed into the mechanics of a princely patronage that was particularly generous toward scholars and men of letters. In Florence and Milan, for instance, humanism and humanists in league with the governing powers served to project and give cultural expression to the policies of centralization of the emergent *signorie* (the Medici family in Florence; the Sforzas in Milan), whose interest lay in dividing and disbanding the compact and powerful jurist class.

There were few "humanists" among the Italian jurists. Aside from Bolognini, we can count Ludovico Pontano (d. 1439) in Rome, Felino Sandeo (1444–1503) in Lucca, Matteo Gribaldi (d. 1564) in Piedmont, Lelio Torelli (1489–1576) in Fano,[6] Mariano Sozzini or Socini (1397–1467) in Siena,[7] and in Naples Alessandro d'Alessandro (1461–1523) and Marino Freccia (1531–1603).

One jurist, Andrea Alciato (1492–1550), is considered the major representative of the humanistic school of Italian jurisprudence. In his work, which is impressive for both its mass and its quality (*Commentaria ad Pandectas, Paradoxa, Parerga, De re militari, Emblemata*,

---

5. There is one important monograph on Bolognini: Severino Caprioli, *Indagini sul Bolognini: Filologia e giurisprudenza nel Quattrocento italiano* (Milan: Giuffrè, 1969).

6. Giovanni Gualandi, "Per la storia della 'editio princeps' delle Pandette fiorentine di Lelio Torelli," in *Le Pandette di Giustiniano: Storia e fortuna di un codice illustre, Due giornate di studio*, Florence, 23–24 June 1983 (Florence: Olschki, 1986), 143–97. On Torelli's three short juridical works, see 149–50.

7. Paolo Nardi, *Mariano Sozzini, giureconsulto senese del Quattrocento* (Milan: Giuffrè, 1974).

and more), Alciato by and large maintained a balance between demands for renewing and refashioning the law and acceptance of the weighty legacy of Italian legal doctrine of the thirteenth and particularly the fourteenth centuries.

5. The "Ancient" Method in Italy: "Bartolism"

Beyond the small, often isolated, and ephemeral areas within which the few Italian jurists attracted by humanism and by the *mos gallicus* expressed themselves, the juridical scene in northern Italy was still largely dominated by a traditional method that recognized Bartolus of Saxoferrato as its figurehead; hence, those who continued Bartolus's work and shared his stance and his vision of the law, either out of interest or from conviction, were known as Bartolists.

On the southern Italian mainland, in Sicily, and in Sardinia the scene was more varied and is even less well known. Aside from the ideas and cultivated curiosity of Lucas of Penna, the *Dies geniales* of Alessandro d'Alessandro,[8] and the modest collected works of Marino Freccia, few significant traces of legal humanism appeared in southern Italy. Furthermore, we need to consider how much those regions were affected (and precisely how) by Spanish innovations in methodology launched by Francisco de Vitoria, the "school" of Salamanca, and the "Secunda Scholastica," a movement that was to dominate much of the European legal scene. We also need to see what role the "system" of Bartolist *ius commune* continued to play in those regions, since for centuries they had been closely connected to the great university schools of northern Italy, and their jurists usually had an early acquaintance with works of the doctrines of the *ius commune*.[9] One example of a practical jurist who was also familiar with these works is a Palermo judge, Tommaso di Carbonito, who, as we know from a donation in 1328, owned a manuscript containing "leges commentatas

---

8. Domenico Maffei, *Alessandro d'Alessandro, giureconsulto umanista (1461–1523)* (Milan: Giuffrè, 1956).

9. This topic was the focus of a "Settimana di lavori" in Erice at the "Ettore Majorana Center for Scientific Culture" in October 1983. The Acts of this workshop are available as *Scuole diritto e società nel Mezzogiorno medievale d'Italia*, ed. Manlio Bellomo, 2 vols. (Studi e ricerche dei "Quaderni Catanesi," 7, Catania: Tringale, 1985–87). For other thoughts on the subject, see Manlio Bellomo, "Cultura giuridica nella Sicilia catalano-aragonese," *Rivista internazionale di diritto commune* 1 (1990): 155–71.

super Digesto veteri" that included a copy of Cinus of Pistoia's *Divina Lectura*, a recent work.[10]

6. "Practical Jurisprudence": Bartolists, Tract-Writers, *Consiliatores*

In much of Europe the potential of the Bartolist "system"—that is, its capacities as a tool in legal practice—are best seen in the massive activity of the practical jurists. When the lawyer or the judge had to think through an act, prepare a defense, or hand down a judgment, he may well have been obliged to apply the law of the *ius proprium*, but he also had to use the *ius commune* in his work, arguing from passages in the *Corpus iuris civilis* or the *Corpus iuris canonici*, citing precedents one by one, and accumulating large numbers of citations in support of his argument or his decision.

This was how the jurist protected himself from an increasingly centralized political power that was becoming organized in increasingly authoritarian ways and was stripping many legal operators (the humbler run of lawyers, employees in the offices of the nascent bureaucracies, court consultants, and so forth) of their autonomy and their freedom of action. It was also how the jurist guaranteed himself and his class a vital and still prestigious social and political position within the princely order.

The *consilium* was the genre that best expressed the great (or would-be great) Italian jurist's sense of his social position. This was a tradition that had originated long before, in the twelfth century, and had given the "commentators" of the fourteenth century matter for study and theoretical elaboration.[11]

The most significant *consilia* from the historical point of view were the ones given by the *doctores*. This is not only because portions of them have been preserved in manuscript codices and printed editions

10. See Domenico Maffei, *La "Lectura super Digesto veteri" di Cino da Pistoia: Studio sui mss. Savigny 22 e Urb.lat.172* (Milan: Giuffrè. 1963), 37 n. 104. On legal libraries in Sicily, see Henri Bresc, *Livre et société en Sicile (1299–1499)* (Palermo: Luxograph, 1971); Bresc, "Egemonia e vita del diritto nello specchio del consumo del libro in Sicilia (1300–1500)," in *Scuole diritto e società*, ed. Bellomo, 1:183–201.

11. On the *consilia*, see Mario Ascheri, *I "consilia" dei giuristi medievali: Per un repertorio-incipitario computerizzato* (Siena: "Il Leccio," 1982); Ascheri, "Rechtsprechungs- und Konsiliensammlungen," in *Handbuch der Quellen*, ed. Coing, vol. 2, pt. 2, 1111–21.

but also because they showed the strict connection between theory and practice more clearly, thanks to the theoretical elaboration called for in teaching, in a focused scholarly output, or in the exercise of practical legal activities on a high level.

This connection is obvious in many instances, but at least two episodes might be recorded here. First, during the first decades of the thirteenth century, Accursius gave a *consilium* in part derived word for word from a gloss taken from an *apparatus* of Azo, part of the substance and the form of which Accursius himself later used for a gloss that eventually appeared in the *Magna glossa*.[12] Second, toward the end of the 1320s Riccardo Malombra, as we have seen,[13] gave a *consilium* at Bologna that only a few years later (with appropriate modifications and along with other *consilia*) passed into the *commentaria* of Bartolus of Saxoferrato.

Consilia were requested and given in a wide variety of forms, but they all documented a strong connection between theory and practice. For instance, a judge or a private citizen formulated a question involving the narration of an event and stating a legal doubt arising from that event; or he might describe an act or event that already had a legal solution and that outlined the litigation that had arisen or was about to arise concerning that solution; or he might formulate a series of legal questions to submit to a jurist for an opinion in the form of a simple affirmative or negative response.

Requests for *consilia* were written on a sheet of parchment, or in a special register that the jurists kept in their studios for the use of clients, or they might arrive in a letter from distant lands. The responses (the *consilia* proper) were expressed in a corresponding form, on the same parchment or paper sheet as the request, in the same register, or in a letter.

These acts and the related documents accumulated rapidly between the thirteenth and the fifteenth centuries. At the same time, *consilia* written not by a single jurist but by various sorts of groups of jurists (more important, by groups of jurists deliberately brought together for that purpose) began to appear. Some *consilia* were signed by a number of colleagues and fellow-jurists; some were written up and

12. See Manlio Bellomo, "Consulenze professionali e dottrine di professori: Un inedito 'consilium domini Accursii,'" *Quaderni Catanesi* 7 (1982): 199–219.
13. See chap. 7, section 18.

signed by one *doctor* and then elaborated upon and linked—perhaps with only a brief phrase or the addition of a citation from the *Corpus iuris civilis* or from canon law—by the *doctor*'s son (himself a *doctor*) or by a pupil in his school. A smaller number of *consilia* were given collegially by an entire corporation. The *consilia* of the colleges of jurist doctors are examples.

The emperor, the pope, and lesser rulers made use of well-known *doctores* to arbitrate quarrels or to help avoid foreseeable controversies. In such cases there was usually a preliminary exchange of letters in which the terms of the questions were clarified, both as to what had happened and as to what legal rules were involved. At an appropriate time, the parties gathered together, the necessary proofs were marshalled, the legal problems were discussed, and possible solutions were tested. Finally the jurist, as the arbiter of important and divergent interests, made his decision, citing Roman and canon law in the text of his *sententia* (opinion).

This entire procedure has left only fragmentary traces, because the letters were lost and no accurate and complete minutes of the discussions or the testimony of witnesses remain. At best we have references and mentions included in the final act stating the decision. Afterwards the decision might easily have been distorted by being inserted, along with many other fragments of various provenance, into a generic collection of *consilia* and *tractatus*. This is what happened, for example, with Vatican codex Vat.lat. 10726, where the compiler quite obviously intended to transfer results of practical activity into the theoretical sphere so that the outcome could be of use to practitioners as well as to theorists.

The price for a *consilium* was always extremely high. Not only did the principal consultant or an entire college of jurists have to have their recompense, but also anyone who had added a signature or a word or two could claim his due. The cost might be as high as the semester's or year's stipend for a professor who taught in the famous and wealthy university schools of the age, and it might even be much larger. For example, at a time when a professor of logic and philosophy in Florence was paid an annual stipend of forty gold florins and a professor of medicine twenty-five, in Bologna one *consilium* could cost as much as one hundred florins! Here, quite evidently, economic data cannot escape having a precise significance, since they express the monetary value of the jurist doctors' power. They also give a concrete sense of how certain decisions could be redirected in one's favor by paying an open, legal price in homage to the power that the *doctores* in law enjoyed.

There were some nondescript collections made by bundling together the *positiones, allegationes,* letters, and consultations of a number of jurists, transcribing them in whole or in part, summarizing their texts or abridging only one portion, on occasion simply omitting references to persons, names, and dates. There were also better-organized collections that concentrated on one jurist (perhaps adding a scattering of writings of his colleagues and adversaries) or related to one topic or one major sector, such as succession, dowries, or criminal law. There were also collections that carefully documented (or attempted to document) the full range of one jurist's activities. At the turn of the fifteenth century, some famous jurists reworked earlier series of *consilia* by jurists whose word still bore weight in collective memory, and they took the opportunity to emphasize anew the essential relationship between what was produced for the courtroom and what was elaborated on the level of doctrine for the guidance of that practical legal activity.

On occasion open and bitter polemics arose. The most famous of these was a quarrel that raged between Andrea Alciato and Tiberio Deciani (d. 1582), which seems to have originated in an apparently innocuous question:[14] Was it useful or harmful that many, perhaps all, jurists published their *consilia,* either out of a passion for celebrity or because they were persuaded that they were making an appreciable scholarly contribution to practice or offering useful and practical professional tools?

It was hardly by coincidence that a "humanist" jurist such as Andrea Alciato was hostile to the practice of printing immense sets of *consilia.* His attack against the rampant tide of *consilia* that were being turned out by the publishers of his day was in fact perfectly consistent with the central thrust of his work, which aimed at stripping the *ius commune* of all potential application to practice and relegating it to the realm of history and "antiquity." With Vico,[15] Alciato held that it

14. On this quarrel, see Francesco Calasso, *Medio Evo del diritto* (Milan: Giuffrè, 1954), vol. 1, *Le fonti,* 593.

15. For Giovan Battista Vico's thoughts on the subject, see Maffei, *Gli inizi dell'umanesimo giuridico,* 160–63.

would be better to give Roman law back to the Romans, which would remove it from the hands of jurists who had made it a trenchant tool in their practice—jurists intent on maintaining their personal position and the prestige of a class that resisted the centralization of the new and authoritarian princely and monarchical orders that absorbed all power to themselves.

7. "Traditional" Jurists in Publishing and the Book Markets

The last great season of the *ius commune* in its fourteenth-century guise took place in practice, inaugurated by works written above all in Italy. Furthermore, it was not only professors and legal consultants who were responsible for this late flowering; a new attempt to prove the "practical" validity of the *ius commune* as Bartolus had constructed and used it came from a completely different quarter, one in which shrewd businessmen made fortunes.

The sixteenth century was a golden age for printing. After Johannes Gutenberg's first successful experiments in Mainz between 1440 and 1455 and the first printers' refined editions (incunabula), book production thrived in a number of cities: Mainz, Frankfurt am Main, Paris, Rome, and, above all, Venice in Italy and Lyons in France.

It is instructive to glance at the catalogues of what the leading printshops of the time produced, or at the lists of their best clients, the jurists. In the middle of an age of juridical reform, between legal humanism and the "Secunda Scholastica," the great works of the recent past were republished repeatedly. If there were acid-tongued humanists who vented their critical humors by coining picturesque insults for the jurists of the thirteenth and the fourteenth centuries (Accursius and Bartolus in particular), there were also energetic printer-publishers ready to invest capital and labor and to run the entrepreneurial risk of printing the *Magna glossa* of Accursius or the *Commentaria* of Bartolus of Saxoferrato, Baldus de Ubaldis, Johannes Andreae, and many others. In other words, the publishing business took over the scholarly production of jurists from the recent and the not-so-recent past and printed thousands of copies of their works. It was obviously good business to put on the market works that embodied the "system" of the *ius commune* from the thirteenth to the fifteenth centuries.

Everything was published, not only the greatest works. We cannot say that this publishing boom resulted from the humanists' ardent desire for a knowledge of ancient Roman law that shifted to an interest in legal works of the more recent past as a way to trace the legal vestiges of a great civilization. This may have happened in some cases. Some publishers may have been interested in offering "historical" testimony of the past, and their efforts may have coincided with a similar interest on the part of the reader. If that had indeed been the case, however, few copies would have been produced and even fewer sold.

The fact is, however, that thousands of copies of Accursius's *Magna glossa* were printed (in five large folio volumes in the richest editions; in quarto format for less luxurious editions), and equal numbers of the immense *commentaria* and the lesser works of Bartolus of Saxoferrato (a total of ten folio volumes!). Hence it is obvious that the public for these works cannot have been made up only of a handful of cultivated humanists eager to know the past; it must have included judges, lawyers, professors, and students, who used that rich legacy of works in their everyday activities and who used them as tools and as a vital part of their present, not their past. This is even clearer with such works as Azo's *Summa*, a work that went back to the twelfth century and that was offered as a volume of manageable size still extremely useful in the courtroom; or the *Speculum iudiciale* of Guillielmus Durantis, a thirteenth-century work that in practical application even became *Speculum iuris*, or the great *glossae ordinariae* to the texts of the *Corpus iuris canonici*. I might also note that in 1582 the *correctores Romani* gave their approval to print the most important glossed edition of the *Corpus iuris civilis* of its day.

For nearly two centuries, the printing presses worked ceaselessly to print works on the *ius commune*, slowing only in the 1620s or 30s. No judge or lawyer of any prominence failed to own in his personal library at least one glossed corpus of civil law and of canon law.

Everything was printed, at times with little success, which meant that some examples of the older writings became rare (and are even rarer today). Among these were the *Lecturae* of Odofredus Denariis (a thirteenth-century work) and the *summae* on the *Code* and the *Institutes* of an even older jurist, Placentinus (twelfth century).

Some of the books that were printed—collections of scattered materials and uncertain and incomplete depositions gathered together and reworked—contained writings not originally conceived as one work. As far as we know in the current state of scholarship, this was how the *commentaria* of Jacobus de Arena and Jacobus Buttrigarius the Elder were "constructed," and, in all probability, those of Baldus de Ubaldis (taken from his *lecturae* from a number of years) as well—all jurists of the thirteenth and the fourteenth centuries.

Works that the older jurists had never written were also printed—forgeries, works falsely and surreptitiously attributed to famous jurists. Obviously there were people who sought them and bought them.[16] The authorship of a work might be changed if the publisher thought it convenient: thus a *lectura* on the *Code* by Jacques de Révigny (Jacobus de Ravanis, thirteenth century) was attributed to Pierre de Belleperche (Petrus de Bellapertica).[17]

"Historical concentration" was particularly intense concerning works published under the name of Bartolus—which simply demonstrates the continuing importance of "Bartolism" in Europe, particularly for practical jurists, who earned and spent money and who formed the market for legal publishing in the sixteenth and seventeenth centuries and guaranteed its success, both in cultural and economic terms.

8. The "Reception" of the *Ius commune* in Germany

The "market" for legal works further broadened in the late fifteenth century. This wider demand came from new customers who lived and worked in the German-speaking lands of central Europe. What remained of the "Holy Roman Empire" had taken root in Germany, where empire provided a backdrop for clashes between German princes and, after the "Golden Bull" of 1356, for the "great electors" of the emperor.

In 1495 the imperial supreme court, the *Reichskammergericht*, was founded; it respected the time-honored structures but brought them up to date and bound them more closely to German lands. This court was composed of *assessores*, one-half of whom were *doctores in iure* and the other half aristocrats and experts in judicial procedures. The first sat on the "learned bench," the second on the "noble bench." The

16. Domenico Maffei, *Giuristi medievali e falsifacazioni editoriali del primo Cinquecento: Iacopo di Belviso in Provenza?* (Frankfurt am Main: Klostermann, 1979).

17. Hans Kiefner, "Zur gedruckten Codexlectura des Jacques de Révigny," *Tijdschrift voor Rechtsgeshiendenis/Revue d'histoire de droit* 31 (1963): 5–38.

structure of the court was coherent with a policy of giving the *ius commune* priority among the normative systems that could be applied—in particular, with giving it precedence over local customary laws. The supreme court was to decide cases and set sentences primarily "according to the common law of the empire," hence the judges had to know Justinian law and canon law, according to the Roman principle of *iura novit curia* (the court knows the law). In this sense, the *ius commune* was the "norm" of the imperial order, and as such it was to be respected and applied.

Local law was in quite a different position. It was at base customary law or was derived from customary law. Judges were not obliged to know it, and for that reason it did not fall under the principle of *iura novit curia*. If one of the parties to the legal action requested its application, however, the judges were obligated to admit local law if it could be "proved" (like any other fact), and, if this proof was positive, it was to be taken into account and applied, but only insofar as it was consonant with the relevant precepts of the *ius commune*.[18]

This was how an event of capital importance in the history of the *ius commune* in the early modern age took place. Historiography calls it the "reception" of the *ius commune* (which means the Roman law) in Germany.

In carrying out this operation, the strong jurist class that backed up the German princes, barons, and city oligarchies in the administrations of the small, compact local governments showed proof of intuition and political talent. For some three centuries jurists had grown in numbers, many of them trained *in terra aliena* (in foreign lands), particularly in Italy, where the *natio teutonica* (German nation) in fourteenth-century Bologna is known to have been so numerous and to have carried such weight that the sources called it the *membrum precipuum* (principal part) of the entire *universitas ultramontanorum*,[19] and Padua had been and continued to be so popular among German-speaking students that life in that city took on many Germanic ways. By the mid-fourteenth century a tightly-knit network of new univer-

---

18. See, in particular, Umberto Santarelli, "Recezione (storia)," *Enciclopedia del Diritto* (Milan: Giuffrè, 1958-), vol. 39 (1988), 58–68 and the literature cited therein.

19. Bologna, Statutes of the German Nation, 1345–48, rubr.28 *De vocatione nobilium ad universitatem per procuratores facienda*, in *Statuta nationis Germanicae Universitatis Bononiae (1292–1750)*, ed. Paolo Colliva (Bologna: Associazione Italo-Tedesca, 1975).

sities had developed throughout German-speaking lands: as we have already seen (chap. 5), they included the universities of Prague (founded 1348), Vienna (1365), Heidelberg (1386), Cologne (1388), Erfurt (1392), Leipzig (1409), Rostock (1419), Freiburg (1457), Basel (1460), Tübingen (1477), and more. Within a century, and often after only a few years, one broad cultural area after another had a center where young people could pursue their intellectual and professional training in their own lands. Young Germans interested in the law studied the *ius commune*, civil and canon, in ways very similar to the ways the law was studied in Italy. They even studied analogous problems of the connection and coordination of the norms of the *ius proprium* and the *ius commune*—problems that were felt even more strongly in German lands because everyone knew that the empire was "Germanic," and in German lands the emperor's law could not help but have the force of positive law.

Thus, as we consider the vicissitudes of the "reception" of Roman law in German lands, we need to keep an eye on the jurist class. Even more, the proliferation of new universities also needs to be considered in relation to the solid social and political position that the jurist class had achieved; it also needs to be regarded as one of that class's most efficient ways to consolidate its position, replenishing its ranks as time went by and calling attention to itself as a unique political force in European society.

The "reception" of Roman law and the "pre-reception" that some scholars see as preceding it were in reality aspects of a slow and continuous historical process that affected students first—hence, that affected German jurists in the great university centers of Italy and France. It was a historical process that gradually soldered differing peoples together into one cultural and professional amalgam by means of a common method based in the use of one language—Latin—and by an appeal to common legal concepts, doctrines, and institutions.

Working within this historical process, promoting it and nourishing it, there were jurists with a strong group identity who banded together in active corporations. As they used the *ius commune* as an instrument for controlling the normative systems of the particular laws and as an all-inclusive "system," such jurists were quite capable of sensing the political potential in it.

It is no coincidence that in the early sixteenth century the "received" Roman law was greeted with hostility by another powerful group. The portions of the feudal forces that were most strongly entrenched in defense of seigniorial customary law felt threatened by the *ius commune* and by the jurists who held a monopoly on it. From any objective point of view they were in fact threatened, and in an incisive manner that left its mark. Use of the *ius commune* reinforced the social connotation of jurists as a class definitively immersed in urban civilization and strongly connected to the city patriciates. They analyzed the theoretical roots of power, offered their services as its privileged interpreters, and displayed their solidarity by writing in justification of power. Thus we can readily understand why the stronger the hostility became, the more the rural populations coupled "jurists" and "Christians" in such shouted insults as "Juristen böse Christen!" (Jurists are bad Christians). This was their way of defending the "culture" of their custom-based juridical world and of sharing in the protests of Martin Luther, which, as is known, spread like wildfire throughout Germany after 1517.

9. From Italian "Practical Jurisprudence" to the *Usus modernus Pandectarum* in Germany

While the "reception" of the *ius commune* was making headway in Germany between the fifteenth and the sixteenth centuries, in Italy the times were ripe for "practical jurisprudence." This movement drew strength from the method known as the *mos italicus* (to distinguish it from the *mos gallicus*), a method rooted in the perennial legacy of Bartolus and the commentators and *consiliatores* of the fourteenth and the fifteenth centuries. But in the new climate that was forming in Europe during the sixteenth and the seventeenth centuries, new voices were raised, and figures who differed substantially from the founding tradition of the *ius commune* rose to prominence and blazed new paths.

The first trend to emerge and become consolidated was known as "practical jurisprudence." It preceded a second movement, the *Usus modernus Pandectarum*, with which it was in part intertwined. "Practical jurisprudence" nonetheless deserves separate consideration.

One major Italian jurist of "practical jurisprudence" was Giovan

Battisa De Luca (1613–83),[20] born in Venosa but Roman by adoption
and a cardinal of the Holy Roman Church in the period of its greatest
religious intransigence, expressed by the Counter Reformation and
its operational arm, the Holy Inquisition. Giovan Battista De Luca
went his own way, however. Above all, in the composition of his
works he alternated between the use of the "vulgar" language (Italian) and Latin, which was already a revolutionary novelty in the official culture of Europe. His most widely read work, *Il Dottor Volgare*
(written in Italian) was a sober and balanced work that took up the
legal problems of civil coexistence and reorganized the "institutes" of
private law. De Luca had two basic guiding principles: one must always be a "person of good sense," and one must listen to the voice
not only of "reason" but also of "reasonableness."

All the "practical" currents in Italian and European jurisprudence
merged in De Luca's thought, especially in the monumental collection of jurisprudential "maxims" that he extrapolated from an immense number of judicial decisions. The work was entitled, signifi-
cantly, *Theatrum veritatis ac iustitiae*, almost as if the author wanted
to dramatize truth and justice in a world in search of guidelines for
everyday life. It is that "practical" side that we need to keep in mind
if we are to understand the methodological tendencies that brought
homogeneity to a large part of continental jurisprudence.

After 1495 "practical jurisprudence" found a large audience in Germany as well, but following particular lines of investigation reserved
to certain sectors of jurisprudence, limited fields within which we can
identify principles and figures specific to a microsystem. Even so,
German juridical culture was not isolated from other European currents of the time, nor can it be seen apart from what it inherited from
various other parts of Europe. Thus, for instance, if problems in commercial law seem to be specific to Germany, they were not a totally
new phenomenon: both on the Iberian Peninsula, principally in Catalonia and Portugal,[21] and in Italy, commercial law had been devel-
oping as an autonomous branch of law for some time. In the sixteenth

---

20. Agostino Lauro, *Il Cardinale Giovan Battista De Luca: Diritto e riforme nello Stato
della Chiesa (1676–1683)* (Naples: Jovene, 1991), xxxvii–xxxviii.

21. See Domenico Maffei, "Il giureconsulto portoghese Pedro de Santarém, autore
del primo trattato sulle assicurazioni (1488)," in *Estudos em Homenagem aos Profs. Man-
uel Paulo Merêa e Guilherme Braga da Cruz* (Coimbra: Universidad, 1983), 703–28.

century there were major figures in commercial law, men such as Benvenuto Stracca (1509–78) of Ancona, or Sigismondo Scaccia in Genoa, who were followed in the seventeenth century by Ansaldo degli Ansaldi in Florence and, bridging the seventeenth and eighteenth centuries, Giuseppe Maria Casaregi in Genoa.[22] There were also major figures in civil and criminal trial law and in criminal law: Benedikt Carpzov (1595–1666) in Leipzig, who was preceded by such men as Giulio Claro (1525–75) in Alessandria and Prospero Farinaccio (1554–1618) in Rome.

This jurisprudence was occupied, constantly and on a daily basis, with solving the problem of using both the local laws (*iura propria*) and the common law (*ius commune*). It concentrated on discerning the elements of local law—content, form, principle, or legal institution—that were consonant with the *ius commune*; it took on the task of evaluating the *ius proprium*; it tended toward serious consideration of the *ius commune*, but in ways that permitted giving particular weight to specific legal situations and that heeded the need to reorganize into homogeneous sections the arguments and institutes that were scattered in the Justinian compilation.

The second methodological trend, the *Usus modernus Pandectarum*, began in Germany after the "reception" of Roman law in 1495. The name of this event came from an expression coined considerably later by Samuel Stryk, a jurist who lived from 1640 to 1710 and was a professor at Frankfurt an der Oder and at Halle, a famous work of whose was entitled *Usus modernus Pandectarum* (roughly, "Romanistic Practice Brought into Line with the Needs of the Times").[23]

The *Usus modernus Pandectarum* put its stamp on a long period in German jurisprudence that included prestigious names, among them Hermann Conring (1606–81).[24] The jurists who proposed an *usus modernus* of Justinian's Pandects praised German jurisprudence for its powers of assimilation. They stressed the "national" character of the

22. Vito Piergiovanni, ed., *The Courts and the Development of Commercial Law*, Comparative Studies in Continental and Anglo-American Legal History, 2 (Berlin: Duncker & Humblot, 1987).

23. Umberto Santarelli, in Franz Wieacker, *Storia del diritto privato moderno*, trans. Umberto Santarelli and Sandro Angelo Fusco, 2 vols. (Milan: Giuffrè, 1980), 1:307, the Italian translation of Wieacker, *Privatrechtsgeschichte der Neuzeit unter besonderer Berücksichtigung der deutschen Entwicklung*, 2d ed. (Göttingen: Vandenboeck und Ruprecht, 1967).

24. See Wieacker, *Privatrechtsgeschichte der Neuzeit*, 1:303ff.

new law and pointed to the way that "German" jurisprudence had adapted to new needs while utilizing the ancient law. Part of this adaptation process was an ingrained habit of using the *ius commune*, made "national" by the everyday activities of judges and lawyers. It was also the result of theoretical reflection, however, capable of reinterpreting the norms and doctrines of the *ius commune*, of transferring them to a new cultural terrain, and of reorganizing them sector by sector.

If European jurisprudence remained "systematic," and if the very idea of "system," as it had been experienced and practiced for centuries, could function in the nineteenth century as a central motive force and a cardinal sign presiding over the relaunching of legal science on the European continent, it owed it to the remodeling and the perpetuation of the institutions and the experiences of the grand tradition of Italian legal doctrine, as these were relived and reinterpreted in the rich German experience of the *Usus modernus Pandectarum*.

10. A European Jurisprudence

We need to summarize. During the sixteenth century the principal currents in European jurisprudence began to branch off from one another. Each one ended up not only as the expression of an institutional reality that was consonant with that jurisprudence and supported it but also as the projection of aspirations and political programs aimed at universal domination.

While the British Isles went their own way (as they had been doing for centuries), a substantively distinct continental law came to be divided into several broad cultural areas. One of these was "old" Italy, where the "Bartolisti" and the system of the *ius commune*, in a crisis of adaptation, took the path of experimentation and reelaboration in legal practice. While the Italian jurists continued to follow the tradition of Bartolus, they were also sensitive to "practical jurisprudence," whose techniques and methods they knew and at times followed.

For centuries, vast German-speaking regions had stable connections with Italy, especially after 1495 and the "reception" in Germany of the common law and the methodology long practiced in Italian jurisprudence. In France, the national monarchy became firmly established, and along with it the humanistic tendencies in harmony with it. At the same time, however, all of these large areas suffered internal divisions and were lacerated by religious strife between Protestants, followers of Martin Luther (1483–1546) or John Calvin (1509–64), and the Catholic faithful, who resisted Protestantism and grew increasingly radical and intolerant. The excesses of the Holy Inquisition were a result.

We need to remember, however, that defining cultural areas in Europe is a schematic exercise that suffers from the limitations and rigidities of all schemes. We might do better to consider the "areas" involved less as concrete physical and geographical entities and more as ideal moments, moments of the mind, or attitudes toward method on the part of those who professed jurisprudence. In fact, it is obvious that the various movements—legal humanism, Italian Bartolism, "practical jurisprudence," German *Usus modernus Pandectarum*, the "Secunda Scholastica"—were all European in scope and were present everywhere. There were Bartolists in Spain, legal humanists in Italy and Germany, and representatives of the "Secunda Scholastica" in Holland and Italy.

11. The "Secunda Scholastica"

Between the fifteenth and the sixteenth centuries, between "practical jurisprudence" and humanistic jurisprudence, and at a time when the first results of the "reception" of Roman law in 1495 were becoming clear, attitudes toward the *ius commune* were undergoing constant review. The compactness of the new principalities and absolute monarchies urged them to adopt a view of legal phenomenology that gave the *ius commune* a value of *ratio scripta* (written reason) rather than of positive law in its everyday contrast with the flourishing legislative programs of the various governments. Whether the reasoning of the "practical" jurists turned the tide or whether it was the arguments of the humanists who were attempting to "restore" Justinian's law to ancient Rome and the ancient Romans, in any event, conditions were in place for a new discussion of the functions of the *ius commune*, which was still such an integral and substantive part of the law that it could not be completely eliminated but which needed redefinition vis-à-vis the various particular laws. All the various currents—the jurisprudence that followed the old Bartolist ways or the currents that sought new ways in legal humanism, practical jurisprudence, or the

Usus modernus Pandectarum—continued to study the *ius commune*, albeit with different approaches and methodologies.

If we look to Spain, however, and in particular to Salamanca, the picture changes radically. In the early sixteenth century a totally new and original legal culture formed and developed in Spain, which then expanded and took hold throughout Europe among the dominant currents of legal thought.

This new jurisprudence was based on the *Summa Theologica* of St. Thomas Aquinas and on the theoretical approach that had long been known as scholasticism. Historiography thus calls this revival "Late Scholasticism" or "Second Scholasticism"—the "Secunda Scholastica." I prefer the latter term because it removes all ambiguity concerning the profound novelty of Spanish legal doctrine in the sixteenth and seventeenth centuries.

These were, what is more, the centuries in which Spain was the most important area of all Europe. Between the late fifteenth century and the seventeenth century Spain truly lived its golden age—*El Siglo de oro*—not only for the splendor of the reigns of Isabella of Castile (1451–1504) and Ferdinand of Aragon (1452–1558) and later for the power and size of the empire of Charles V (1500–58) and Philip II (1527–98), but also for its wealth, accumulated by plundering the subjected "savage" populations of West Africa and the "Indies" (the Americas) and from the extraordinary profits it made from the slave trade and the exploitation of the economic resources of the "new worlds" (gold, and especially silver).

There is no better observation point for understanding what was new on the European scene between the late fifteenth and the sixteenth centuries or for getting an overall view of Europe than the Spain of Isabella and Ferdinand, Charles V, and Philip II. This is particularly true if we use that privileged vantage point not to return to the history of the Mediterranean and the European continent but rather to understand how general problems (legal problems in particular) fitted into the mentality and the culture of the leading figures in the broad span of imperial history when, for the first time, they found themselves face to face with unknown lands and "savage" and "infidel" peoples.

One thing is certain: not only in the economic sphere but also in social thought, Spain felt the pull of the "Indies," which Christopher

Columbus had discovered and claimed in the name of Castile in 1492, and of Africa, circumnavigated by Vasco da Gama in 1498.

It may be that the discoverers' first thought regarding the "Indians" on the other side of the Atlantic and the "savages" of Africa was for the health of their souls and for their eternal salvation rather than for their destinies in this life. Theology was a branch of knowledge that was cultivated intensely: the problems of colonialism gave it an anthropological tinge, but as a discipline it was honored all the more as the political thrust of imperial expansionism in Europe met with resistance from what had become sovereign states and clashed with religious reform on the part of Lutherans and Calvinists in Germany, Switzerland, and Holland.

12. Leading Figures in the "Secunda Scholastica"

In Spain of the Golden Age, Salamanca and its university served as the focal point for the new spiritual forces and the ideas that were turning the old Europe upside down.

In Salamanca, theology was the sovereign discipline, and Francisco de Vitoria emerged to head one leading school. Probably born in Vitoria (in the province of Alava) about 1492, Vitoria spent much of the period of his cultural formation in Paris, where from 1506 to 1523 he studied theology in the tradition of the first scholasticism—that is, studying the *Summa Theologica* of Thomas Aquinas, a work composed long before, around 1265. He took it over as the basic text for the first great phase in a theological revival. Although important humanists were present in Paris at the time, Francisco de Vitoria was by and large unaffected by humanism. He was more sensitive to the religious ardor of Erasmus of Rotterdam (1466–1536) than to Erasmus's thought and acts as a leading figure in European humanism. What he sought was a regeneration of civil customs and a restoration of the faith, the need for which seemed all the more acute as the preconditions for Martin Luther's "protest" in 1517 intensified and as that "protest" raged. Luther was excommunicated in 1521, precisely during the time that Vitoria was in Paris.

Francisco de Vitoria's work was centered on quintessentially theological interests, but his theology was open to the world and he was intensely curious about the savage "souls" of populations little known at the time. As he wrote, "The office and calling of a theologian is so wide, that no argument on any subject can be considered foreign to his profession."[25]

The investigation of nature was an investigation into the way in which God had modeled nature. The task of the jurist-theologian was to seek the will of God in nature, and to make himself its interpreter. He must find ways to create social structures and set up legal norms for the legislator that corresponded to that nature.

A theological basis of thought thus encouraged a vision of human law that was both a projection of divine will and a creation of man, but only to the extent that man was capable of receiving and interpreting the signs of the divine will that were impressed in nature: "The primitive origin of human cities and commonwealths was not a human invention or contrivance to be numbered among the artefacts of craft [*inter artificiata*], but a device implanted by Nature in man for his own safety and survival."[26]

This central point in the legal theology of Salamanca had various consequences, and it was connected with a large number of solutions in the fields of both public and private law. Attentive observation of nature necessarily led, these jurists argued, to giving up the fantastic idea that all men were equal and might enjoy the same rights and powers: God had never willed that "all men are equal." It followed that the more worthy and the more able should command and govern others who were by nature inferior. Divine will was providential: "If all members of society were equal and subject to no other person, each man would pull in his own direction as opinion or whim directed, and the commonwealth [*respublica*] would necessarily be torn apart. The civil community [*civitas*] would be sundered."[27] In order

---

25. Francisco de Vitoria, *in principio* "De potestate civili" (1528), in Francisco de Vitoria, *Relectiones Theologicae XII in duos Tomos divisae* (1528), 2 vols. (Lugduni 1557), 174: "Officium ac munus Theologici tam late patet, ut nullum argumentum, nulla disputatio, nullus locus alienus videatur a theologica professione et instituto," quoted in the text from Francisco de Vitoria, *Political Writings*, ed. Anthony Pagden and Jeremy Lawrance (Cambridge and New York: Cambridge University Press, 1991), "On Civil Power," Prologue, 3.

26. Vitoria, "De potestate civili," no. 5, 181: "Patet ergo quod fons et origo civitatum rerumque publicarum non inventum esse hominum, neque inter artificiata numerandum, sed tamquam a natura profectum, quae ad mortalium tutelam et conservationum hanc rationem mortalibus suggessit"; "On Civil Power," Question 1, article 2, paragraph 5, p. 9.

27. Francisco de Vitoria, "De potestate civili," no. 5, 181–82: "Si enim omnes aequales essent et nulli potestati subditi, unoquoque ex sua sententia et arbitrio in diversita-

to keep *civitas* from dissolving and the *regnum* (kingdom) from falling apart as a result of internal divisions, nature required a *gubernator* with the power to command and make appropriate decisions: "Such partnerships cannot exist without some overseeing power or governing force."[28]

Furthermore, if, as some theologians held, it was by divine will that men were not equal, it followed that some men were of superior *status* and others of inferior *status*, some free and others slaves, some rich and others poor. This provided a theoretical justification for *dominium* not only over things (which brought wealth to the more able and poverty to the less) but also over persons in the legal institution of slavery.

Anchoring his argument in *natura* (a concept that would later be reinterpreted by the Dutch school of natural law) enabled Vitoria, as both theologian and jurist, to apply reason to an evaluation of what was in *natura* and to act as an interpreter of the divine will that had created that *natura* and given it specific form. Transporting the law into the vast, all-encompassing, and dominant field of theology had the effect (but was also a presupposition) of moving the jurist's role into the spheres of religion and of the universal church that governed religion. Thus the jurist (and theologian) was in a position to support the actions and fortunes of the church in a world whose confines, both physical and ideal, were expanding extraordinarily and in which Christianity had become one *provincia* of the terrestrial globe.

Francisco de Vitoria saw and understood the entire known world, old lands and new regions and continents alike, as a whole and as a entity consisting of Christian republics: "Any commonwealth is part of the world as a whole, and in particular . . . any Christian country is part of the Christian commonwealth."[29]

---

tem tendente, necessario distraheretur respublica, dissolveretur civitas"; "On Civil Power," 9, edited. Vitoria continues: "Omne enim regnum in seipsum divisum desolabitur. Et ubi non est gubernator (ut ait sapiens) dissipabitur populus," "De potestate civili," 182; " 'Every kingdom divided against itself is brought to desolation' (Matt. 12:25), and 'where there is no ruler the people perish,' as Solomon says," "On Civil Power," 9.

28. Francisco de Vitoria, "De potestate civili," 181–82, "Societas nulla consistere potest sine vi aliqua et potestate gubernante et providente"; "On Civil Power," 9.

29. Francisco de Vitoria, "De potestate civili," no. 13, 193: "Cum una respublica sit pars totius orbis, et maxime Christiana provincia pars totius reipublicae, si bellum utile sit uni provinciae aut reipublicae cum damno orbis aut Christianitatis, puto eo ipso bellum iniustum"; "On Civil Power," Question 1, article 9, paragraph 13, p. 21: "Since

The field of observation had been enlarged: this was the age in which the "Indians" had appeared, but also, after the fall of Constantinople in 1453, it was the age in which "barbarous" Turks loomed on the eastern horizon and threatened Europe.

In the "world-wide" perspective of Vitoria, of the famous Salamanca school that started with him, and of the current of thought that we call the "Secunda Scholastica,"[30] the system of the *ius commune* was inadequate to express and interpret the new notions elicited by a new world in formation. The world had previously been conceived of as an empire and a church with fixed confines, a closed world that embraced only the *fideles Christi*; jurists had been indifferent to what was happening outside Christian lands and distrustful of anything new, or at most interested in "infidels" only in order to exclude them from both civil society and the religious community. Problems of religious transgression had arisen only within the compass of the church, where they were viewed and judged as problems of heresy and deviations from orthodoxy. Now, just as the religious "protest" of Martin Luther and John Calvin was exploding throughout Europe and offering alternative projects for the religious governance of humanity to those of the Roman Catholic Church, Europe became aware of the great masses of the "Indians," the Africans, and the Turks, scattered and "savage" peoples who were presented and conceived of as hostile and violent. They raised problems, however: By what law had those masses lived and did they continue to live? Above all, by what law could and should they live in the future?

Thus the missionary movement was unleashed. The faith and the "Holy Inquisition" became more intransigent. The models for a plurality of Christian *iura propria* that could be (and had been) connected with a Christian *ius commune* disappeared from the spiritual and cultural horizon.

Now, almost unexpectedly but hardly by chance, after centuries in

---

any commonwealth is part of the world as a whole, and in particular since any Christian country is part of the Christian commonwealth, I should regard any war which is useful to one commonwealth or kingdom but of proven harm to the world or Christendom as, by that very token, unjust."

30. The term appropriately provides the title of an important volume, the acts of a conference that took place in Florence, 16–19 October 1972: *La Seconda Scolastica nella formazione del diritto privato moderno: Incontro di studio,* ed. Paolo Grossi (Milan: Giuffrè, 1973).

which the laws of Justinian had been not only accepted but regarded as sacred texts, authoritative, complete, and perfect (that is, without real internal *contrarietates*—contradictions), the content of those laws was discovered to have defects and their organization was denounced as chaotic (a criticism that to some extent echoed the conclusions of legal humanism).

A return to *natura* and a trust in reason to interpret that "nature" became the guidelines of the new political and spiritual reality. The "Secunda Scholastica" developed precipitously on this front. Its leading figures, beside Francisco de Vitoria (who died young in 1546), were Domingo Soto (1495–1560), Martín Aspelcueta, called Doctor Navarrus (1493–1586), and Melchior Cano (1509–60), whose interests were more strictly juridical, Fernando Vasquez (d. 1568), and in particular Diego Covarruvias (1512–77). Juan de Sepúlveda (1490–1573) and Bartolomé de Las Casas (1474–1566) also played important roles in defining the cultural scenario of the "Secunda Scholastica."

Juan Ginés de Sepúlveda was both a courtier and a man of the church. Historian to Charles V, preceptor to Philip II, in 1547 he offered a radical solution to the problem of the conversion of the "Indians" to Catholicism. He wrote a work whose long and eloquent subtitle gave a foretaste of conclusions sufficiently harsh to lead to the work's being censured by the Academy of Alcalá and the University of Salamanca. The book's themes were typical of the "Secunda Scholastica": its subtitle began, "Whether it is Just to Continue the War Against the Indians, and Take their Dominions and Possessions and Worldly Goods, and to Kill Them if they Offer Resistance." The continuation of the subtitle hinted that the author's answer was affirmative, justifying the greatest atrocities by the end that violence against persons and things should serve: ". . . in Order that They [the "Indians"], Despoiled of their Things and Subjected, Will be Persuaded more Easily to the Faith and be Converted by the Work of the Preaching Fathers."[31]

It is undeniable that Sepúlveda grasped the true nexus of the great debate that shook and involved the conscience and the thought of his

---

31. The long subtitle of the *Democrates secundus* reads: *seu de iustis belli causis, an liceat bello Indios prosequi, auferendo ab eis dominia possessionesque et bona temporalia, et occidendo eos, si resistentiam opposuerint, ut sic spoliati et subiecti facilius per Predicatores suadeatur eis fides.*

century. The ensuing events were further proof of this, and they offer an excellent means for understanding the general atmosphere that pervaded sixteenth-century Europe, turning it toward problems that either did not exist before that time or had gone unnoticed.

Juan de Sepúlveda was convinced that men were unequal, that their inequality was willed by God and was God's work, that it was therefore just that different legal systems should give concrete form to that diversity, and that slavery was a just legal consequence of the inherent natural defects of the slaves. Up to this point he interpreted the classical themes of the "Secunda Scholastica" in orthodox fashion. He then took several steps beyond the accepted limits by proposing cruel and extreme solutions. He stated that it was just to wage war against the "Indians" because they were inferior beings; that it was just to strip them of all they owned; that it was necessary and licit to use every means, even violence, to compel their primitive minds to try to understand the grandeur of the Catholic faith and the Catholic Church; that it was licit to kill those who resisted evangelization. The easiest way to reach the goal of converting to Catholicism entire populations of savages and infidels was by the example of depriving the "Indians" of their goods, throwing them into subjection as slaves, and, failing all else, by the extreme example of inflicting death on all who resisted.

Juan de Sepúlveda expressed similar ideas in an important work, *Apologia pro libro de iustis belli causis*, published in Rome in 1550. In this work he defended the theses he had expressed in 1547 in the earlier work that the Academy had blocked. The *Apologia* gave Domingo Soto the opportunity to organize a public debate in Rome between Juan de Sepúlveda and Bartolomé de Las Casas, an adversary of Sepúlveda's and a critic of his ideas. Other persons were also named to defend the opposing theses. Sepúlveda was considered the loser in the debate, but he was defended with such great skill by Bernardino Arévalo that the confrontation ended with no victor and no vanquished—further confirmation of how intensely felt and how widely diffused Sepúlveda's radical and violent ideas were in the mind-set and the shared culture of the times.

There is a sequel to the story. In 1552 Bartolomé de Las Casas wrote up his response to Sepúlveda in a work that is important in itself but that also offers important proof of the vitality of the ideas that Las Casas opposed. A balanced and incisive work, the *Brevisima relación de la destrucción de las Indias* is justly considered one of the bulwarks of political and religious culture in sixteenth-century Spain.[32] Once more the attention, the thought, and the conscience of Europe was focused on the "Indies" and the war on the "Indians."

13. Hugo Grotius and the Doctrine of Natural Law

When Hugo Grotius (1583–1645) appeared on the European scene in the early seventeenth century, the confines of the known world had broadened enormously and international trade was weaving dense and profitable exchange networks between the Atlantic coasts of Europe (Portugal, Spain, France, Holland, and England) and West Africa and the Americas.

Triangular trade routes among these three geographical areas brought immense riches. Merchandise of little intrinsic worth left from European ports to be exchanged in Africa for merchandise of much higher value; in that "black continent" young men and women were hunted down pitilessly, thrown into chains, put onto ships, and sent to the Americas. There they fetched high prices as manpower for immense and rapidly multiplying plantations (of sugar cane, for the most part), and the space they had occupied in the ships was then filled with American agricultural products that were carried back to Europe. Thus with one round-trip voyage a ship could turn a high commercial profit three times.

The capture of African and American men, navigation over nearly uncharted seas, landings in regions inhabited by "savage Indians" and pagans all left their mark on the cultural level when it came to pursuing in greater depth legal problems that already figured prominently in the thought of the "Secunda Scholastica."

We have seen the Salamanca jurists' intense intellectual curiosity and their efforts to deal with questions of war, peace, plunder, and the extermination of entire non-Christian populations. Although Hugo Grotius is usually credited with being the founder of international law, in reality the prevalent historiographic perspective often (but not always) oversimplifies the complex vicissitudes of European

32. Las Casas, *Brevisima relación* was published in Seville in 1552. On Vitoria and Las Casas, see James Muldoon, *Popes, Lawyers, and Infidels: The Church and the Non-Christian World 1250–1550* (Philadelphia: University of Pennsylvania Press, 1979), chaps. 6 and 7.

thought and the European scene between the sixteenth and seventeenth centuries. For one thing, before Grotius, themes inherent to international law were very much present in the doctrines of the "Secunda Scholastica," to the point of furnishing titles for several works of that school and of suggesting Francisco de Vitoria as a candidate for father of international law. For another, Grotius outlined and experimented with an original systematics in which he found a place not only for the problems of war, peace, and international law but also all the legal "institutions" that regulated the civil life of a society.

Hugo Grotius lived in the years of the rise of a number of extremely powerful mercantile "companies": the East India Companies of England (1600) and Holland (1602), and the Dutch West India Company (1621). It was this economic reality that gave urgency to Grotius's consideration of the legal problems of navigation and the spoils that could be won in the course of long and adventurous sea voyages.

Grotius's first work, published anonymously in 1609, bore the significant title of *Mare liberum* and was conceived as an autonomous chapter of a much larger treatise, *De iure praedae*. As is known, however, Grotius's fame rests on the vast fresco of his *De iure belli ac pacis*, published in Paris in 1625 after a period when he was pursued by personal troubles that included being sentenced to prison for life in Holland and fleeing, under perilous circumstances, to freedom in Paris.

De iure belli ac pacis was in large part written during Grotius's prison years, and it draws largely on the Spanish legal literature of the sixteenth century, which Grotius had been able to study in depth even though he was incarcerated. Although he amply and ably exploited the possibilities that the new methodology had opened up and borrowed relevant reflections from the "Secunda Scholastica," he reinterpreted them with originality and set them within his own comprehensive, synthetic, and systematic vision of the law.

The matrix of Spanish ideas and methodology is particularly evident in the way in which all Hugo Grotius's institutional thought is anchored in the concept of nature. From this basic point of departure and this pivotal idea, Grotius derived a carefully articulated vision of the legal "institutions," following an organization that radically and definitively rejected the sequence of books and titles in Justinian's *Digest* and even the three-part linear division of the Roman institutional scheme of the *Institutes*.

In Grotius's thought, however, the aims of religious expression shifted. A man who reflected on nature was also a man who reflected on his own nature, on his own instincts, and on the need to control those instincts and subject them to discipline. He was admittedly a man who entrusts himself to the nature willed by God, but for precisely that reason he first must trust himself, his own individual nature, and his own capacity for seeing and comprehending. In this fashion, nature took on the colors of "human reason" and was itself fundamentally the reason of the man who investigates and who knows. The age of Descartes was drawing near: that famous French philosopher's *Discourse on Method* was published in 1637.

It is often said that European natural law doctrine was born with Grotius. In any case, Grotius had many and famous successors and followers, among whom Samuel Pufendorf (1632–94) was one of the most important.

14. In the Guise of a Conclusion

With humanism, the "Secunda Scholastica," and the doctrine of natural law, new paths were open for a critical evaluation of the *ius commune*. Such evaluations were not always historiographical judgments, as was intended; at times they were polemical attacks and at other times projects aiming at revision of problematics, of legal "institutions," or of systematics. Those viewpoints gained such broad circulation that they became dominant in European culture of the seventeenth and eighteenth centuries.

Thus we have returned to our point of departure. Now we can understand what lay behind the harsher attacks on the "system" of the *ius commune* on the part of some concerned representatives of legal humanism, the more carefully thought out and historiographically more productive positions of other currents of legal humanism, and the radically new approaches of the "Secunda Scholastica" and the doctrine of natural law. We can also measure how wrongly and rashly many historians of our own century have adopted critical historiographical judgments of the *ius commune* that were rooted in specific movements for reform and that were the image and reflection, the reason and end, of those movements.

Even today, if we follow the anxieties and the bitter controversies of the sixteenth, seventeenth, and eighteenth centuries and follow them as insiders, taking them as vital questions today just as if the "system" of the *ius commune* were still a genuine hindrance for contemporary jurisprudence, we cannot avoid falsifying the historical perspective and limiting ourselves to a scanty comprehension of entire centuries of the law in Europe. Those centuries had their own unique, legitimate and vital experience, an experience just as legitimate and just as vital as those of later ages.

Thus we have returned to a clearer view of the *ius commune* after attempting to shatter the distorting lenses that the programs of past attempts at legal reform have imposed on our vision during the last two centuries.

It may even be that recalling these historical developments can be of use in the construction of a new European common law.

Bibliographical Note

1. Specific bibliography on the common law is both endless and quite limited. And this is not a paradox.

It is quite limited because few works have directly posed the problem of understanding the internal dynamics of the *ius commune* (the *utrumque ius*) or the dynamics of the systematic relationships between the *ius commune* and the *ius proprium*. It is endless because there are thousands of studies and monographs devoted to individual jurists, particular themes, circumscribed circles, and tendencies in legal thought. Such works generally presuppose an idea or a concept of the *ius commune* that is not expressed explicitly, that is often unclear, and that cannot be deduced from the concrete historiographical experience. Other works are indifferent to the problem, and even though they provide excellent data and give food for thought, they seem (because in fact they are) totally impermeable to the general problematics of the *ius commune* and its system.

In the last fifty years alone, there have been a number of bibliographical surveys (even recent ones) that may be of use although they concern studies in the general history of jurisprudence rather than the *ius commune* in particular.

They are: Bruno Paradisi, "Gli studi di storia del diritto italiano dal 1896 al 1946" (1946–47), "I nuovi orizzonti della storia giuridica" (1950–52), and "Indirizzi e problemi della più recente storiografia giuridica italiana" (1963–71), all now available in Paradisi, *Apologia della storia giuridica* (Bologna: Il Mulino, 1973); Ennio Cortese, "Storia del diritto italiano," in *Cinquanta anni di esperienza giuridica in Italia*, Atti del Congresso di Taormina, 3–8 November 1981 (Milan: Giuffrè, 1982), 785–858; Adriano Cavanna, *La storia del diritto moderno (secoli XVI–XVIII) nella più recente storiografia italiana* (Milan: Giuffrè, 1983). There is ample bibliography (not specific to the *ius commune*, however) in Adriano Cavanna, *Storia del diritto moderno in Europa* (Milan: Giuffrè, 1979), vol. 1, *Le fonti e il pensiero giuridico*, 617ff.; Helmut Coing, ed., *Handbuch der Quellen und Literatur der neueren europäischen Privatrechtsgeschichte*, 3 vols. in 8 (Munich: Beck, 1973–87), vol. 1, *Mittelalter (1100–1500); die gelehrten Rechte und die Gesetzgebung* (1973), vol. 2, pt. 1, *Neuere Zeit (1500–*

1800), *das Zeitalter des gemeinen Rechts* (1977), pt. 2, *Gesetzgebung und Recht-sprechung* (1976).

2. For guides to the history of the *ius commune* in particular, there is biblio-graphical information (not recent, however) in Giuseppe Ermini, *Corso di diritto comune*, 3d ed. (Milan: Giuffrè, 1952), vol. 1, *Genesi ed evoluzione storica: Elementi costitutivi: Fonti*, xi and 123–41.

It should be noted that the most important turning point in the history of the *ius commune* in this century occurred in 1934 with the publication of Francesco Calasso, "Il concetto di diritto comune," published along with later essays in Calasso, *Introduzione al diritto comune* (Milan: Giuffrè, 1951). Other studies by Calasso on specific topics are republished in Calasso, *Stori-cità del diritto*, ed. Piero Fiorelli (Milan: Giuffrè, 1966), 201–337. Finally, Ca-lasso's *Medio Evo del diritto* (Milan: Giuffrè, 1954), vol. 1, *Le fonti*, is still a fundamental resource, particularly 345–629.

Another broad summary with a different (and less fertile) approach is Paul Koschaker, *Europa und das römische Recht*, 3d ed. (Munich: Beck, 1958), in Italian translation as *L'Europa e il diritto romano* (Florence: G. C. Sansoni, 1962), intro. Francesco Calasso, trans. Arnaldo Biscardi.

Other works that might be consulted are: Enrico Besta, *Fonti: Legislazione e scienza giuridica*, 2 vols., in *Storia del diritto italiano*, ed. Pasquale Del Giu-dice (Milan: Hoepli, 1923–25); reprint (Frankfurt am Main: Saur und Auver-mann KG, and Florence: O. Gozzini, 1969); Hermann Kantorowicz, *Studies in the Glossators of the Roman Law* (Cambridge: Cambridge University Press, 1938), reprinted with additions and corrections by Peter Weimar (Aalen: Sci-entia-Verlag, 1969); Franz Wieacker, *Privatrechtsgeschichte der Neuzeit unter besonderer Berüchsichtigung der deutschen Entwicklung*, 2d ed. (Göttingen: Vandenboeck und Ruprecht, 1967), in Italian translation as *Storia del diritto privato moderno con particolare riguardo alla Germania*, trans. Umberto San-tarelli and Sandro Angelo Fusco, 2 vols. (Milan: Giuffrè, 1980); Manlio Bel-lomo, *Società e istituzioni dal medioevo agli inizi dell'età moderna* (1976), 6th ed. (Rome: Il Cigno Galileo Galilei, 1993), 327–513; Bellomo, *Saggio sull'Univer-sità nell'età del diritto comune* (Catania: Giannotta, 1979; 2d ed. Rome: Il Cigno Galileo Galilei, 1992).

There are two works that concentrate on the *ius commune*, but both their approach and their information is out of date, hence they are of limited use: Giuseppe Ermini, *Corso di diritto comune*, 3d ed. (Milan: Giuffrè, 1952), vol. 1, *Genesi ed evoluzione storica: Elementi costitutivi: Fonti*; Giovanni Cassandro, *Lezioni di diritto comune* (Naples: Edizioni Scientifiche Italiane, 1974).

Riccardo Orestano, *Introduzione allo studio del diritto romano* (Bologna: Il Mulino, 1987) is overly theoretical and reliant on preconceptions. Alan Wat-son, *The Making of the Civil Law* (Cambridge, Mass.: Harvard University Press, 1981) is misleading, unreliable, and confused, and it is difficult to see why the work should ever have been translated into Italian: Watson, *La formazione del diritto civile*, trans. Nicoletta Sarti (Bologna: Il Mulino, 1986). On this work, see the strongly negative review by Paolo Grossi, *Quaderni Fiorentini* 17 (1988): 483.

Eltjo J. H. Schrage and Jean H. Dondorp, *Utrumque Ius: Eine Einführung in das Studium der Quellen des mittelalterlichen gelehrten Rechts* (Schriften zur europäischen Rechts- und Verfassungsgeschichte, 8; Berlin: Duncker und Humblot, 1992), has lacunae in its information and is lacking in ideas. The sweeping phenomenon of the *ius commune*, mentioned in only a few insufficient and antiquated pages, is substantially ignored in the new edition of Carlo Augusto Cannata and Antonio Gambaro, *Lineamenti di storia della giurisprudenza europea*, vol. 2, *Dal medioevo all'epoca contemporanea*, 4th ed. (Turin: Giappichelli, 1989), 11–29.

Bartolomé Clavero, *Derecho común*, Temas de Historia del Derecho (Seville: Secretariado de publicacciones de la Universidad, 1977) gives a brief summary of the *ius commune*. The problems are better selected in Adriana Campitelli, *Europeenses: Presupposti storici e genesi del diritto comune* (Bari: Cacucci, 1990).

3. Works that belong only partially to the literature on the *ius commune* despite their titles are Arrigo Solmi, *Contributi alla storia del diritto comune* (Rome: Società editrice del "Foro italiano," 1937); Giuseppe Ermini, *Scritti di diritto comune*, ed. Danilo Segoloni, 2 vols. (Padua: CEDAM, 1976, and Perugia: Libreria editrice universitaria, 1980).

There are several collections of studies of great importance for a specific approach to the *ius commune*: Eduard Maurits Meijers, *Etudes d'histoire du droit*, ed. Robert Feenstra and H. F. W. D. Fischer, 3 vols. (Leiden: Universitaire Pers Leiden, 1956–59), vol. 3, *Le droit romain au Moyen Age*; Stephan Kuttner, *Gratian and the Schools of Law: 1140–1234* (Aldershot: Variorum Reprints, 1993); Kuttner, *The History of Ideas and Doctrines of Canon Law in the Middle Ages*, 2d ed. (Aldershot: Variorum Reprints, 1992); Kuttner, *Medieval Councils, Decretals and Collections of Canon Law: Selected Essays*, 2d ed. (Aldershot: Variorum Reprints, 1992); Kuttner, *Studies in the History of Medieval Canon Law* (Aldershot: Variorum Reprints, 1990); Brian Tierney, *Church Law and Constitutional Thought in the Middle Ages* (London: Variorum Reprints, 1979); Jean Gaudemet, *La formation du droit canonique médiéval* (London: Variorum Reprints, 1980); André Gouron, *La science du droit dans le Midi de la France au Moyen Age* (London: Variorum Reprints, 1984). For a different and older general approach to the problems of the *ius commune*, see Robert Feenstra, *Le droit savant au Moyen Age et sa vulgarisation* (London: Variorum Reprints, 1986).

There are a number of Acts of colloquia, conferences, and workshops that refer directly or indirectly to the *ius commune*. The more important of these are: *Bartolo da Sassoferrato: Studi e documenti per il VI Centenario*, Atti del Congresso di Perugia 1–5 April 1959, 2 vols. (Milan: Giuffrè, 1962); *Atti del Convegno internazionale di studi accursiani*, Bologna 21–26 October 1963, ed. Guido Rossi, 3 vols. (Milan: Giuffrè, 1968); *Confluence des droits savants et des pratiques juridiques*, Actes du Colloque de Montpellier 12–14 December 1977 (Milan: Giuffrè, 1979); *Diritto comune e diritti locali nella storia dell'Europa*, Atti del Convegno di Varenna 12–15 June 1979 (Milan: Giuffrè, 1980); *Il diritto comune e la tradizione giuridica europea*, Atti del convegno di studi, ed.

Danilo Segoloni (Perugia: Libreria universitaria, 1980, distribution Rimini: Maggioli); *Scuole diritto e società nel Mezzogiorno medievale d'Italia*, the Acts of a "Settimana di lavori" on the topic "Cultura giuridica e circolazione libraria nel Mezzogiorno medievale d'Italia," Erice 23–30 October 1983 (Studi e ricerche dei "Quaderni Catanesi," 7–8), ed. Manlio Bellomo, 2 vols. (Catania: Tringale, 1985–87); *España y Europa: Un pasado jurídico común*, Actas del I Simposio Internacional del Instituto de Derecho Común, Murcia 26–28 March 1985, ed. Antonio Pérez Martín (Murcia: Instituto de Derecho Común, Universidad de Murcia, 1986).

4. Reviews that focus on the *ius commune* are, for civil law: *Ius Commune*, Frankfurt am Main, 1 (1967), founded by Helmut Coing and now directed by Dieter Simon and Walter Wilhelm. For canon law, *Zeitschrift der Savigny-Stiftung für Rechtsgeschichte, Kanonistische Abteilung*, founded by Ulrich Stutz and now directed by Theo Mayer-Maly, Dieter Nörr, Wolfgang Waldstein, Adolf Laufs, Werner Ogris, Martin Heckel, Paul Mikat, and Knut Wolfgang Nörr; *Studia Gratiana* 1 (1954), founded and directed by Giuseppe Forchielli and Alfonso Maria Stickler, after 1972 directed by Stickler alone; *Bulletin of Medieval Canon Law*, n. s. (1971), founded and directed by Stephan Kuttner until 1989, now directed by Kenneth Pennington and Peter Landau. For the field of the *ius commune* in general, see *Rivista Internazionale di Diritto Comune* 1 (1990), founded and directed by Manlio Bellomo.

5. For fundamental resources and an introduction to research in the doctrinal sources of the *ius commune*, see: Stephan Kuttner, *Repertorium der Kanonistik (1140–1234)* (Vatican City: Biblioteca Apostolica Vaticana, 1937, reprint 1973); Gero Dolezalek and Hans van de Wouw, *Verzeichnis der Handschriften zum römischen Recht bis 1600*, 4 vols. (Frankfurt am Main: Max-Planck- Institut für europäische Rechtsgeschichte, 1972); Gero Dolezalek and Laurent Mayali, *Repertorium manuscriptorum veterum Codicis Iustiniani*, 2 vols. (Frankfurt am Main: V. Klostermann, 1985).

Today an extremely rich range of microfilms of doctrinal sources is available to the scholar interested in specific topics. For canonistic doctrine and the Vatican manuscripts in particular there is the collection at the Institute of Medieval Canon Law at the University of California, Berkeley (Stephan Kuttner, emeritus director)that was moved to Munich (Germany) under the directorship of Peter Landau; for civil law doctrine (and some canon law manuscripts) there is the collection of the Max-Planck-Institut für europäische Rechtsgeschichte in Frankfurt am Main, founded by Helmut Coing and directed by Dieter Simon and Michael Stolleis. There are also collections at the Istituto di Storia del Diritto Italiano directed by Antonio Padoa Schioppa, Università Statale, Milan, and connected with the Seminario Giuridico, a section of Storia del Diritto Italiano e di Diritto Comune, director Manlio Bellomo, Catania, Università di Catania, which has a particularly extensive collection of microfilms not only of manuscripts but also of incunabula of civil and canon law.

Index

The Common Legal Past of Europe, 1000–1800
was composed in 10/12 Galliard by World Composition Services, Inc.,
Sterling, Virginia; printed on 60-pound Glatfelter Supple Opaque Recycled and
bound by Thomson-Shore, Inc., Dexter Michigan; and designed and produced
by Kachergis Book Design, Pittsboro, North Carolina.